"Markow's book is a comprehensive and practical e
tional behavior, culture, and health. Seminaries shou
this book for *every* student. Nonprofit leaders should
leaders through several sections of this book, especially the chapters on emotional intelligence, emerging approaches to leadership, and organizational culture."

—**Craig Domeck**, Palm Beach Atlantic University (retired);
founder and principal, 3-D Leadership Development

"If you are looking to create a safe and thriving culture within your church, look no further than *Organizational Behavior in Christian Perspective*. Use it to create generative conversations that will take your teams to a higher level."

—**Jay Gary**, Oral Roberts University

"In seminary, I had the privilege of studying organizational leadership under Markow. The principles, practices, and concepts of leadership and organizational health and behavior I gleaned from his teachings were immediately applicable to pastoral ministry and provided helpful tools for me to lead, develop, and empower others more effectively. Many of these profound insights are captured in this book and are sure to better equip any pastor or ministry leader to lead healthier, more fruitful organizations."

—**Jelani Lewis**, campus pastor, Gateway Church, Southlake, Texas

"Markow is a brilliant thinker who understands organizational behavior at a core level that few can. For years now, students at The King's University have benefited from this skill and gift that he brings to the classroom. We are excited for the release of Markow's book because it will allow the rest of the world to experience the deep insights that we at TKU have grown so accustomed to. *Organizational Behavior in Christian Perspective* is the perfect blend of academic, practical, and biblical truths that every organizational leader can benefit from. I highly recommend taking a serious look at this book."

—**Jon Chasteen**, The King's University (former president);
lead pastor, Victory Church

"This book brings together some of the best ideas from the field of organizational behavior, offers scriptural support and insight, and helps Christian leaders create healthy organizations. A well-presented book, this text offers—for pastors, executive pastors, and all who lead organizations with a heart for the kingdom—a way to create positive work environments where everyone wins."

—**Roxanne Helm-Stevens**, Azusa Pacific University

"Highly relevant, timely, and practical, *Organizational Behavior in Christian Perspective* provides leaders with clarity on the heart of any organization—its people. Markow's simple but brilliant five-level model is built on years of research and practice, addressing the long-neglected leadership issues in churches and ministry organizations. You will want to give this book to your leadership team to strengthen their tool kit, successfully navigate challenges, increase effectiveness, and provide hope for the next generation of faith-based leaders!"

—**Angie Richey**, Life Pacific University

"Working with people in organizations is complex and vital work. This book provides insightful reflection on the nature of healthy leadership and organizational practice. Engaging the best of the organizational behavior literature, Markow reflects on and applies this literature in a way that is relevant not only to business leaders but also to nonprofit and church leaders. Based on his many years of leadership and educational experience, Markow is well-positioned to provide an important voice on leadership and organizational practice from a Christian perspective. I'm grateful for the work he has put into this project that I'm sure will benefit students and practitioners alike."

—**Justin A. Irving**, The Southern Baptist Theological Seminary; author of *Healthy Leadership for Thriving Organizations*

"It is difficult to not be effusive about this incredible book. I have taught leadership for thirty-five years, and this is hands-down the best leadership textbook I have ever read. Markow expertly weaves the Christian faith into his research and writing. A must-have book for any faith-based business or leadership program. His analysis of past and current leadership issues is both deep and thorough, a masterful combination of the theoretical and the practical. His case studies bring life to his material. It is like James MacGregor Burns and Patrick Lencioni combined forces to create the perfect leadership text. Absolute genius."

—**Michael M. Whyte**, Azusa Pacific University (emeritus); president, Global Academy for Transformational Leadership

"Leading a healthy organization is the primary responsibility of every leader. The challenge is understanding how organizational behavior impacts the leader's ability to build and maintain an organization. Markow has a unique ability to explain in secular and spiritual terms how an organization should behave and the best perspectives and practices that can help it grow. His scholarship is prominent, and his practicality is masterful."

—**Ricky Temple**, pastor, Overcoming by Faith Ministries, Savannah, Georgia

"Markow connects the dots between complex organizational theory, practical application, and thoughtful theological perspective. As challenging as this is, he does it in seamless style. From the first page I was entirely engaged, as the book distinguishes itself as thought-provoking, witty, and always workable. The science and craft of leadership is shown to be achievable. Somehow Markow intermingles organizations and the ever-present human mystery while being entertaining along the way. Think about it: how often have you been *charmed* to learn challenging and often perplexing lessons?"

—**Sam Rockwell**, Pepperdine University (adjunct); principal, Rockwell & Company

ORGANIZATIONAL
BEHAVIOR
in Christian Perspective

ORGANIZATIONAL
BEHAVIOR
in Christian Perspective

Theory *and* Practice *for* Church
and Ministry Leaders

FRANKLIN A. MARKOW

Baker Academic

a division of Baker Publishing Group
Grand Rapids, Michigan

Published by Baker Academic
a division of Baker Publishing Group
Grand Rapids, Michigan
BakerAcademic.com

Printed in the United States of America

Library of Congress Cataloging-in-Publication Data
Names: Markow, Frank A., author.
Title: Organizational behavior in Christian perspective : theory and practice for church and ministry leaders / Franklin A. Markow.
Description: Grand Rapids, Michigan : Baker Academic, a division of Baker Publishing Group, [2024] | Includes bibliographical references and index.
Identifiers: LCCN 2023053575 | ISBN 9781540968029 (paperback) | ISBN 9781540968036 (casebound) | ISBN 9781493446834 (ebook) | ISBN 9781493446841 (pdf)
Subjects: LCSH: Christian leadership. | Organizational behavior.
Classification: LCC BV652.1 .M3594 2024 | DDC 253—dc23/eng/20240213
LC record available at https://lccn.loc.gov/2023053575

Cover design by Gayle Raymer

Baker Publishing Group publications use paper produced from sustainable forestry practices and postconsumer waste whenever possible.

24   25   26   27   28   29   30   7   6   5   4   3   2   1

To the One who saves and sets us free,
and to those who labor
to advance the coming of his kingdom

Contents

Preface

This book is the product of many accumulated years of studying and teaching on the topic of organizational behavior, mostly for graduate students in Christian universities and seminaries. I have seen the lights go on for hundreds of students over the years as they have encountered ideas that give insight into things they have seen and experienced but that they had not previously articulated or known how to address. You may find that many of the ideas in this book seem familiar but have been mysterious or problematic. My hope and prayer is that I will give you a coherent and thorough way to think about organizations and piece them together in your own mind and practice. In today's contemporary landscape, I feel it is vital that leaders become students not just of leadership but of organizations and that they learn how organizations function well. We must learn comprehensive and grounded ways of seeing and articulating what we encounter that go beyond the latest pop trends or ideas of leadership. This book will give you just such a perspective, with the aim of helping you become a more effective leader so that you may advance the kingdom in the corner of the world to which you have been called.

There are many folks to thank here for the personal and professional help they have lent along the way. I thank my beautiful wife, Gina, for encouraging and supporting me over the years and for helping me pursue my dream, and I thank my wonderful adult children Jacob, Benjamin, Abigail, and Matthew, all of whom I am extremely proud. I thank the various leaders who have allowed me to hone and put into practice my own thinking and teaching over the years, including Gary Moncher, Jim J. Adams, Jon Chasteen, Jon Huntzinger, David Moore, David Cole, Robert Morris, and my ministry partners at Gateway Church in Southlake, Texas. This book also owes much to all my professorial colleagues at The King's University and Life Pacific University, who have inspired and encouraged my endeavors to teach and do research. Thanks to all my students over the years—undergraduate, graduate, and doctoral—who patiently listened to my teaching both live and on video and shared their own leadership experiences and challenges, helping me see what was valuable and how these ideas impacted their own churches and ministries. Kurt Dahlin (Water Wells for Africa), Todd Lane (Gateway Church), Mundo Meneses (The Life Church), Angie Richey (Life Pacific University), Dale Swanson (Victory Church), and a couple unnamed sources provided research interviews for this book. I also offer thanks to all the friendly baristas at Roots Coffee in North Richland Hills, Texas, for keeping me well caffeinated during the five months when I was writing this book. Last but not least, thanks to my Savior Jesus, who found an aimless twenty-five-year-old kid and gave him a hope and a future, a calling and a blessed life.

Introduction to Organizational Behavior

Introduction

We have been hearing about leadership in the church for decades now. The writings of Christian authors such as John C. Maxwell and George Barna, mainstream leadership writers like Jim Collins and Patrick Lencioni, and scores of others have all become part of our common vernacular in and outside the church. There seems to be a nonstop flow of books, seminars, and gurus. Seemingly, every corporate executive, winning sports coach, or leader of a megachurch has written a book or has a podcast on the subject. Yet despite this deluge of information on leadership, and despite the leadership industry being a billion-dollar-a-year enterprise,[1] why is it that our churches and ministries still struggle to grow and thrive? Why haven't we figured it out yet? And why another book for leaders? Is this the one that finally gets it right and answers all the big issues we face?

My contention and premise are simple: our organizations still struggle with leadership issues because we do not understand the context from which the study of leadership has originated—namely, *organizational behavior* (OB). Leadership does not happen in a vacuum. It happens in a blender! That blender is the ever-changing, dynamic, and messy context of an organization. People, with their warts and all, make up our churches, and people are messy, complex, and hard to understand. This book can help you see the nature of the church as an organization comprising people and the way those people relate to you, to one another, and to the organization itself. When people come together in a common cause, as they do in a church, by definition there is an organization. In churches, businesses, and nonprofit organizations, people are people, and when setting and accomplishing goals together, we all face the same set of challenges, no matter the origins and goals of the organization.

This is not a how-to book or Markow's Ten Easy Principles to Help Your Church Grow. In my estimation, one reason for the malaise in the contemporary church is an overdependence on quick fixes and one-size-fits-all solutions, which sends people running from one seminar to the next and looking for the fabled silver bullet. Leadership in churches, as in all organizations, is complex and often defies easy fixes. In addition to the normal concerns, such as balancing order and innovation and achieving proper alignment to the mission, we must factor in the complexity of an institution that is over two thousand years old; has morphed into a thousand different shapes, sizes, denominations, and microcultures; and has a theological and spiritually rooted essence. One can easily see why leading a healthy church is such a daunting challenge. Yet it is my contention that the field of OB can provide an important part of the answer. Organizational behavior is a well-developed and theoretically and empirically based set of ideas that have currency in all organizations, even the church.

Organizational Behavior and the Church

At this point some may protest, "But since the church is a spiritual entity, we cannot or should not apply secular business principles or psychology to help us." First, let's deal with the concept of "secular business principles" in a church context. True, a church is not a business in the traditional sense—that is, an entity created by a human founder to sell a product or service for a profit. We have a spiritual foundation, an eternal mission, and an ever-present Founder who promised to always be with us (Matt. 28:19–20). Nevertheless, a church has to deal with many of the same issues and challenges faced by other organizations. The primary reason is this: the church is, at the end of the day, made up of people. As well-meaning and God-fearing as Christians may be, people in Christian organizations think, feel, and behave much the same way as people do in any other organization.

In a similar vein, consider the "secular business principles" that most churches incorporate regularly without thinking twice. Insurance, payroll and accounting, legal help, building and facilities, and maintenance are but a few of the aspects of secular business from which churches benefit every day. Imagine a church that contended, "We don't follow any of those secular business principles in our accounting department. We just throw all the money and receipts in a box and let the bean counters deal with it once a year." There is a term for this: "malfeasance," the misuse of public trust. Or consider a church building that is not up to city code. How safe would you feel bringing your children into a facility that did not bother with those "secular business principles"? In a similar way, churches must understand the ideas of OB just as they understand accounting and construction principles in order to avoid neglecting and abusing the very people they claim to serve. To not do so, in my opinion, is leadership malfeasance. Sadly, this happens every day in countless churches across the world as they limp along and struggle to do good. It is the aim of this book to help correct this neglect and to help leaders understand and apply some of the underlying principles of organizational behavior, of which a moderate amount of study can pay priceless dividends for perhaps eternity.

This book follows a model I have developed over the years in my teaching, a model that helps categorize organizational phenomena based on five different levels. Sometimes we can see organizations as a mysterious and big "black box" of activity and ideas. My hope is this five-level model will help you understand how these things fit together and give you a mental model for thinking about the different organizational issues you encounter every day, a schema to help you, as a leader, think through the various issues you face on a regular basis and pinpoint where an issue may lie. While principles may have their place, the field of OB is built on organizational theory. Theories are, in essence, "laws" that have been demonstrated to be effective in a variety of settings, over a period of time, with the use of sound research methodologies. Some organizational theories have more time and testing, some are emerging, and some are more conceptual constructs. Nevertheless, organizational theory seeks to utilize underlying principles of psychology, sociology, anthropology, and a variety of social sciences to back up their claims. To the extent to which we can truly predict anything about humans and their behavior, the study of OB can give leaders more confidence in how their own behavior and actions will impact those they seek to lead. To be certain, there is a lot of "art and craft" to leadership that defies easy description. But this book aims to give leaders needed theoretical and scientific balance to their artful practice.

What Is Organizational Behavior?

Organizational behavior is the study of people in organizations—how they relate to one another in an organizational context, how they relate to the organization itself, and how the organization relates to its people. While many of the management disciplines look at the "hard" side of organizations (e.g., finance, administrative process and policy, legal compliance), OB looks at the "soft" side, the skills needed to effectively lead and manage people. Yet while I refer to these as the soft side, good OB is not merely a subjective matter. Rather, it is built on a foundation of academic disciplines that help us understand the social nature of people and society. Individual psychology, social psychology, sociology, anthropology, and other traditional academic fields constitute much of the fabric of contemporary OB study and understanding. Thus, we can say that OB is a dependent and synthesizing discipline. It borrows from what we know about human behavior from a variety of sources of knowledge and incorporates that information into an organizational context. And while it has scholarly foundations, it is ultimately an applied discipline. OB exists to help practitioners—managers and leaders at all levels of organizations—in their daily practice. The field of inquiry into OB is rich and diverse. Many books and academic journals are filled with OB concepts and theories, with mounds of empirical data to test these theories, and new ideas are emerging over time. While some may argue that OB can become too theoretical, many of these ideas ultimately trickle into the vernacular and into the hands of nonacademics, giving impetus to best practices for running their departments and organizations. If you have ever uttered a phrase such as "get the right people on the bus" (from the concept of "fit"—see chap. 2) or "he's just a maintainer" (from the concept of "leadership versus management"—see chap. 8), you have experienced OB seeping into your own thinking about leadership.

Metaphors for Organizations

An important starting point for thinking about the nature of organizations was offered by Gareth Morgan in his seminal work *Images of Organization*.[2] Morgan challenged us to change the way we think about organizations by using a variety of metaphors, visual pictures, or ideas that represent an organization. The standard metaphor most are familiar with is the organization as a machine. Machines have parts, run well, are predictable and stable, and are designed to accomplish a specific purpose. They may break, but they can also be fixed by replacing or rearranging parts. Using this metaphor, we see organizations as rational and purposeful entities, ones that the savvy leader can tinker with and change via the right know-how and technical expertise. Strategy, goals, policy, processes, and regulations are all the jargon and substrata of the organization as machine. Sounds familiar, right?

While this is the conventional wisdom of organizations—that they are rational and fixable entities—Morgan challenges us to think with more complexity about organizations by introducing a new set of metaphors. He argues that using a metaphor is a way of thinking but also a way of *not thinking* about organizations, and he says that we can become stuck in one metaphor. This "stuckness" can introduce distortion and blind us from seeing reality in new and important ways. So, what are some of the other metaphors we can use to help us understand organizations? Consider these:

- Organism: The organization is a living, growing entity that lives in a natural symbiosis and needs to adapt to its environment as part of an open system. It goes through stages of life, from birth, through infancy, to maturity. The organization can become sick and need healing, and it may eventually, like all other organisms, die.
- Brain: Brains are self-referential, learning, and self-organizing entities. Using this metaphor, we can see our organization as something that looks into itself and thinks about ways to learn from its

experience, rearranging itself by using plasticity in the face of new challenges and opportunities.

- Culture: The organization is a value-based entity with a history, symbols, and symbolic meanings. Over time it has developed into something wholly unique, with its own set of ideals and challenges. A culture defies easy fixes or changes but gives people a rich sense of shared community and history to which they are proud to belong.

Morgan also posits some "darker" metaphors: political systems, psychic prisons, flux and transformation, and instruments of domination. Using these metaphors, we can see the controlling and ambivalent nature of organizations, entities populated with members vying for power and scarce resources and keeping people in their places, entities subject to the whims of a powerful few. We in the church rarely "go there," but if we are honest we can see that these, too, can help us explore some of the dysfunctions that keep us trapped in harmful cycles.

Reframing: Bolman and Deal

Another valuable and memorable schema for helping us understand the nature of organizations is one posed by Lee G. Bolman and Terrence E. Deal in *Reframing Organizations*.[3] In this model organizations can be viewed through four different frames:

- The structural frame: In this frame we see organizations as factories, similar to Morgan's machine metaphor—rational, logical, well-designed, and fixable entities. Organizational charts ("org charts"), policies, and vision statements reflect this frame. This frame is easy to see, and most people think of this when they think of an organization.
- The human-resources frame: This frame focuses on the human side of organizations and sees them as families, with father and mother figures who help the family get along and work together and who provide support and mentorship. Trust and loyalty to the family are a requisite commodity for being part of the shared community. Ideas such as people skills and levels of trust, along with

approaches to motivation and the concept of leadership styles, reflect this frame.

- The symbolic frame: This frame, which is similar to Morgan's cultural metaphor, views organizations as temples, rich in meaning and values, with an important purpose in society and in members' lives. Members share their rich history as a foundation of meaning and purpose, and they are indoctrinated into the lore and ways of the organization through stories, myths, and rituals. The idea of "how things really work around here" reflects this frame.
- The political frame: Through this lens, we see organizations as jungles, potentially scary places populated by a variety of creatures roaming and seeking power, dominance, and resources. The saying about "who you know and not what you know" reflects this frame.

Through a variety of mental models and frames, we can challenge our assumptions and allow our thinking about organizations to become much more complex and nuanced. I cannot tell you how many times I have witnessed a church leader say or write something like "The church is not an organization; it is an organism!" and expect everyone to thwack their foreheads with their palms as they realize the brilliance of this revelation, now truly understanding where they had gone wrong. An organism is but one of a myriad of helpful metaphors we can use to give us insight. When I hear my students say, "Our church is really an organism," or, "Our church is really a family," I do a different palm-to-forehead thwack, thinking, "No, an organism or family is but one of several ways you should be thinking about your church." If you insist that it *is* an organism or a family, or only think about it as such, you will overlook the richness and importance that a brain metaphor or a machine metaphor or a jungle metaphor can bring to your thinking and practices. These all can be creative and helpful ways for us to reimagine how we think about our organizations and can help us develop new language and new ways of reflecting on challenges. I encourage all leaders to complexify their thinking by using a rich set of metaphors. You can even create your own—how about "Our church is like Noah's ark, with lots of strange animals running around who need feeding and sure poop a lot"? The possibilities are endless.

*The Changing Nature of Organizational Behavior
and Management Sciences*

Our thinking about organizations has changed radically over the past century. It has transitioned from being an approach (primarily) benefiting the organization to being one that appreciates and values the individual, realizing that happy people make for happy organizations. The following are several of the main streams of development and their relative contributions to the field.

WEBER AND TAYLOR: SCIENTIFIC MANAGEMENT

The earliest efforts at organization science are typified by the thinking of Max Weber, a nineteenth-century German sociologist and political economist, and Frederick W. Taylor, a US-born inventor and engineer. Weber's concept of *bureaucratic management* helped organizations become orderly and methodical entities. Ideas such as rules, standardized processes, technical competence, documentation, division of labor, the organizational hierarchy of relationships, and appointments to offices based on qualifications are all part of Weber's concept of bureaucracy. He contrasted these with then-prevalent forms of organization, such as those based on tradition (e.g., monarchies and feudal systems with lords) or charismatic or despotic leadership. Taylor introduced the concept of *scientific management*, the notion that work should be done in the most efficient way possible, getting the most from both people and resource materials. Time-and-motion studies were conducted to ensure management was getting the most from their personnel. Taylorism led to the development of the assembly line and mass production, the impetus to modern production practices still used to this day.

Bureaucracy has become somewhat of a dirty word conjuring up images of paperwork or being stuck in line at the Department of Motor Vehicles. While these realities are a drag, to be sure, Weber's and Taylor's contributions to efficient organization cannot be underestimated, and even many churches and ministries incorporate these bureaucratic practices to help them be good stewards of their resources. Yet it is not hard to see how this approach largely favors the organization. People become cogs in the machinery, doing as their role prescribes and doing it with maximum efficiency.

LEWIN AND MAYO: THE HUMAN-RESOURCES TURN

The tide began to turn in OB with the thinking of Kurt Lewin, a German American sociologist, and Elton Mayo, a professor of the industrial research department at Harvard University. Lewin recognized the connection between people and their environment, and he pioneered group studies and dynamics. He felt that groups were most productive in the long term not when they were led by autocrats but, rather, when they were democratically led and the people were given a say in decisions that would impact them. Mayo led a research team through the seminal Hawthorne Studies. These studies began as Taylor-like time-and-motion studies but took a revolutionary turn when it was discovered that production improved not because of physical changes to the work environment itself (e.g., the placement of tables, the amount of lighting) but because the workers themselves were involved in the changes and their feelings were considered. This was a novel idea at the time, when management alone was responsible for decision-making and the workers did as they were told. As it turns out, people, their efforts, and their feelings are also an important part of the success of an organization. It is now commonplace to think about emotional intelligence, human motivations, trust, conflict, group cohesion, and other such matters as part of the management and leadership recipe for success.

THE HEART AND THE SOUL AT WORK

Today the concepts of bureaucracy, democratic leadership, and emotions are well-worn territory and are taken for granted in our ideas about how organizations should be run. Over the past twenty years, emerging yet potent ideas have been developing regarding the role of spirit and soul at work. While Christians have understood the nature of spirituality, transcendence, and ultimate meaning for millennia, the notion that work must have purpose is taking root in mainstream organizational thinking and practice. The advent of the Management, Spirituality and Religion interest group of the Academy of Management,[4] along with books such as Margaret Benefiel's *Soul at Work*, has promoted the idea that people are not only rational and emotional beings but are also spiritual and transcendent beings who seek integrity between themselves and their work.[5] Thus, the workplace should be one that recognizes and values the spiritual dimension of the workforce and pays attention to matters beyond efficiency or the bottom-line profit margins. Practicing one's religion at work can be a controversial topic in our pluralistic society. Nevertheless, many organizations are recognizing the need to make spirituality and common human values part of their corporate culture. This is expressed in a variety of ways, such as corporate-social-responsibility initiatives and the advent of the chief spiritual officer and corporate chaplain.

The Benefits of a Good Understanding of Organizational Behavior

Now that we have defined OB and looked at its historical roots and lineage, it is fair to ask what the value of OB is and how it can help people be better stewards of those entrusted to them in the church. As you read this book, you will no doubt be inspired in countless ways, but here are a few big takeaways that OB can help you engender in your workforce.

As most seasoned leaders know, organizational life can be a tough grind, and people can find themselves feeling alone or isolated for a variety of reasons. While OB is not a silver bullet, a better grasp of OB topics can help us address our people's sense of satisfaction and engagement with their work and ministry. Research shows a connection between workplace thriving and people's sense of connection to, commitment to, and engagement with work. People need to feel challenged at work, to find meaning in their work. What they do needs to have purpose and be fulfilling beyond just a paycheck. While one can assume that working in a church, ministry, or other values-driven organization is inherently fulfilling, we know that even people working in these types of organizations also suffer from isolation and a lack of engaging or meaningful work. Particularly in a church, where there is often constant pressure to prepare for the next big event, where people's souls are seemingly in our hands, and where the concerns of life and death and the challenges of an apathetic and even hostile society weigh on us, work can feel discouraging and relentless rather than satisfying. Church leaders must be equipped to faithfully steward their people, and OB can be an important part of their conceptual tool kit, helping them steward more effectively.

Further, OB itself is a leadership-development endeavor. When we learn how to empower people, help them engage with their work, create healthy cultures, make the work itself motivating, involve people in decision-making, manage conflict, and improve communication, we are developing others' ability to lead. Thus, OB can be part of a church's approach not only to personal development at all levels but also to the development of the leadership pipeline, as it provides tools leaders can use to create healthy cultures and processes by which people thrive and give of themselves. If leading healthy churches and organizations is your goal and developing your leadership pipeline is important, OB knowledge and good OB practices should be part of what you bring to the table.

Organizational Behavior and Theology

I have briefly addressed some possible objections above, but now I will offer a further thought on a larger conceptual scale to help us consider the nature of the church.

Early on in the theologizing of the church, Christians wrestled with the nature of Christ. Was he human, divine, or some combination of these? Various factions in early Christianity argued for one position or the other, and the victorious position was that Jesus was, in fact, fully human *and* fully divine. We can clearly see both of these natures in Scripture for ourselves. Jesus did divine miracles and was himself raised from the dead by the power of the Spirit. And yet he also seemed to suffer thirst, got tired, and expressed human emotions such as anger and sadness. Paul reminds us of these things in various writings, particularly Philippians 2:6–11, where he speaks of the divine and human natures of Jesus and the necessity of this combination in accomplishing his salvific work.

Similarly, consider the nature of Scripture itself. Again you will find factions vying for a variety of positions on the divine nature of Scripture. While wanting to avoid opening the can of worms that the topic of inerrancy can be, I believe it is safe to say that regardless of people's position on the inerrancy of Scripture, most in the church believe it has both divine and human qualities. It is a wholly divine book in that it is "God-breathed" (2 Tim. 3:16) and is God's divine, expressed will for his creation, inspired and inspiring unlike any other book. And while this is true, we can also see that God used human authors as the vessels by which he communicated his will. The various authors all show distinct writing styles, as the biblical documents were written over a span of at least a thousand years by people from a variety of backgrounds—priests, kings, doctors, and fishermen. There is also a variety of genres, from legal code to poetic and artistic expression to precise historical account. Yet it has a continuity that transcends this diversity of time and authorship. The Bible itself is a marvelous and miraculous book that shows both divine and human fingerprints coming together to express the highest form of revelation we know.

Now consider the nature of the church. Scripture itself is clear that the church (*ecclesia*) is the body of believers Jesus himself ordained into existence and that he is its very cornerstone (e.g., Eph. 2:20). It is a spiritual entity created by God to be a place for the gathering of his people and to spread God's message to the ends of the earth. And yet, while all this is true, we are also aware, sometimes painfully, that the church is a very human entity. It is populated by redeemed yet flawed human beings. Each of us brings something unique and important, not only our spiritual gifts but also, by virtue of the diversity God has given to his body, our varied cultures, experiences, skills, and intellectual capacities, as well as a whole host of other characteristics that make us human.

While we have a clear understanding and theology of the divine nature of the church—well-reasoned ecclesiologies, polities, and qualifications for eldership—it is my contention that we have a very underdeveloped understanding of the human nature of the church. We have done little to investigate and understand how it is that people work together and do the work to which God has called them in the forms and structures we have developed. I have often wondered over the fact that besides the mention of various church offices (e.g., Eph. 4:11 names "the apostles, the prophets, the evangelists, the pastors and teachers") and qualifications for eldership (e.g., 1 Tim. 3:1–7), the Bible is largely silent on actual church organization and its form. Over time Christians have developed a few basic forms of polity—namely, the episcopal, presbyterian, and congregational forms, each with various permutations. And biblical values inform church practices to a certain degree. But otherwise, the church has largely been a wild west of organizational forms, structures, cultures, and organizational practices. Some closely follow contemporary corporate structures and hierarchies, thanks to Weber's invisible presence even in our churches; some resemble family businesses; and some are, frankly, organized chaos!

What can we conclude about this? While the Bible gives us all we need for life and godliness and gives us the needed divine message of the gospel for all time for all people, God has seemingly allowed us to figure out the details of how we are to run our churches. Could this be because he understands the situatedness of the local church and knows that each church is by definition an expression of its own local era and context? Further, does he allow us to demonstrate our God-given creativity and initiative when it comes to the best way to organize? We can only speculate here, but for better or worse, how we organize and how we choose to run our churches and Christian organizations seems largely left to us. Thus, insert OB into the vacuum. As you will see, I am not advocating for the wholesale and stringent adoption of OB practice in the church. Rather, I am suggesting that OB can help fill the void that can lead to organizationally underdeveloped churches. The concepts of OB can be an important handmaiden to the church as it seeks to become the beautiful bride, the solid building built on the foundation of the apostles and the prophets, and the healthy body composed of the wonderful and diverse set of gifts God has given his people.

Myriads of well-meaning and highly spiritual leaders often fly by the seat of their pants when it comes to leadership, and the result is at least non-thriving churches and, at worst, churches that leave masses of people hurt or distraught. Look no further than the cautionary tale of the defunct Mars Hill Church in Seattle for an example of not only a leader but an entire system and culture of malaise. As a leadership and OB teacher, when I heard the details of this story I could see various missteps made along the way that OB could have addressed through healthy leadership, alignment of values, good personnel evaluation, and proper ethics management, all of which are marks of healthy churches. I am not saying a good Christian OB book would have prevented this fiasco. But I am saying that the more we can get these concepts into the minds and hands of church leaders at all levels, the greater will be our chances of building healthy, thriving, and successful churches and ministries. This is a hope that helped propel the authoring of this book.

Models of Organizations

Before we begin an in-depth exploration of the various topics of OB, I will set forth the big picture of organizations and a model that can serve as a scaffolding for our thinking about organizational phenomena and the topics of this book. As mentioned earlier, organizations can seem overwhelmingly complex and complicated, like big black boxes filled with mysterious things going on all at once. Models, in a way similar to metaphors, are essentially pictorial representations of abstract concepts or ideas that help us connect concepts to one another in a memorable way. The purpose of this model is to help you break down some of this complexity and mystery, gain a way to isolate and think about various issues, and achieve a better perspective and diagnostic ability. (The term "diagnostic ability" refers to a person's ability to figure out what the organization's issue is in order to better address it.) Part of my goal for this book is to give you a rich set of conceptual tools that will help you think about your organization at a deeper and more nuanced level. The old adage that "to the one with a hammer, everything is a nail" is appropriate here. If one has no model, or limited models, by which to think of an organization, the approach to dealing with organizational issues may be heavy-handed or misguided—that person may try hammering a thumbtack with a sledgehammer, breaking the tack and breaking their thumb in the process! Thus, I will introduce various models along the way, and the first model will set the stage for the rest of the concepts in this book and will be referred to from time to time.

The Five-Level Model of Organizations

We can think of OB phenomena as happening at five distinct levels:

1. Individual level
2. Interpersonal level
3. Group level
4. Organizational level
5. Interorganizational level

This approach moves from the micro level to the macro level of organizational concerns and can be represented by figure 1.1. Each circle represents a smaller unit of analysis—that is, something that should bring an issue into focus. Throughout this book we will explore in depth a variety of issues primarily in the first four levels.

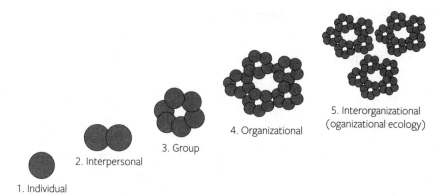

5. Interorganizational
(oganizational ecology)

4. Organizational

3. Group

2. Interpersonal

1. Individual

Fig. 1.1

The Five Levels

Levels	Chapter/Topic
Individual	2 / Individual Differences
Individual	3 / Emotions, Attitudes, and Perceptions
Individual	4 / Motivation, Evaluation, and Rewards
Interpersonal	5 / Interpersonal Relationships in Organizations
Interpersonal/Group	6 / Groups and Teams
Individual/Interpersonal	7 / Conflict Management
Organizational	8 / Leadership, Part 1
Organizational	9 / Leadership, Part 2
Organizational	10 / Organizational Culture

About This Book

This book attempts to explore the world of OB in a way that is relatable to those who serve in leadership and administrative roles in the church, parachurch ministries, and other Christian nonprofit organizations. The needs of these organizations are unique and complex and differ from those of organizations in the for-profit sector, at which most OB books are seemingly aimed. For example, churches and ministries have these five characteristics:

- They are values-driven, existing to accomplish an enduring mission in the world based on Scripture.

- The needs of the local community drive the action.
- They utilize a large, diverse volunteer force to accomplish work.
- Their goals are often spiritual and transcendent and thus challenging to measure.
- Members conflate their work life and community with their spiritual life and community.

Because of these and other complexities, the way OB is discussed in a church or ministry context will differ from the way it is discussed in a standard business-focused OB text, as helpful as those are. The applications and insights needed by leaders in these Christian settings will be different. For example, when discussing personal evaluation and rewards, the perspective on volunteers should differ from the perspective on paid staff, and leaders should consider the theological aspects of rewards, including both God's role and the church's role. Likewise, the dynamics of a multiethnic congregation or of intergenerational leadership may lead to unique challenges. This book will attempt to address the needs and perspectives of churches and help you find value in a way that is relevant and meaningful to your context.

This book will not attempt to cover in depth every area treated in a typical OB textbook but will, rather, focus on the areas felt to be most relevant for church leaders and church contexts. Conversely, some areas not explored in typical OB textbooks will also be addressed here—such as founders and elders, volunteers, one's sense of calling, and spiritual gifts—as they are common in church settings. And of course, Scripture will be utilized as appropriate to support or illustrate various concepts.

Chapters include examples and illustrations along the way to help you think about and apply concepts. To the same end they will conclude with a set of Practical Leadership Application Questions. A case study is also included in most chapters—a fictional, relatable, and challenging scenario accompanied by questions that will help you process the information in the chapter. Further, several chapters include sidebars on the way contemporary churches and ministries are addressing OB topics discussed in the chapter. Endnotes are included for further reference.

It is my hope that, as you read this book, you will be inspired and challenged to consider the ideas as they pertain to your own context.

OB is a broad and insightful field, and while not every idea will work for every church in every situation, there is much value here. As stated previously, this is not a how-to book, and OB is not a silver bullet for all your church woes. We all need divine help and wisdom if we are to lead the complex and robust churches and ministries God has called us to. But perhaps this book can inspire you and give you some needed wisdom and insight as well.

▪ Practical Leadership Application Questions ▪

Consider the following for deeper reflection:

- What are sources of knowledge for you as you lead your church or ministry? How widely read are you? What value do you think the larger body of literature on organizations can add to your own thinking on and practice of leadership?
- What are some issues you are currently facing in your organization, and how do you think a fresh OB perspective could give you new insight?
- What metaphor of organizations do you tend to favor, and how can some of the other metaphors discussed in this chapter help you break out of your current mental model and offer fresh insight?
- What secular business principles do you already employ with little or no consternation (e.g., accounting practices, legal compliance)? How might your reliance on these principles help assuage any concern you have about expanding your knowledge base of OB concepts?
- How deeply have you thought about the human side of your church or ministry? Do you tend to default to certain theological assumptions? How has this either helped or hindered your practice of leadership?

▪ Further Reading ▪

Bolsinger, Tod. *Canoeing the Mountains: Christian Leadership in Uncharted Territory.* Downers Grove, IL: IVP Books, 2015.

Green, David. *Leadership Not by the Book: 12 Unconventional Principles to Drive Incredible Results.* With Bill High. Grand Rapids: Baker Books, 2022.

Irving, Justin A. *Healthy Leadership for Thriving Organizations: Creating Contexts Where People Flourish.* Grand Rapids: Baker Academic, 2023.

Irving, Justin A., and Mark L. Strauss. *Leadership in Christian Perspective: Biblical Foundations and Contemporary Practices for Servant Leaders.* Grand Rapids: Baker Academic, 2019.

Sanders, J. Oswald. *Spiritual Leadership: Principles of Excellence for Every Believer.* Chicago: Moody, 2017.

Stott, John. *Basic Christian Leadership: Biblical Models of Church, Gospel and Ministry.* Downers Grove, IL: InterVarsity, 2002.

2

Individual Differences

Introduction

Leaders tend to look at their organizations as large groups of people all pulling together to do the work of ministry. And while that is true to a certain degree, the basic unit of analysis and interest is the individual, as individuals make up every department, task force, committee, board of elders, and strategic decision-making body, at every level and rank throughout the organization. Thus, understanding people is primary and a good point of departure for OB studies. At this level we are looking at the trees and not the forest of an organization, aiming to see what makes all these wonderful people tick. That is a mixed metaphor, but I trust you get the point!

People are complex, and the way we think about them should be equally complex. While leaders are not necessarily called to be psychologists or spend inordinate amounts of time considering the peculiarities and idiosyncrasies of every individual in their organization, they should nonetheless have a good understanding of human behavior as it relates to people in their work setting.

There are several categories of individual differences that are relevant when we think about individuals and their behavior in organizations. The following sections will review the most important of these: diversity factors, personality, abilities and skills, locus of control, and self-efficacy, as well as calling, spiritual gifts, and creativity.

Diversity Factors

It is no secret that our working world has become richer and more diverse than in the past, with people who differ in color, gender, age, and abilities all working and serving together. People of all ages and socioeconomic backgrounds constitute many of our churches and ministries, in public ministry roles and behind-the-scenes staff and volunteers. An understanding of and appreciation for a diverse work population is vital for leaders in contemporary ministry and can help us showcase the diversity of heaven before a watching world, which often accuses the church world of being monolithic and segregated.

The term "diversity" is not synonymous with equal-employment opportunities or, simply, minorities. It refers to the multiplicity of factors, such as culture, gender, and age, that make people different from others. Moreover, diversity factors are an important part of people's identities— that is, how people refer to and think about themselves in terms of the groups they belong to. Social identity deals with how individuals define their own self-concept through their connections and relationships with social groups.[1] Though our identity in Christ is foremost for Christians, people form identity in other ways as well. For example, an individual who is a woman might also identify with other groups of people, such as African Americans, women pastors, lovers of goldendoodles, and victims of child abuse. To varying degrees, a person's many social identities contribute to who they are as a diverse and unique individual. Because social identity is an important part of a person's psychological makeup, understanding social identity in a work context is crucial, as individual identity is connected to the larger group identity.

Leaders who understand and value the rich diversity in the contemporary church can appreciate a variety of perspectives and needs. Most of us tend to default to our own background and perspective and assume that others see the world the same way we do and want the same things we want. Especially if a leader is part of a majority culture, they may have become immune to the way their own perspective and worldview drives some of the assumptions they make about other people. In a ministry context, becoming aware of others' perspectives can help leaders reduce miscommunication, enhance decision quality, and develop more creative ideas and solutions.

Personality and the Big Five Model

Each of us possesses a unique set of qualities, traits, behaviors, and so on—our personality. Whether it is genetically given (each of us is "fearfully and wonderfully made," Ps. 139:14) or developed over time through experience, a person's personality impacts their behavior in a work context. "Personality" can be defined as a relatively stable set of personal characteristics that have been formed by both genetic and environmental factors over one's lifetime. There have been many theories and models of personality offered over the years; this is one of the more well-worn territories of the field of personal psychology. One popular model is the Myers-Briggs Type Indicator, with its four-letter description of one's personality (I am an INTJ, in case you are wondering). The Enneagram assessment is another popular approach, and it identifies each person with a number between 1 and 9, along with a "wing" number (I am a 9 wing 1).[2] Personality assessments such as these have been effectively used in the workplace for decades and can be used for determining why people behave or react differently to the same situations. For example, why do some people get excited about initiating a new ministry, while others look at the prospect with dread? The answer is that some folks are more open to experience and agreeable, while others are less open and more disagreeable. These are all important personality traits and are discussed below.

Another useful approach to personality in the workplace has been the Big Five theory of personality. It seeks to incorporate the most prevalent traits from a variety of different models, the ones that tend to be shared among them. The five personality characteristics common to most models of personality, called the Big Five, are as follows:

1. Conscientiousness: the ability to stay focused on a few tasks and have good follow-through
2. Extroversion: comfortableness in social situations and the tendency to derive energy from such situations

3. Agreeableness: the ability to get along with others and have pleasant social interactions

4. Emotional stability: the tendency to be consistent in one's mood or disposition

5. Openness to experience: the tendency to explore and like new ideas and projects

Understanding personality can have many benefits in a workplace context. A major application is the area of "job fit," which has to do with whether or not leaders are putting someone in a role that, due to their basic psychological makeup, they are equipped to succeed in. Consider the following examples.

1. *If a role requires attention to detail* and follow-through, someone high in conscientiousness will do better than someone who is low in this area. High conscientiousness is a desirable characteristic in those being considered for promotion to higher levels of management, as they will make sure the job gets done. However, sometimes these people can struggle in areas of leadership that require a bigger-picture mentality that may require some degree of risk and uncertainty. Highly conscientious people want to predict and count on outcomes.

2. *If a role requires someone to be in public* and around people frequently, an extrovert will thrive, while an introvert may struggle and quickly grow weary. While there is a lot of middle ground here and ambiverts can thrive in any situation, understanding who thrives when being with people and who does not thrive, or requires a substantial amount of recovery time, is important.

3. *If a team has too many disagreeable people*, they will invariably work against smooth social functioning. Considering the social makeup of the team and ensuring it has enough agreeable people may help it work properly.

4. *If a person has low emotional stability*, they may have a hard time finding satisfaction in their work regardless of motivational approaches or incentives. Be prepared to give extra attention to helping them find contentment in their work.

5. *If an organization needs a creative spark*, those who are high in openness may be able to help. They can be more adventuresome, and you will hear "But we've never done it that way" a lot less. This is also a great leadership characteristic, as leaders need the ability to dream and cast audacious visions, which requires one to be open when faced with an uncertain future.

In addition to helping with individual role assignments and job fit, understanding personality can help us see that interpersonal and/or group conflict often comes from a clash of personalities. For example, why did Elder Ed get excited and jump on board with the pastor's new vision, while Deacon Debbie did not and gave ten reasons why the church should not head in that direction? Our tendency is to cast her as Debbie Downer or maybe as someone who has less faith than others. The reality may be that she simply is less open to experience or higher in conscientiousness by personality. A clash of personalities like this can in fact be a blessing, as those who are seemingly dream killers are often those who think through vital details that the visionary dreamers do not. The challenge for leaders is to avoid the temptation to castigate those who are different or disagree with them as the bad guys and, instead, to value personality-based perspectives as an asset to the team, one that helps the group see ideas or decisions from many important angles. Be intentional about whom you bring onto the team. Do not pick only those who always agree with you; include those with different personalities and perspectives. This can bring balance and perspective in countless ways. We will discuss group and team composition in depth in chapter 6.

Abilities and Skills

Because we seek to employ those who are skilled in their work and will perform well in their roles, we naturally tend to see a variety of skills and abilities, noticing both the *type* of the skills and the *level* of the skills. Further, because people learn on the job, they will naturally progress and develop in time, opening up new opportunities for both the individual and the organization. Leaders should recognize this variety in skills and abilities, making appropriate room for those who are growing and training those who need development.

In a church context, which utilizes a host of volunteers, we will invariably see people with a wide range of skills and abilities who seek to participate in ministry. It is wise to assess these skills and abilities before making ministry assignments. Consider, for example, listing the required skills and abilities necessary for a particular role and then determining the degree to which each volunteer fits. Sometimes, particularly in smaller churches when the need is greater, we fill slots regardless of ability. When we place someone in a role for which they are not equipped and expect them to learn on the job, we may be setting them up for frustration and failure. If a position involves running the church media system on Sunday morning and you place a willing but unable volunteer in that role, they will be stressed and the service will not go smoothly. Of course, many skills are acquirable, and if the church has adequate time and resources, training someone may work well. Just be prepared for the time and investment that will be required.

Locus of Control

Locus of control (LOC) refers to whether individuals tend to think that things happen, or do not happen, based on their own effort (internal LOC) or outside factors (external LOC). This is considered a relatively stable characteristic, whether it comes from genetics or environment, similar to personality characteristics. Those with an internal LOC tend to believe that a good performance is due to their own skill and hard work. They made it happen. Those with an external LOC tend to believe that other forces, irrespective of their own personal effort, controlled the outcome. In a work context, those with an internal LOC will tend to take more responsibility for their actions and understand how their work leads, or does not lead, to desired results. On the other hand, when those with an external LOC find that their efforts did not achieve the desired results, they will tend to find other explanations. Sentiments such as "We would have been successful if only the budget team had approved the additional funding we requested" or "The executive pastor always favors the other ministries, and that is why ours is failing" can be heard from the lips of "externals." LOC is not necessarily a prescriptive concept, as it is not possible to train someone to be one or the other. However, once you understand this concept, you will see it play out in conversations all the time, and leaders need to be able to discern when the externals are putting too much blame on "boogie men" as excuses for other factors, such as bad strategy or poor execution.

Self-Efficacy

Self-efficacy (SE) is the level of confidence one has in accomplishing a certain task. Those with high self-efficacy will tend to have a can-do attitude and take on their assignments with enthusiasm. On the other hand, those with low self-efficacy tend to drag their feet or doubt their own ability, maybe even giving up before they begin, as they are not confident that they will succeed. Unlike LOC, SE can be developed in time. Leaders need to help low-SE folks start a large task by breaking it down into smaller, more accomplishable tasks so that they can see themselves succeed at first. Then the leader should give them tasks with ever-increasing degrees of difficulty. For example, imagine you are tasking someone who you feel has the ability to run an event, but they have never done so before and are afraid, because of their low SE, that they will not succeed. Begin by giving them small pieces of the process at first, such as scheduling a meeting with another team leader just to talk about the event. Then have them invite five people to a planning meeting to discover ideas from others. They will begin to see themselves succeed in small ways. The cumulative effect will build their SE, and while they may stumble at points, they will come to see that they can, in fact, handle this responsibility.

Calling

The sense that one has a calling, or has been called, is a powerful and important individual difference in a ministry context. A call can be viewed as one's perception of being marked for a specific vocation (from the Latin *vocare*, meaning "voice") or something else. While the concept of calling developed in the Christian tradition, it has transcended religious contexts and can be applied to those who feel led to pursue a profession such as medicine or visual art. Calling is held to be a primary source of purpose and vision in pastoral leadership and typically sets the course of one's life as a minister.[3] It can give a person long-term resilience in the face of obstacles and can clarify the direction of one's life work.

As such, recognizing and affirming a calling in the lives of those who serve in our ministries is a vital leadership activity. While many pastors no doubt can relate to the awkward situation in which a parishioner professes a calling that has no basis in reality, when we see a genuine call, we need to give it credence and value, help nurture it, and give the person opportunities to grow in the relevant areas. Some people may be early on in recognizing and developing a sense of calling, while others may be mature and fully engaged in the work to which they are called. Seeking to help people engage in their calling is difficult at times but can also be one of the most rewarding parts of leadership, as we enable them to fulfill their God-given destiny and see them flourish in our midst.

While a calling may give purpose and vitality to one's work, there can be negative consequences to working in an area of one's call, particularly for those who are strongly driven or have a type A personality (we will discuss this concept fully in chap. 3). Their strong sense of commitment can make it difficult to distinguish work from other important areas of life, such as family, or recognize the need to disconnect from work and recharge. A blurring (or demolishing) of healthy work-life boundaries makes one feel that they are always "on," needing to be constantly available to their teams, checking email, supervising all events and activities, and inordinately carrying the weight of responsibility on their shoulders for the success of the work. For these folks, finding a healthy balance and making time to be off work is important to maintaining long-term success.

Spiritual Gifts

Perhaps the most biblical of all the individual differences I will discuss in this chapter are spiritual gifts—namely, those found in Ephesians 4, Romans 12, and 1 Corinthians 12. People working in ministry will likely cite both their calling and their gifting as foundational to their ministry and will be serving in roles that incorporate both. In fact, we are admonished to do so: "For just as each of us has one body with many members, and these members do not all have the same function, so in Christ we, though many, form one body, and each member belongs to all the others" (Rom. 12:4–5). One could cite this idea, which has to do with a proper fit for those serving in the church, as a biblical OB concept.

Ephesians 4:11–12 recognizes five primary gifts that are common in a ministry context: apostle, prophet, evangelist, pastor, and teacher. Romans 12:6–8 adds leadership and teaching, and 1 Corinthians 12:28 includes apostles, prophets, teachers, workers of miracles, and helpers. It is not the purpose of this book to exegete the passages or give nuanced interpretations of what these gifts look like; suffice it to say that we should recognize these gifts as important differences between individuals and should assist our people in working in areas that incorporate their gifts. Particularly when working with people who are new to the ministry (e.g., volunteers), leaders should view gift recognition as an important teaching task, as it can help set the course for those just beginning to understand and enter into their role in the body of Christ. When people recognize and begin to operate in their area of giftedness, it brings great blessings to them as well as others.

Creativity

The ability to create is powerful and wonderful. In Scripture, creating is the first act we see God undertaking (Gen. 1). He is the ultimate Creator, having made everything we can see (John 1:3), and as those made in his image, we also share in this creative ability and impulse. While many people generate new things or ideas, we can see this creative ability more strongly in some people than in others, thus making creativity an important area of difference between individuals in a ministry context. In a work context creativity is the ability to break away from habits and routines, to innovate and see things in new ways. Leadership, as having to do with vision and change, must have an element of creativity in order to help drive the organization forward.

The need for creativity across an organization has become an important competency to think about strategically. In fact, in a competitive marketplace, hiring for and empowering creativity can become a competitive advantage. Of course, churches typically do not think in terms of competitive advantage, but many churches sure could use a good dose of creativity in terms of how they think about reaching their communities and changing to meet new needs and new generations. Recognizing and empowering the creative impulse in people may help unleash lots of new "possibility thinking" that may, in turn, lead to novel approaches to ministry. Instead of being tradition bound or fearful of change, consider how your organization can tap into the creative potential in your ministry workforce. Leading creative people and giving space for innovation can, of course, be challenging, and routine and stability are indeed called for. Nevertheless, recognize and appreciate those who bring new ideas to the table, give space for new ideas in appropriate ways, and watch how these people thrive and the organization stays fresh.

Putting It All Together: Individual Differences and Job, Role, and Organizational Fit

So far we have discussed the individual differences between people in a work context. Now we will discuss how these differences can help people serve with maximum effectiveness and how the organization can align its practice of placing its people. Praying for those we have chosen to include as ministry partners is a given, and any and all attempts to determine fit should include ample time of prayer on behalf of those who "work hard among you" (1 Thess. 5:12). It is my hope that the following section will give you practical advice that will help you place those in your ministry well.

"Fit" is the OB term used to describe how one is incorporated into the organization in a healthy and optimal way. Just as clothing should fit, a person should fit into the organization at multiple levels. The following model can help leaders think through the variety of ways in which people can and should fit into the organization.

To determine fit at various levels, ask the following:

- Functional/role fit: Does this role give the person opportunities that are aligned with their personality, skills, gifts, and abilities, as well as where they are in their development trajectory? Do they have the skills for this role, or can they acquire them?
- Task fit: Do they regularly perform routines and activities that require their skills, and are these tasks motivating? Are they naturally good at these tasks?
- Interpersonal/relational fit: Do their relationships with their supervisor and direct reports encourage them to be their best?

- Organizational fit: Does the organization itself allow opportunities for them to thrive, grow, and make a difference with what is important to them? Do they fit with the cultural norms and values of the organization?
- Calling and career fit: Does this role fit with their general passions, disposition, and calling? Is it compatible with their personality and disposition for things like stress, risk, stability, and so on?

Fit can be determined at various points. Initially, leaders should seek to determine fit up front, in the preboarding or onboarding stages of hiring or volunteer placement. Some candidates will "inflate" their experience to fit the role if they are eager to get the job, so basic questions in an interview may not help much. Many organizations use a variety of professional personality assessments, such as the Myers-Briggs Type Indicator, versions of which are tailor-made for organizations and job functions. Additionally, conducting interviews at multiple levels of the organization can help you determine fit from a variety of vantage points. While these processes may cost time and money, they can, in the long run, save untold amounts of time and money, not to mention hurt and frustration, by determining who will fit with the roles and needs of the organization. Particularly for managerial and leadership roles, verifying qualities such as conscientiousness as well as relevant work skills is critical, as a misstep here runs the risk of subjecting good people to poor or unqualified oversight.

Determining "calling fit" up front may be tricky, though new candidates should be asked about their sense of calling, as appropriate. It may become clear right away whether the role is a good fit or not. Often, people will get their foot in the door of a church or organization in the hopes of moving to a better job and fulfilling their long-term calling aspirations, only to painfully find later on that the opportunity they thought was there did not materialize. In higher education I have, on numerous occasions, seen people hired for administrative roles and found out later they really wanted to become teachers and saw this initial role as their way in. In a church context, people may apply for an administrative role, with aspirations to pastor their own congregation. While these are, of course, important and noble aspirations, we should try to determine them early on, be clear about whether the initial role will fulfill their aspirations, and be honest about foreseeable growth opportunities. This can save both parties time and heartache.

Determining culture and organization fit is also not easy but can be done by paying attention to what candidates naturally talk about early on. Most will likely be aware of the organization and make sure it is a good choice for them before applying or joining, but some may look only

---

CURRENT ISSUES

The Five Seasons of Calling Development Model

The focus of my doctoral dissertation was calling and leader identity.* I explored the life stories of long-term successful pastors and ministry leaders in order to determine how their sense of calling developed over their life in various seasons and how it impacted their own identity. The conventional wisdom about calling is that it is a one-time, perhaps supernatural encounter that people have in which they hear a voice, have a vision, or experience some other encounter of biblical proportions—think of Moses and the burning bush (Exod. 3) or Paul on the road to Damascus (Acts 9:1–9). While this prototypical calling experience does happen, my research revealed the more subtle and pervasive ways in which calling was realized and experienced over the entire life of the leader. The typical sequence can be seen in what I call the five seasons of calling:

1. Awaiting: experiences in childhood or youth that, in hindsight, were precursors of one's eventual life calling
2. Awareness: the recognition of the call through spiritual awakening and involvement, sometimes including signs and wonders or a deep sense of conviction gained through the day-in and day-out satisfaction of serving
3. Actualizing: the actualization of the call through experience, mentoring, and preparation for vocational service (this is how the calling is further refined and prepared for)
4. Anguishing: a struggle to separate from previous relationships, roles, and identities—an internal struggle to fulfill the calling that

at the job, irrespective of the organization. Leaders should be up front about the organization's culture and its values early on. Conversely, while culture congruity may seem like an obvious benefit, some organizations are intentional about seeking an outside perspective for certain roles and are open to those who may, on the surface, not seem like a good fit culturally. Organizations run the risk of becoming myopic or inbred if

comes from the expectations of others, expectations of themselves, and/or a competing identity
5. Acceptance: the integration of identity and the merging of faith and work, yet accompanied by ongoing wrestling with preferred roles and possible selves

This research shows another important facet to what it means to be called: calling is not necessarily a one-and-done experience that brings complete certainty and satisfaction with one's ministry role. Rather, my model suggests that calling can be more developmental and ambiguous, something that adapts over time to new experiences and realizations. Further, it may be normal for people to revisit and reenvision their calling during different seasons of life.

This approach to understanding calling can be helpful for leaders seeking to onboard and develop their staff and volunteers. Instead of asking, for example, "Does this person have a call on their life?" (a one-and-done mentality), consider asking questions such as these:

- How is the person's calling manifest during this season of life?
- How can we help them fully explore their calling and give them opportunities to realize it in our ministry?
- Can we provide the type of mentoring and training that will help them fulfill their call?
- Are they wrestling with their calling, and can we help them find clarity, certainty, and acceptance in this season with us?

* Frank Markow, "Calling and Leader Identity: Utilizing Narrative Analysis to Construct a Stage Model of Calling Development" (PhD diss., Regent University, 2007).

they hire only those who are like them and shut out those whom the Lord might bring in to offer them new ideas, skills, and vision. We will more fully discuss organizational culture in chapter 10.

In addition to undertaking the initial process of determining fit, leaders and managers need to be cognizant of fit at all levels as an ongoing process. They need to reassess various fits and make room for and encourage growth as people develop. How well people fit should become clear in time, but being intentional at various points is important. Performance evaluation or review time is an obvious occasion for this intentionality. In addition, good feedback and an open-door approach can help both the employee and management know how well the employee fits into the role and the organization. Of course, people change and grow, and they desire more from their roles or want more interesting and challenging roles over time. This is natural and should be expected. A forward-thinking organization needs to anticipate and allow for this. A real challenge to keeping talented people can be accommodating staff members' growth paths and their calling or career aspirations. There may be more desire than room to fulfill these aspirations. But having a strategic and intentional approach that acknowledges and makes room for people's growth is vital in developing a healthy work environment where people want to stay for the long haul.

While some of these fit factors can be addressed by the organization, some cannot. For example, leaders can seek to determine how well one's personality, skills, and abilities fit into their tasks. They can also help ensure people are in a group and setting that bring out their best. Yet some are beyond the organization's ability to change, and they require appropriate honesty. For example, if a person has a sense of calling that cannot be met in the organization (at least not at that time), or if the role is too demanding for their disposition and personality, an honest conversation may be needed. Prospective staff may not be a good fit for the ministry at a variety of levels. Differences in philosophy of ministry, or leadership and management style, are not likely to change on the organization's end, and leaders may not want to hire "prophets" who see it as their mission to challenge the system. Of course, all organizations need to be open to the input of its people and seek appropriate change, but some differences are deep and intractable, and it may be best to encourage people who differ from the organization in this way to find a place to serve that is more in keeping with their deeply held sensibilities.

■ Practical Leadership Application Questions ■

- How sensitive have you been to the diversity in your organization? How has this diversity been a blessing, and in what ways has it been challenging?
- How aware of individual personality are you? Are you intentional in matching people's roles to their personality? Have personality differences led to conflict in your organization? If so, how have you dealt with it?
- Does your organization assess the skill level of personnel or volunteers before placing them in roles? Do you seek people with existing skills, or do you train them on the job?
- How do you seek to help people fulfill their calling in your organization? Are you intentional in this area, or does it catch you by surprise when people share their calling? How do you help people use their spiritual gifts in their assignments?
- How well does your organization determine job, role, organizational, or cultural fit in the hiring process? What is being done to reassess these kinds of fit throughout people's tenure in the organization?

CASE STUDY

Right Person, Wrong Role

Erik was a rising star in the youth group. He attended the group every week, volunteered for almost every opportunity and outreach initiative, and was faithful in his commitment to the church. Moreover, all the other kids loved him. He was a kid magnet and was always bringing new, unchurched youth to the services each week, and he would invest in them personally throughout the week. During breakout groups his was always the largest, as the other kids wanted to be part of his group—it was always fun and exciting. His gifting and talent did not go unrecognized by the church leadership either. Erik was frequently a point of discussion at staff meetings, and several people mentioned that they would love to bring him on staff in the future.

Then, one day, the opportunity arose. One of the longtime staff youth leaders decided to leave for a full-time senior pastorate in another city, and the church needed to hire someone to take her place. Together, the staff agreed that Erik should be the number one candidate. It was a no-brainer to them—or at least *most* of them. Karla was not so sure he would be a good fit.

She protested that since the previous role was filled by a female, the new role should go to a female, just to keep the gender balance in place and show the female population of the youth group that women were valued as leaders in the church. She also felt that while Erik was indeed a charming young man and showed potential, he had not proven himself in some areas that were included in the role, such as planning events, recruiting and training new leaders, and dealing with the tough issues of youth ministry, like angry parents, kids who misbehaved behind the church building during services, and cooperation with other staff.

The staff consensus prevailed, and despite Karla's concerns, Erik was hired. Everyone was excited, especially the youth, who saw Erik as a new type of leader. He was exciting and "one of them." He brought a new energy and vision to the group and began talking about all he wanted to accomplish in the future.

But after a couple of months, some cracks began to show in Erik's shiny new armor. For example, he dropped the ball on some important items in planning for the next outreach event. Parental-consent forms were overlooked, so the church was opened to liability; he booked accommodations too late, so some kids were unable to go, much to their disappointment; and the event came in way over budget. Further, he was having some personality issues with some of the other youth leaders: he tended to dominate conversations, would not try to build consensus, and was always seemingly flying by the seat of his pants in terms of planning for each week's youth group. "Let's just see what the Lord does" was his mantra. Some saw him as very spiritual and liked his spontaneity. Yet others saw his approach as an excuse for laziness or an inability to think through how a service should go, and many other leaders were left scrambling to finish their preparations before youth group.

In time, the youth leadership pool began to dwindle, and the group therefore began to lose attendance. The youth-department issues were taking more time at staff meetings, and Erik was frequently absent. Parents were complaining about the youth group, and the administrative staff always had issues with the department— forms not being completed, receipts not being turned in, and so on. Erik himself was also seemingly less than happy these days and began taking on more speaking engagements at local churches that desired to bring his charismatic fire to their group as well. He was heard telling others, "I've been called to preach, not do a bunch of paperwork!"

Karla tried hard not to give the other staff an "I told you so," but it was clear that her concerns had been warranted. Some of the other staff members continued to support this rising star and would cover for him, but it was now obvious to all—Erik was a problem and needed to be dealt with.

Questions for Discussion

- Using the individual differences introduced in this chapter, how would you describe Erik? Consider, for example, personality, skills, and calling.
- What could have been done up front, before Erik was hired, to make sure he was a good fit for the role?
- Were the staff justified in their enthusiasm for Erik, or were they shortsighted and mesmerized by his charisma? How could Karla have made a better case for her concerns?
- What can the church do to keep Erik and help him perform better—or should they cut their losses and let him go?

▪ Further Reading ▪

Dawson, Patrick, and Constantine Andriopoulos. *Managing Change, Creativity and Innovation*. 4th ed. Thousand Oaks, CA: Sage, 2021.

Klein, William W., and Daniel J. Steiner. *What Is My Calling? A Biblical and Theological Exploration of Christian Identity*. Grand Rapids: Baker Academic, 2022.

Loritts, Bryan. *Insider Outsider: My Journey as a Stranger in White Evangelicalism and My Hope for Us All*. Grand Rapids: Zondervan, 2018.

Lussier, Robert N., and John R. Hendon. *Human Resource Management: Functions, Applications, and Skill Development*. 4th ed. Thousand Oaks, CA: Sage, 2021.

Wilson, Todd. *The Enneagram Goes to Church: Wisdom for Leadership, Worship, and Congregational Life*. Downers Grove, IL: InterVarsity, 2021.

3

Emotions, Attitudes, and Perceptions

Introduction

The previous chapter explored the variety of ways leaders can consider the uniqueness of the individuals in their churches and ministries. We are all unique and can make important contributions to the workplace because of this uniqueness. In addition to understanding these individual-difference factors, it is important to recognize the affective dimension of our workforce. "Affect" is the term used in OB to describe feelings, inclinations, and dispositions—the less tangible and more subjective dimension of individuals that is a driver of much behavior that is relevant to work performance. As those made in the image of God, people possess a full range of complex emotions and attitudes that lead them to perceive the world around them in fascinating and important ways. We make a mistake if we overlook this important dimension of people in our ministries, assuming they are simply rational working-units that are there to complete assigned tasks. When we envision people showing up to work, whether they are staff or volunteers, we should visualize them walking in with a suitcase—their emotional and attitudinal baggage—which, in time, they will unpack in one way or another. The baggage will impact how they perceive us as leaders, how they respond to and interact with their coworkers, how they adapt to their work environment, and what challenges and stresses they will face. This chapter will explore the emotions, attitudes, and perceptions that people bring with them every day and will hopefully give you a new awareness and appreciation of these factors so you can be more effective in sailing through the sometimes turbulent and challenging waters they may bring.

Emotion, Mood, and Emotional Contagion

"Emotion" can be defined as "a state of physiological arousal accompanied by changes in facial expressions, gestures, posture, and subjective feeling."[1] Primary emotions are those such as surprise, joy, anger, fear, sadness, anticipation, and jealousy. The workplace itself may elicit such emotions in people on a regular basis. For example, consider the following scenario:

> Senior Pastor Paul walks in, very upbeat, filled with excitement and enthusiasm. He says, "Today, ladies and gentlemen, I'd like to share with you a new vision I feel the Lord has given me for the next season of our church," and then proceeds to give some broad brushstrokes for his new vision. While Stacey is swept up in the excitement and enthusiasm and indeed senses the Lord's leading in this, she is also feeling other emotions. For example, she senses some fear, wondering what all this means for her job and for her team. Will she be reassigned? Will her team be broken up? She is also a little angry. This new vision, in reality, is something she brought to him over a year ago. Why is he not giving her some credit here? Overall, the new vision is a mixed bag for her emotionally.

The above scenario highlights that emotions at work can be complex and challenging. Sometimes emotions are clear-cut—people are excited or angry. And while we know what we *should* feel in the above scenario (of course, we should share in the pastor's enthusiasm), what we actually feel is more complex. Excitement and fear, enthusiasm and dread, are all competing for emotional space in our hearts. "Should" is a tough mandate when it comes to feelings. The way people feel may be at odds with expected responses, particularly in a Christian work context, where there may be an expectation, either explicit or implicit, to "consider it pure joy" (James 1:2) and put a happy spin on any news or event. An impassive Christian stoicism that suppresses our true feelings is a dangerous attitude to harbor personally or engender in a workforce. Leaders in churches and Christian ministries need to recognize the power emotions have and should make an appropriate place for them to be expressed. If we sweep emotional issues under the rug, eventually someone will trip over the bump! Further, we should not assume everyone will respond to circumstances the same way. The goal should be to develop healthy and open places for honest dialogue and to try to prevent the common "stuff and bury it" attitude that stifles true liberty in the workplace. Of course, there are appropriate times and places for sharing emotions. Typically, one-on-one meetings work best unless the group has developed high levels of trust and transparency over time. Regardless, leaders should seek to develop a culture that is sensitive to feelings and allows people the freedom to feel and express those feelings.

A mood is similar to feelings but is described as a more generalized state that is a *result* of feelings and that can last longer than the inciting emotion. For example, one may become fearful of upcoming changes in the organizational structure or have a tense encounter with a co-worker that goes unresolved. The emotion or emotions generated by the experience lead to a more pervasive sense of anxiety, maybe even minor depression, until the issue is resolved satisfactorily. Moods such as "anxious," "frustrated," "calm," or "bored" are common. Some people are more prone to mood swings or moodiness due to personality factors such as those described in chapter 2 or due to personality issues. If a leader thinks a staff member has a consistent mood that negatively impacts their work or workplace, it may be beyond the leader's skill or place to help, and they may—appropriately, through human resources—encourage counseling. While our churches may be filled with healthy and joyful personalities, they may also attract those with mood and personality issues that are challenging to deal with. While seeking to be warm and open, leaders should always maintain appropriate emotional distance and not endeavor to counsel. The leader is there to lead, not be a counselor or personal confidant, and a confusion of these roles can get both parties into emotional and legal trouble.

"Emotional contagion" is the idea that emotions can be spread to others in the workplace. For example, a leader who is upbeat and positive will generally impact the mood of the team positively. On the other hand, a leader who is angry or fearful will likely impact the team negatively, and the effect may spread to others as well. This is why—particularly for those leading others—a person's emotions and moods should be in check and considered before they engage others. If, for example, you are scheduled to lead a team in a creative brainstorming session and you just received some bad news before walking into the meeting, be sure to allow yourself space to deal with this news before you enter the room. If you enter the room in a state of anger or frustration, the emotions will spread quickly, and you will not get the best from your people in a meeting designed to get them thinking creatively. Try to set the appropriate emotional tone at the beginning of one-on-one or group meetings. Getting people engaged in positive and upbeat topics before a meeting will break the ice. A small amount of effort in seeding "good vibes" up front will go a long way in making a meeting healthy and productive.

Is it ever appropriate to share negative emotions in a workplace setting? Sometimes. We can harness negative emotions to motivate our people. For example, if a leader and/or their executive team have learned of a serious event that suggests the organization needs to make some changes quickly, expressing their own emotions can get the attention of others and let them know that the situation is serious. If a leader enters a serious meeting with a light or smiley affect, people may not take the circumstances as seriously as they should. While I am not advocating leading through fear or anger and am not suggesting you make this your default approach to getting people's attention, expressing a sense of fear or anger can, at times, be an effective motivator. Even Jesus expressed righteous anger and got the attention of the entire crowd and religious establishment (John 2:13–17). Fear does motivate—but use it sparingly.

Emotional and Social Intelligence

Emotional intelligence has gained a great deal of popularity and generated much conversation over the past thirty years, and it has almost become conventional wisdom in the workplace. Daniel Goleman popularized the topic in the 1990s with his books *Emotional Intelligence* and *Working with Emotional Intelligence*.[2] Later, along with Richard Boyatzis and Annie McKee, he popularized the concept for leadership with the book *Primal Leadership*.[3] "Emotional intelligence" (referred to as EI or EQ) is typically defined as the ability to do the following things:

- Be aware of one's own feelings
- Manage one's emotions
- Motivate oneself
- Express sympathy toward others
- Handle relationships with others

A person with high EI is self-aware and can manage their own emotions at any given moment. While we typically think of emotion as something that hijacks rational thought and action (and indeed it can), EI suggests that people can prevent this from happening by monitoring and controlling emotions rather than being controlled by them. Expressing emotions can be helpful, but unchecked emotions, particularly in leaders, can lead to disaster. Some leaders are oblivious to their own emotional state and are unable to control themselves when their buttons are pushed, and they are seemingly incapable of understanding their own or others' emotions. Psychopathy, an extreme form of emotional disconnection, is a disorder that may be impacting leaders who are callous toward the feelings of others and who advance in leadership by ingratiating themselves with their superiors.[4] These types of leaders are no fun to work for, and they often self-destruct when upper management begins to understand the damage they are inflicting. However, such people are anomalies, and most of us can become more aware of, and control, our emotions in the workplace. Here are a few points and instructions to consider:

- Emotional changes happen because of your brain chemistry changing and sending out different signals so your body can react. They are God's way of preparing us to take action.
- Become more aware of your own physiological changes under stress. For example, is your heart rate speeding up, or do you feel blood rushing to your head? This is a sign of emotions rising.
- At the onset of such a change, name the emotion. Are you feeling angry or sad or jealous or confused? Ask the Lord to help you identify and name the emotion.
- Mentally step away from the emotion. You can recognize it, but it does not need to force a reaction. Say to yourself things like, "Lord,

help me stay in the game here." Take a few breaths and, if needed, calmly walk out for a minute to compose yourself.

You cannot stop your emotions, but you can stop them from dictating the way you behave. Learn to recognize what your body is telling your heart, and—in Jesus's name—tell your heart to be calm!

Social intelligence (SI) refers to the same ideas but in a broader group context. It involves understanding the mood of the room. Consider this second part of the scenario with Pastor Paul:

> As Pastor Paul winds down his enthusiastic speech, he notices several people with perplexed and anxious looks on their faces. Thinking for a moment, he continues, "While I feel certain this is the best move for us as a church, I'm sure it must raise questions and concerns for some of you. I want to assure you, we will do all we can to keep everyone in their current roles and will consider your own thoughts and concerns during this transition. We are a team, and all voices are welcome." Stacey immediately takes a breath and relaxes. She knows Paul's heart. They have gone through changes before, and she is reassured by his acknowledgment of her unspoken concerns and welcomes the chance to be involved in the planning for this new change.

With just a small amount of social intelligence, Pastor Paul goes a long way to calm the fears of Stacey and, no doubt, others in the room. Being aware of and sensitive to people's feelings is a vital leadership skill and helps build trust and rapport among the team (for more on building trust, see chap. 5).

EI and SI are considered to be learnable skills, not static personality traits. While some people have more natural or acquired EI or SI, they can be developed with attention and practice, and leaders can go a long way in serving their people well by acquiring both. If you have ever seen those with high EI or SI in action, you will know that it is a beautiful thing to see and brings peace and liberty to others in a God-honoring way.

Emotional Labor

Emotional labor refers to the type of work that requires one to assume a happy posture even in circumstances that are not always happy. Of course, those in ministry never face this (I hope you can detect my tongue in my cheek here!). Emotional labor requires that we enhance, fake, or suppress our true emotions, and this in turn can lead to stress. In secular business, it is often required in customer-facing roles, where frontline staff are trained that "the customer is always right."[5] In ministry we might think of our parishioners here. While being stern or frank occasionally has its place for leaders, more often than not one is tasked with helping people see the bright side of situations, making lemonade from lemons, and generally seeing the way forward. Those in ministry are often in unpleasant situations that require them to keep things positive and upbeat. We serve a God who is for us, who is with us, and who makes a way for us in all circumstances. Nevertheless, even those with a strong and genuine faith in the goodness of God may become "weary in doing good," despite the biblical admonishment not to do so (Gal. 6:9). This weariness leads to stress and burnout for many in the church, who are constantly "on" and feel the need to have the right answer and a cheerful disposition at all times.

Stress and Burnout

Organizational stress is a very real concern in contemporary organizations, particularly busy churches and ministries. In addition to the normal stresses of life we all face (e.g., parenting, marital issues, financial issues) and the above-mentioned emotional labor, those in ministry often encounter stress due to their roles. While we may think of stress as an emotional reaction, it is biologically rooted. Stress occurs when a person's adaptive response to a stimulus places excessive psychological or physical demands on that person. When a stressor is encountered, chemicals such as adrenaline and cortisol are produced to make them mentally and physical prepared for a threat. This is a natural process and can help people in emergencies, but prolonged stress may cause serious problems and lead to physical symptoms like high blood pressure and headaches and psychological symptoms like anxiety and depression. This leads to changes in behavior; we can become irritable, withdraw, have outbursts of anger, or have difficulty sleeping.[6] Even in contemporary civilization our brains have a hard time distinguishing between a primal or physical threat and a non-life-threatening demand placed on us by our job.

Workplace Stress Factors

Stress in the workplace is typically caused by the following factors:

- Task demands: those associated with the specific job a person has
- Physical demands: those associated with the job's physical setting and requirements
- Role demands: those associated with the expected behaviors of a particular position in a group or organization
- Interpersonal demands: group pressures, leadership responsibilities, personality conflicts, and so forth

In ministry, there is a multitude of stressors that are simply part of the work. In addition to the constant grind of preparing for weekly services, there are seasonal events (e.g., holidays), special-occasion events (e.g., weddings, funerals, commissioning services), special productions, and outreach initiatives. Moreover, there is the ever-present reality of dealing with crises, staff conflicts, boards and committees, deadlines, a lack of boundaries, the tendency to carry others' burdens, and a sense of urgency toward the work to which they feel called. Ministry is not for the fainthearted!

We all deal with stress differently. Some are more optimistic and tend to feel that things will work out. Thus, they do not typically stress as much. Conversely, those who are pessimistic feel that the worst will happen and therefore experience more stress. In addition, type A and type B personality types respond to stress differently. People with type A personalities famously tend to be competitive and highly committed to work and have a strong sense of urgency. People with type B personalities, on the other hand, are less competitive and committed and have a weaker sense of urgency. Finally, hardiness is one's ability to effectively deal with and manage the stress that life's demands generate. In short, we can say that some people are more likely than others to place stress on themselves and/or more able than others to deal with stress effectively.

While stress is generally considered a bad thing in the workplace, too little stress can also be a negative factor. For example, consider the motivating influence of an impending deadline or event. Without these deadlines or looming tasks, we tend to procrastinate and not engage. "Eustress" is good stress, an optimal level of stress, between too much and too little, and it is important for leaders to consider in the workplace. So, too, is the value of setting motivating deadlines and assigning tasks that are appropriately demanding and move people to action.

An extreme form of stress, burnout, is a major concern for those in the contemporary workplace in general and ministry in particular. In addition to facing the demanding nature of ministry work, those in ministry typically are highly committed and identify with their work. Contemporary ministries are often event driven and oriented toward serving people. Those serving a large church may feel the constant pressure of the next event and the weight of throngs of people and tasks demanding attention, all while dealing with many other typical professional pressures such as budgets and staffing problems. A ministry colleague commented to me that up to half of his church staff were on the verge of burnout at any given moment.

Archibald Hart has done extensive research and writing on burnout and clergy. He describes burnout as a psychological process in which work stress leads to emotional exhaustion, which in turn causes the person to become withdrawn and to lack confidence in themselves and in God.[7] Additionally, those experiencing burnout suffer from depersonalization and low personal accomplishment, struggle to deal with problems, and no longer have the joy of their work.[8]

While it is beyond the scope of this book to give a full treatment of burnout, leaders need to be able to spot the symptoms in themselves and those they lead. We may see changes in behavior that are indicative of extreme stress problems. For example, if a normally gregarious staff member is becoming withdrawn, excessively tardy or absent, discourteous, or unable to make good decisions, they may be showing symptoms of burnout. We can help by being aware of demands placed on people and by considering the person's fit with the role and work culture, giving adequate recovery time after stressful events or seasons, helping to set appropriate boundaries, and encouraging and allowing for regular physical exercise. These practices are foundational to helping others deal with stress and avoid burnout. Some churches even offer people in key leadership roles a sabbatical, an extended period away from work during which the person can recuperate and prepare for a new season.

Attitudes

While the term "attitude" has become synonymous for "bad attitude" in the common vernacular—as in "She was sportin' a 'tude!"—attitude is an important concept in OB and refers to a mental state of readiness that has been learned and optimized over time through experience. Attitudes are important, as they can be determinants of behavior and are linked to a host of other psychological factors such as emotions, personality, and motivations (see chap. 4 on motivation). Attitudes are learned yet can change over time. They are the emotional basis for relationships with others and are thus important to understand in organizational contexts, which so heavily rely on smooth interpersonal relationships. Attitudes have a cognitive, emotional, and behavioral component. In other words, they impact how we think and rationalize, how we feel, and how we act in certain situations and contexts. Some important attitudes in an organizational context are described in the following paragraphs.

Attribution and Attribution Errors

Attribution has to do with what we perceive to be the reasons behind certain outcomes. We *attribute* causes to certain behaviors or events. Self-enhancement is the tendency to enhance our own self-perceptions (e.g., our abilities, performance, looks) in comparison to another reference group, and our self-serving bias gives us credit for successes and blames external forces for failure. Conversely, the "fundamental attribution error" suggests that if something goes wrong for other people, it was their fault and not the result of external factors. In a work context, these factors can play out in a variety of ways. For example, they may influence the way a team describes its performance. If the team is successful, the members will give themselves credit based on their own contributions. If they fail, they will blame external factors, such as other people or circumstances. We tend to blame others based on their characteristics—"If he wasn't so lazy he would have been better prepared"—and give ourselves undue credit—"Of course I got the new ministry assignment; I worked harder than everyone else." Understanding and recognizing these types of attitudes is important in matters of fairness, and it helps people avoid making biased judgments.

Bias, Stereotypes, and Prejudice

People tend to inaccurately categorize and characterize people according to the groups of which they are a part. Bias and stereotypes attribute people's performance and character to factors outside the individual, based largely on misperceptions of an overall group. Common (and misguided) workplace biases are attitudes about women and members of historical minority groups such as Hispanics and African Americans.

Prejudice is another attitude seen in organizations, particularly when the work involves crossing cultural or racial lines. It is a largely fixed attitude, belief, or emotion held by an individual about another individual or group, based on faulty or unsubstantiated data. It involves inflexible generalizations that are resistant to change or evidence and is self-oriented rather than other-oriented. Leaders should face the challenge of dealing with their own prejudices and those of followers, and skilled leaders need to find ways to appropriately interact with followers from different cultural backgrounds.[9] Our larger US cultural conversation has, in recent years, become sensitized to and centered around this important topic, and workplace inclusion and antiracism efforts are becoming commonplace. Churches are places where members of all groups should be welcome and included and should excel, and church leaders should seek to determine whether and how bias or stereotypes might be negatively impacting their workforce.

Cognitive Dissonance and Distortions

Have you ever encountered a situation that required you to believe two or more competing truths at the same time? For example, imagine a pastor who has personally treated you very well over the years, has cared for you and your family generously, and has led the church through many years of ministry success. Then you find out he is being accused of inappropriate conduct with some female parishioners. The revelation leaves you mentally and emotionally torn: You have love and respect for someone who, as it turns out, was not a decent person in ways that matter. How can you, a genuinely decent person, love and respect someone like that?

This is cognitive dissonance, the discomfort that comes from facing the fact that two competing ideas are true at the same time. This comes into play organizationally when, as in the above example, we encounter moral or ethical dilemmas that require us to challenge our preconceived ideas about someone or something. When we are faced with this dissonance, there are different options for reducing it and the negative feelings it brings: we can change our previous conceptions (e.g., "Now that I think about it, the pastor was always a bit of a jerk; this does not surprise me"), challenge the accusations themselves (e.g., "I'm sure these women are overreacting to the pastor's affection"), or "shoot the messenger" (e.g., "Boy, the rumor mill is really cranked up over this one; I'm sure they will get to the bottom of this and find the truth here").

Cognitive *distortions* are a more recent topic of discussion in the psychological field and have significance for understanding the way people's attitudes manifest themselves in the workplace. Here is a list of the most common cognitive distortions:

1. All-or-nothing thinking: You see things in black-and-white categories. If your performance falls short of perfect, you see yourself as a total failure.
2. Overgeneralization: You see a single negative event as a never-ending pattern of defeat.
3. Mental filters: You pick out a single negative detail and dwell on it exclusively, with the result that your vision of all reality becomes darkened.
4. Disqualifying the positive: You reject positive experiences by insisting they do not count for some reason or another.
5. Jumping to conclusions: You make a negative interpretation even though there are no definite facts that convincingly support it. Related are the following:
   a. Mind reading: You arbitrarily conclude that someone is reacting negatively to you and do not bother to look into the matter.
   b. The fortune-teller error: You anticipate that things will turn out badly and feel convinced that your prediction is an already-established fact.
6. Magnification (catastrophizing) or minimization: You exaggerate the importance of things (such as your mistake), or you inappropriately shrink things until they appear tiny, such as your own desirable

qualities or another person's imperfections. This is also called the "binocular trick."

7. Emotional reasoning: You assume that your negative emotions necessarily reflect the way things really are: "I feel it; therefore, it must be true."

8. "Should" statements: You try to motivate yourself with "shoulds" and "shouldn'ts," as if you need to be whipped and punished before you can be expected to do anything. "Musts" and "oughts" are similar offenders. The emotional consequence is guilt. When you direct "should" statements toward others, you feel anger, frustration, and resentment.

9. Labeling and mislabeling: This is an extreme form of overgeneralization. Instead of describing your *error*, you attach a negative label to *yourself*: "I'm a loser." When someone else's behavior rubs you the wrong way, you attach a negative label to them: "He's a jerk."

10. Personalization: You see yourself as the cause of some negative external event for which, in fact, you were not primarily responsible.[10]

The way these cognitive distortions can impact workplace behavior should be obvious. Take mental filtering as an example. If the organization tried something in the past but was unsuccessful, an employee might distort the truth by thinking, "We are no good at this type of endeavor. Let's not go there again." Or take magnification. On a micro level, a leader might see one small clerical error as indicative that a worker is careless or unable to do a certain job well and might conclude that they should not be trusted or promoted. Leaders should be on the lookout for the ways they and their staff can cognitively distort organizational issues and should try to bring balance and proper perspective. Moreover, while caution is always called for, being aware of how some of those misperceptions can be spread, like emotional contagion, is vital in a group or meeting situation.

Job Satisfaction

Everyone wants to be a valued and respected member of an organization that pays them fairly, gives them opportunities and challenges, offers collegiality among coworkers, and recognizes achievements. This is, of course, true in a church or ministry setting. When these needs are met, along with a host of others, job satisfaction can be achieved. Job satisfaction is an attitude that results from the perception that the person fits into the organization well and has a future there. Job satisfaction is one of the more well-researched variables in the OB literature and is often the dependent variable that researchers use when measuring how other factors impact those in the workplace.

Many factors are considered to be important to one's job satisfaction—pay and benefits, work conditions, job security, opportunities for advancement, and social environment. Job satisfaction is generally associated with job performance: satisfied workers perform better than dissatisfied workers. Thus, a major concern for management thinkers and practitioners has been how they can promote job satisfaction. Research has shown more nuanced approaches to understanding satisfaction, such as Frederick Herzberg's dual-factor theory of motivation (see chap. 4), and some have questioned how important job satisfaction is to performance. Nevertheless, helping workers find satisfaction should be a concern for those in ministry leadership.

Job dissatisfaction, by contrast, leads to a host of problematic attitudes and behaviors, such as lower performance, nonconformity, intentions to leave, and, ultimately, quitting. It has been said that people do not leave bad jobs; they leave bad bosses.[11] Thus, leaders have much to do with how satisfied their staff are, and they can unintentionally alienate people and cause dissatisfaction. While there are a host of reasons for staying or leaving—and the bulk of OB (and this textbook) addresses many of these issues—here are a few practical ways leaders can help make sure they are not the reason people quit:

- Share your style of management with your team so they understand your intentions.
- Assign your team goals and objectives and give reasonable time frames for hitting benchmarks.
- Mean what you say, and say what you mean. People desire consistency, direction, and honest feedback.
- Lead by example. Roll up your sleeves, get out from behind your desk, and do some of the less glamorous work.

- Hold yourself to the highest standards. If you expect a lot from people, expect a lot from yourself as well.
- Reward people when they do a good job, publicly and privately. A well-deserved and earnest word of recognition goes a long way to help people feel valued.
- When you are wrong, admit you are wrong. It is all right to be human and laugh at yourself. Self-deprecating humor helps people relate to you—and want to continue working with you.[12]

Organizational Citizenship Behavior

When a person goes above and beyond the requirements of their job, they are engaging in organizational citizenship behavior (OCB). OCB was first recognized and researched in the 1980s and has since become recognized as an important attitudinal factor in OB and something church leaders should consider.[13] OCB is the discretionary effort people give toward other people and the organization. It is something that is not strictly demanded or part of their role or tasks. Examples include helping a new coworker learn about the organization, volunteering to serve on committees, doing special projects for a supervisor, or coming in on a day off to do extra work. Simply picking up a piece of trash floating in the parking lot is indicative of OCB. The person sees a need, and because of their commitment to the organization, they take discretionary initiative.

Church leaders might assume that because they are highly committed to the church and make plenty of discretionary efforts on a regular basis and because their people are all committed believers, everyone else is (or should be) a model organizational citizen. While this may be true, even church leaders should not take this for granted. When getting people to do anything extra is like pulling teeth, or when few people show up to special events or activities, we may suspect problems in the culture. On the other hand, strong OCB is a lagging indicator that a church is being led well and has a healthy culture. OCB is not, however, something that can be promoted directly. As soon as leaders attempt to fix an OCB deficiency directly, what used to be a voluntary task now becomes a perceived job demand. Therefore, while there are various factors both within the organization's control and outside of it that can lead to OCB, such as personality and other individual differences, leaders should primarily *observe* OCB instead of trying to generate it through policy or programs. Chapter 10 will discuss the leader's role in creating a healthy culture, which, among other things, can lead to high levels of OCB.

Perceived Organizational Support

How do your people think about the way the organization cares for them? Do they think the organization is for them, notices them, and will treat them fairly and offer justice? If they do, then there is perceived organizational support (POS). POS is the general attitude that the organization cares for one's well-being. The organization treats them fairly, their supervisors support them, they are rewarded for their work, and they are given favorable job conditions.[14] Like job satisfaction, positive POS among workers leads to good outcomes, such as high performance and the intention to stay. Unlike OCB, this is something that is clearly linked to policies and practices of the organization.

In a church or ministry it may be tempting to write this off as a worldly concern or take for granted that POS is present. Do not do that! As with OCB, people with a strong sense of POS, even in a church, will be more motivated to work hard and stay for a long time if they sense the church is there for them in both tangible and intangible ways. Leaders in a church can and should attend to POS. How do your staff and volunteers perceive the organization? Look inward to things such as management style, review and reward practices, and working conditions. Of all organizations, churches should excel in making people feel supported and valued. Our heavenly Father supports and cares for us (1 Pet. 5:7); so, too, should we support and care for those who have chosen to give their service to our ministries.

CURRENT ISSUES

Understanding the Human Side of Staff and Setting the Right Tone

Angie Richey is the president of Life Pacific University in San Dimas, California. The university was founded by the female evangelist Aimee Semple McPherson, and Richey serves as the first female president since "Sister Aimee" began the school over a hundred years ago. Richey brings a unique approach to leadership as a trained counselor and someone with high EI and sensitivity to her people. She encourages leaders to start with curiosity about their people and the problem behaviors they may exhibit. She encourages leaders to, instead of laying blame, start by asking questions, such as, Can you tell me about what's going on? How did you interpret that situation? How are you feeling about this? What do you think about that? What do you need? A genuine curiosity can help break down typical walls between the leader and subordinates and help develop a bond of trust, which is so important to healthy working relationships.

As for being a female leader in a historically male-dominated profession, she knows firsthand the challenges women can face. Yet she has a strong internal locus of control and feels responsible for her own success, having learned from supportive and concerned leaders, both men and women, in her role as university president. She is also aware of how leaders set the tone for a culture, both for better and for worse. Sister Aimee was a wonderful role model of an empowered and dynamic female leader, entrepreneurial and culturally engaged. But she was also a workaholic who suffered strained family relationships. These tendencies can be felt generations later among those who carry on a leader's work, and it is difficult to break cycles—for example, the practice of taking on too many new initiatives or not pressing through challenges when starting new things. Regarding setting the cultural tone, Richey states, "Even though we are a Christian university, a university is not a church and should not be run as a church. While still grounded in our faith, ideas such as professionalism in communication, policies and business practices, and even dress code are all important in helping keep a culture in line with our mission and commitments to both the academic world as well as the church world."

■ Practical Leadership Application Questions ■

- How would you rate your own EI? How about the EI of some of your key staff and leaders?
- How can the idea of emotional contagion be helpful in the way you lead and set the mood for events and meetings, both corporate and one-on-one?
- How effective do you think your staff are at managing stress? Are there organizational stressors that you can address to make it more manageable?
- Have you seen bias or stereotyping in action in your context? What can you do, both personally and organizationally, to help reduce the negative impact they have?
- How might cognitive distortions be a factor in the way you and/or key staff perceive current situations or challenges?
- How can you better use the concepts of job satisfaction, OCB, and POS to gauge the current health of your culture?

CASE STUDY

The Emotionally Hijacked Meeting

Karla was excited about the meeting. The staff were going to discuss how to implement some of the new ideas that had been developed during the recent strategic-planning process. This process had taken about three months, and while it had been challenging to pull together so many different departments and personalities, as the new executive pastor she felt that everyone had worked together well and had come up with ideas and initiatives that would help propel the ministry into its next season of growth and fruitfulness. Many of the staff had put in overtime while working on their parts of the plan. Everyone at the meeting was eager, and notepads, laptops, and coffee cups were strewn across the large conference table. Warren, the senior pastor, sat at the head of the table, next to Karla. They had conferred beforehand, and she felt that the two of them were in sync on how they hoped the meeting would go.

Things went well—at first. Each department weighed in on its specific part of the strategic plan, Pastor Warren gave feedback along the way, and everyone seemed highly engaged. Then Albert had his turn. Albert had been with the ministry for over twenty years, and while some thought he was past his prime, he was still highly respected by most of the staff for his many years of service, having been close to the founding pastor when the church began. His current role was overseeing the pastoral care ministry, which did much of the hands-on follow-up with parishioners and which provided counseling, grief care, and many other important aspects of pastoral ministry. "Pastor," he started, "I have been sitting, listening patiently for over an hour, and while I appreciate all the enthusiasm of the younger staff members, I just don't know if I am on board with all this. When this ministry began twenty years ago, we didn't need all this planning, and things went well. Now we have to discuss and debate every little detail. We tried all this planning stuff in the past, and it never amounted to much. Why will this time be any different? I really feel in my heart that this is a waste of time. You're the senior pastor. Why don't you just let us know how you want things run? I am getting quite frustrated here, listening to all these inexperienced newbies try to run things. Anyhow, that's my two cents. I'll shut up now." And with a nervous chuckle, he sat down, fumbled through his notes, and checked his watch, looking impatient and irritated. The room became very quiet.

This was the last thing Karla wanted to happen. She knew Albert was something of a loose cannon but did not anticipate him going off like this. And she knew Pastor Warren was fully on board with the strategic planning and the approach. In fact, he explicitly told her to get the staff more engaged in the planning and execution of initiatives; he did not want to be the autocratic leader he felt his predecessor was. As Karla looked around the room, she could see and sense a shift in the mood. It went from being engaging and fun to being stern and quiet. Albert had sucked all the oxygen out of the room with his speech, and most of the staff felt conflicted and did not know how to respond. They were excited about their ideas yet respectful of Albert. Moreover, many were seemingly afraid to continue, knowing he did not approve of what was going on. There was an awkward silence, and all eyes, including Pastor Warren's, turned to Karla.

Questions for Discussion

- How was OCB demonstrated among the staff in this situation?
- How can the idea of emotional contagion explain what happened in this situation? How would you rate Albert's EI? How about Karla's EI?
- How can cognitive distortions explain what happened with Albert's attitudes and responses?
- How could Karla respond to this situation?

■ Further Reading ■

Chapman, Gary, and Paul E. White. *The Five Languages of Appreciation in the Workplace: Empowering Organizations by Encouraging People.* Chicago: Moody, 2011.

Goleman, Daniel, Richard Boyatzis, and Annie McKee. *Primal Leadership: Unleashing the Power of Emotional Intelligence.* 10th anniv. ed. Boston: Harvard Business Review Press, 2013.

Hart, Archibald D. *Adrenaline and Stress: The Exciting New Breakthrough That Helps You Overcome Stress Damage.* Nashville: Thomas Nelson, 1995.

Meier, Paul D., Frank B. Minirth, Frank B. Wichern, and Donald E. Ratcliff. *Introduction to Psychology and Counseling: Christian Perspectives and Applications.* Grand Rapids: Baker Books, 2010.

Oakes, Penelope J., S. Alexander Haslam, and John C. Turner. *Stereotyping and Social Reality.* Cambridge, MA: Blackwell, 1994.

Scazzero, Peter. *The Emotionally Healthy Leader: How Transforming Your Inner Life Will Deeply Transform Your Church, Team, and the World.* Grand Rapids: Zondervan, 2015.

Steinke, Peter L. *How Your Church Family Works: Understanding Congregations as Emotional Systems.* Lanham, MD: Rowman & Littlefield, 2006.

4

Motivation, Evaluation, and Rewards

Introduction

Why are you reading this book? Why do you serve in your organization? Why do other people serve (or why do they not serve) in your organization? While these might seem like mundane questions, the truth is that behind every action is a reason—a motivation that leads to a reward—that puts us into motion. There is a seemingly endless number of activities we could engage in, but for some reason, here we are, doing what we are doing. In a work context, understanding what motivates people is vital for leaders who want to create healthy organizations, ones that attract and retain talented people and give them opportunities to use their God-given gifts and reach their full potential. This is the subject of this chapter.

Various theories of motivation have been offered over the years, and motivation has been a subject of research in psychology since the 1940s, when Abraham Maslow published his pioneering work on the subject (discussed further below), and in the OB field since the 1950s. Management thinkers were initially interested in how to help people engage in and sustain their work so that they might be more productive and help the organization accomplish more. There are, of course, lots of reasons for wanting workers to be motivated—for example, to help the organization accomplish its mission or to keep people in the game when things get difficult. Thus, motivation can be seen as important for both the organization and the individual.

"Motivation" can be defined as how behavior gets started, is energized, is sustained, is directed, and is stopped; it is the subjective reaction present in the person while all this is going on;[1] and it is a process of making choices among a host of options.[2] Moreover, we can think of motivation as that which leads to some sort of reward, whether it be material or subjective personal satisfaction. In short, we are motivated to action because we believe that acting will lead to certain outcomes we find desirable and/or a reward we want.

Motivation in the Church

At this point you may be thinking, "How does this apply to me and my ministry? My people are here to serve the Lord, and productivity is not our end goal; spiritual growth is. God will reward those who serve him." Further, you may think that being motivated is a sign of one who is overly ambitious or self-promoting. Is this godly? Fair enough. I would concur: people in your ministry are, no doubt, primarily motivated by their sense of commitment to serving the Lord and are fulfilling their calling. Psalm 40:8 says, "I desire to do your will, my God; your law is within my heart." God should be our goal and desire. And Ephesians 6:5–6 tells us, "Slaves [workers, in a modern context], obey your earthly masters with respect and fear, and with sincerity of heart, just as you would obey Christ. Obey them not only to win their favor when their eye is on you, but as slaves of Christ, doing the will of God from your heart." These verses admonish us to serve gladly and wholeheartedly as working for the Lord (Col. 3:23) in all we do. But note that these verses are seemingly about the servant and *the Lord*. The master cannot presume to impose these words on the worker. We err if we use, either explicitly or implicitly, verses and ideas such as these as a spiritual claim to people's time, energy, or contentment in their service to us. Yes, we can expect that people's earnest and good intentions move them to serve with us, but *leaders have an important role and responsibility in the outworking and sustaining of people's tenure with the organization.* Rather than assuming people are perpetually self-motivated, a church, above all other organizations, should seek to understand what motivates people and help them find fulfillment in their roles. Church leaders should have a good working knowledge of theories of motivation in order to bless their people, help them thrive while they serve in the organization, and help them be more productive—not for the sake of profit but for the advancement of the ministry to which the organization is called. God motivates people, but leaders can and should be the instrument God uses to do this and to offer workers rewards for their service.

By not having a good understanding of motivation, leaders may inadvertently demotivate people. I will give all church leaders the benefit of the doubt here, knowing that most are sincere and want to do right by their people. Yet many a leader has, by a lack of understanding of this topic, caused people to feel frustrated and unmotivated and, eventually, to head for greener pastures. In such work situations there are mixed messages, broken promises, and a perceived lack of concern from leadership. While this is no doubt part of God's providential plan for these workers, and while we know he ensures that all things work together for good (Rom. 8:28), I believe leaders need to understand what motivates and what demotivates people so they can avoid giving unnecessary offense, putting up obstacles to people's work, and inadvertently pushing people out the church door. Saying, "Oh well, it will all work for good for Joe as he leaves my church feeling demotivated, unrewarded, and frustrated," should not be part of anyone's philosophy of ministry.

Intrinsic versus Extrinsic Motivation

A foundational way to think about motivation is to compare *extrinsic* and *intrinsic* motivation. This concept undergirds many of the ideas about motivation that will be explored later. Extrinsic motivations, as the name suggests, are things outside of ourselves that motivate us to action. Examples of extrinsic motivators in a work setting are pay and benefits, work conditions, promotions, opportunities for advancement, and recognition. We cannot offer these things to ourselves; rather, they are given to us by others. Conversely, intrinsic motivation relates to activities that we find rewarding regardless of what happens as a result. The reward is a sense of personal satisfaction or enjoyment, not recognition or a material benefit. The activity itself is sufficiently motivating; like the (theoretical) perpetual-motion machine, it does not need fuel but is able to keep itself going through its own energy production. Meaningful experiences, positive emotions and relationships, and work that is challenging, interesting, or amusing may be intrinsically motivating. People will gladly choose to engage in activities that bring these benefits.

At first glance you may notice that the extrinsic motivators are those most commonly associated with work. Pay, benefits, opportunities, challenges, and so on are often found in organizations. In fact, they are the staple of most evaluation and reward systems. The intrinsic motivators may seem more elusive in an organizational context. One typically finds this kind of satisfaction through hobbies or other unpaid activities, and this reality explains why, outside of work hours, people engage in activities like painting, playing music or sports, gathering with friends, or growing gardens.

Can we find challenges or meaning or have positive emotions and relationships at work? Can work be as fun as playing baseball (assuming you are not a professional ball player)? Yes, but most organizations have seemingly more pressing tasks and goals for their workforce. Organizations historically have considered themselves to be places that give people not personal meaning but, rather, job security and a paycheck, with some recognition and opportunities thrown in from time to time. Put another way, someone has to do the heavy lifting and sweating, and it may not be all that personally satisfying!

Thus, for many people, work is a place they spend forty or so hours a week in order to earn enough money to do the things they really want to do. A healthy organizational challenge is to design work and cultures that allow the organization's need for productivity and task accomplishment to converge with the people's need to find meaning and purpose in their work. A church has a mission filled with meaning and purpose—to bring the good news to the ends of the earth so that people might have peace with God—and the church should seek to connect people with roles and tasks that have meaning that is intrinsically motivating. Leaders should not assume that the work people do for the church will automatically motivate them; they should strive to create healthy organizations for which this convergence is a goal.

But how can we accomplish this goal of making work intrinsically motivating? Simply telling people that their work is meaningful is not enough. Enter self-determination theory (SDT). Developed by Edward L.

Deci and Richard M. Ryan, SDT suggests that something is intrinsically motivating when we have autonomy to do it, when we are competent at it, and when it offers pleasant social interactions (relatedness).[3] Using this as a model for designing work, consider the following questions:

- Does a worker have the autonomy to do the work in their own way? Are they allowed to figure out and design tasks their own way? Are they involved in decisions that affect them? Or are they told how, when, and where to do their job? A worker who has autonomy will be more likely to experience intrinsic motivation.

- Is someone competent to do the job they are required to do? Do they have the proper education, skills, and experience needed to do it well? Do they receive adequate training from the organization? Or are they in above their heads and struggling in vain to do a good job? A worker who is competent and prepared will be more likely to experience intrinsic motivation.

- Does the work environment offer social interaction and support? Does the person work with people whom they like and respect, and do their immediate supervisors offer support and concern? Or do they work in isolation or in conflictual situations with little support from others? A worker who has positive social connections in the workplace will be more likely to experience intrinsic motivation.

With this foundation for the "what and why" of motivation, let us now review some of the key theories of motivation, which can help you keep your staff and volunteers motivated.

Theories of Motivation

Theories of motivation are grouped into two categories: content theories and process theories. Content theories are concerned with the factors within a person and the needs they have. They help us understand human behavior from a psychological perspective, seeking to explore the deeper needs and drives people have. Process theories deal more with external factors and help us see how behavior is initiated, sustained, and stopped. While still interested in one's inner world, these theories are more actionable in that they help leaders and managers think about their specific organizational processes and practices and how these things help people do their jobs.

Content Theories

Abraham Maslow's initial theory of motivation set the foundation for some of the earlier theories of motivation in the workplace.[4] His theory suggests that people have a hierarchy of needs and that they seek to fulfill lower-order needs before higher-order ones. Lower-order needs are basic physiological and safety needs, such as food and shelter. Higher-order needs are belonging (social needs), self-esteem (recognition needs), and what he termed "self-actualization." While Maslow's theory is not without its critics,[5] and while some Christians may take issue with Maslow's approach to self-actualization or contend that meeting the lower-order needs for food and clothing is all one needs for contentment (see 1 Tim. 6:6–8), this theory influenced subsequent theories that are based on categories of needs that all people have and seek to satisfy. To use an old expression, there is some meat to Maslow's theory, and one is free to spit out the bones as one wishes.

Frederick Herzberg and his colleagues developed the dual-factor theory of motivation (also called the two-factor theory), which is a practical theory that categorizes needs in ways that are helpful for organizational leaders.[6] The dual-factor theory suggests that there are, broadly speaking, two categories of needs: hygiene needs and motivators. Hygiene needs are not the need for soap and water (though, Lord knows, some folks do need these things!). They are similar to Maslow's lower-order needs—things such as food and shelter. In a work context we may think of, for example, fair pay, decent working conditions, and health benefits as satisfying our hygiene needs. Motivators are the higher-order needs that one has, such as the need for achievement, recognition, responsibility, and opportunities for growth. What makes this approach novel and helpful is the idea that the fulfillment of hygiene needs prevents people from being *dissatisfied* but will not necessarily make them *motivated*. In other words, fulfilling basic human needs is essential, but it does not mean that a person will be motivated in their work. Decent work conditions and fair pay alone will not sufficiently motivate someone. To motivate the worker, the organization needs to meet higher-order needs, such as opportunities, responsibility, and recognition. This can be a very practical and helpful idea when thinking about what can motivate (or bring dissatisfaction to) staff. See case study 1 at the end of this chapter for a real-life scenario that will help you think through the application and challenges of this approach to motivation.

C. P. Alderfer's ERG model[7] suggests that human needs are grouped into three categories:

- Existence needs, which are satisfied by such factors as food, pay, and working conditions
- Relatedness needs, which are satisfied by meaningful social and interpersonal relationships
- Growth needs, which are satisfied by the individual's making creative or productive contributions

While at first glance this may seem to be the same as the dual-factor theory, what makes this model unique and helpful is its idea of the frustration and regression cycle. If one of these three types of needs is not met, people will seek satisfaction in another way. For example, if someone has poor working conditions or poor pay, they may find fulfillment at work through comradery and social interaction with others. Here, using language from Alderfer's model, the fulfillment of an R compensates for the unmet E need. Conversely, a staff member who is not getting along well with their department mates at the moment may throw themselves into their work and skip usual social activities. Because this person's R needs are not being met, they are moving on to an E or G need. This model can also transcend the barriers between work life and personal life. For example, a person may have a dissatisfying home life and therefore work harder in order to find satisfaction. This does not mean that all workaholics are avoiding undesirable home-life situations or not getting along with their coworkers, but the perspective that the ERG model provides can be helpful for leaders as they see new work patterns or behaviors emerging. Further, it can help us ensure that these three different types of needs are being met in any particular role and to think through ways of creating balance when designing work and roles.

The final content theory I will discuss here is David C. McClelland's learned-needs theory.[8] McClelland believes that one's culture at both the macro (e.g., ethnic) and micro (e.g., family) levels is largely responsible for how people develop needs that motivate them, either consciously or unconsciously, to action. There are three primary needs:

- The need for achievement: accomplishing tasks, getting recognition for work, progressing in work, and so on
- The need for affiliation: meeting social needs, cooperating with others
- The need for power: competing, winning arguments, and being in charge

McClelland later added a fourth motivator: avoidance. We are motivated, he said, to avoid certain things, such as people, activities, or events, largely out of fear. If you have ever walked down another hallway to avoid someone you would rather not speak to at the moment, you have experienced this motivator.

Regarding the need for power, it is important to note that we can distinguish between the personal versus institutional need for power. A personal need for power drives someone to seek control over others, whereas an institutional need seeks to organize the efforts of the institution so it can further its goals. The former is not helpful, but the latter can be very helpful for those in leadership roles. While power certainly can be and has been abused, a need for power is not necessarily a bad thing, particularly if the need is institutional. Most in the church have an aversion to discussing power, equating it to lording it over others (see 1 Pet. 5:3) and authoritarian leadership that most people do not like. However, we can see a person's need for power as a desire to exercise leadership, to take control of or influence outcomes, which is appropriate even in a church. Power takes many forms in churches, but some people will have power to accomplish things, and this ability can be used for good. If leaders do not have power, not much will get accomplished. Thus, a motivation to have power can be important in those God has called to, and gifted in, leadership (Rom. 12:8) and has put into positions of authority.

Another implication of McClelland's theory concerns how we appeal to people based on their motivations. Take the Great Commission as an example. It might readily serve as an achievement motivation for some people to get involved in or support missions in the church. But this opportunity for achievement might not motivate everyone, and please resist the temptation to call them unspiritual. Perhaps appealing to a need for affiliation might be more motivating for some. Attending an event with friends to hear about a cross-cultural outreach initiative focused on local families might motivate these folks. We should consider how we can appeal to others based on a variety of motivations and not simply on our own preferred motivator.

Process Theories

In addition to content theories, there are several important process theories of motivation—namely, goal setting and equity theory.

GOAL SETTING

What is the role of setting and accomplishing goals in motivation? Can setting and accomplishing goals motivate? This is the approach to motivation investigated by Edwin Locke and colleagues.[9] "Goals" can be defined as meaningful outcomes one accomplishes. Goal setting can be used by leadership at all levels to help the organization accomplish important tasks.

- Organizations set broad goals, such as the mission and vision, which show why the organization exists.
- Supervisors set department-level goals, which articulate their area's specific part in accomplishing the organization's mission.
- Individuals set very specific goals to help themselves stay on track with the departmental-level and organization-level goals.

Thus, goal setting is a practical and concrete way to think about motivating others in terms of accomplishment at all levels of an organization.

Goal-setting theory is based on the premise that people will work hard to accomplish certain goals under certain conditions. First, a goal must be adequately difficult. A goal that is too difficult will not motivate, as the workers will not think it can be accomplished. For example, imagine your youth group currently has a hundred kids. If you asked the youth-group leadership team to double the size of the group in the next month, they would likely be frustrated and not know how to begin accomplishing the goal (besides praying for revival!). A more reachable goal might be to grow by 10 percent each month. Youth leaders could then encourage all the kids to invite one friend each week, knowing that maybe 10 to 20 percent would do it. This goal would be more likely to be met, and the youth leaders could develop a strategy to accomplish it.

On the other hand, a goal should not be too easy, as such a goal will not motivate either. To continue with the above example, say you asked your leaders to grow the youth group by ten kids in a year. The youth leaders would say, "No problem," and proceed to do absolutely nothing, as they could accomplish this goal with no additional effort. Finding the "sweet spot" of goal setting, between too much and too little, should be a leader's aim.

In addition to considering how difficult the goal is, the goal setter should consider how specific the goal is. Asking the youth-group leaders to "grow" the group is not very specific, but giving them numerical targets, such as 10 percent per month, is specific. Specificity helps to motivate, because the workers can measure the results. If you set a vague goal, like simply "growing," you will not know when you have accomplished it.

A challenge in ministry is that important goals cannot always be easily measured. For example, imagine you asked the youth leaders to help the group grow spiritually rather than numerically. Of course, they could come up with new ideas, such as focusing on studying the Bible or devoting more time to prayer. But how would they know whether kids were actually growing spiritually? This is a perpetual conundrum in ministry. Perhaps a better goal would be to implement two new activities in the Wednesday youth service that involve a spiritual discipline. This is specific and measurable and will give the youth leadership a motivating and accomplishable goal.

Several other factors should be considered in goal setting as motivators: goal acceptance and goal commitment. People must accept a goal as a good and valid one in order for it to be motivating to them. Similarly, one must have a commitment to a goal in order for it to motivate. One way to help ensure the presence of both factors is to allow people to be involved in setting the goals they are asked to accomplish. When people are allowed to determine their own goals (in alignment, of course, with larger organizational goals), they are much more likely to accept and commit to them. After all, they helped create them. Handing people goals for which they gave no input is less likely to motivate them to action. Consider the previous discussion on Deci and Ryan's theory of intrinsic motivation and the role that autonomy plays. If we allow people to create their own goals, they will exercise autonomy, which in turn will lead to more acceptance of and commitment to the goals.

Additionally, leaders should help followers set goals that have rewards the followers actually want. A gift card is fine, but an hour or two off work so workers can spend time with their kids may be more motivating. Leaders should also help people reach goals by coaching and encouraging; followers may lack the expertise they need in order to accomplish the goals and may therefore require help from others. Finally, leaders should, as much as possible, help remove larger organizational obstacles to accomplishing the goals. For example, the project may have a lack of funding that a leader can address but the workers cannot.

Goal setting can be a great way to motivate and incentivize workers, but it requires a delicate balance of leader involvement and support, as well as worker autonomy.

Equity Theory

One final process theory is J. S. Adams's equity theory.[10] It could be called a theory of demotivation, as the focus is on what demotivates people in a work context. It is based on people's perceptions of fair treatment and of whether their ratio of inputs (work) to outcomes (rewards) is similar to that of others. A person will measure how they are being treated in comparison to how their peers are being treated and will feel that an injustice has occurred if they are not treated in a similar manner. This perception of injustice will lead to one of several possible outcomes: the worker will become angry or resentful, reduce their inputs (i.e., work less hard), campaign or complain against leadership, or even quit. To reduce the cognitive dissonance of all this, they may begin to rationalize why the other person is treated better; for example, they may think the other person is, on further reflection, better qualified or has worked harder than they have. Or the worker may recategorize themselves relative to this person. For example, they might think that they are not actually in the same category as the other person and that that is why the other person received preferential treatment.

No doubt, this sentiment occurs in churches, among staff who work hard but do not see the same level of opportunities as others do or who perceive that others get preferential treatment from leaders. Keep in mind that this is based on the *perceptions* people have, not on any objective standard. Yet as the saying goes, perception is reality, and these perceptions will assuredly influence work behavior and motivation.

From time to time, students of mine cite the parable of the workers in the vineyard (Matt. 20:1–16), which shows that it is the prerogative of the landowner to pay the latecomer workers the same wage paid to the others, even if the early-arriving workers felt it was unfair. This must, the students say, be the biblical perspective—that leaders can treat people how they see fit, regardless of how followers feel. I remind them of the point of this parable: Jesus is saying that God will now include gentiles in his plan of salvation even though they are newcomers to his plan in comparison to the nation of Israel, which had been serving him for generations. I do not believe this parable is meant to be management advice, to imply that leaders can treat followers however they want and that followers need to get over it. In fact, one could argue that this parable supports the very idea of a strong internal sense of justice as well as the feeling of being wronged if this sense of justice is violated. As those made in the image of a just God, we share a sense of justice. This sense of justice permeates much of today's larger social conversation on issues such as social justice, race relations, and business ethics.[11] At work, as in life, people want to be treated fairly.

Leaders need to keep all of this in mind when determining compensation, giving promotions, selecting people for assignments and opportunities, and handling a whole host of other organizational issues. Yes, it is the prerogative of senior leadership to make such determinations, but they should keep in mind the likely consequences of making choices that the workers may perceive as unfair. If they make idiosyncratic deals like allowing one staff member, but not the other, to work from home and both do the same job or work in the same department, it is likely that an injustice will be felt, and the results mentioned above could occur. If it persists over time, this type of approach can lead to cultures that lack trust in leadership.

One way to mitigate this problem is to consider a related issue, procedural justice. Procedural justice suggests that the rules for decisions be made explicit so that everyone knows what they are. For example, when it comes to pay increases or benefits or opportunities, people should know the qualifications for certain roles or how advancement occurs. If the rules are made explicit, even though people may not like an outcome, they are more likely to accept it and less likely to see it as unfair. Another example is the hiring and promotion of family members of current staff, which may be seen as nepotism and is often considered unfair. The qualifications for a role should be made known, the family member should be hired based on these qualifications and not on the grounds of being related to a church leader, and nonrelatives should be involved in the final decision to hire. These and other attempts at procedural justice will go a long way in helping reduce a sense of unfairness in the workplace.

Practical Applications and Managerial Practices

Theories provide a strong foundation for understanding motivation, as the above overview shows. Now that we have surveyed the more prevalent theories about motivation, let's discuss some more practical applications to bring these theories together in actionable ways.

Job Design and Fit

In chapter 2 we discussed the importance of individual differences and job fit, which have to do with how people's personal characteristics will contribute to their success in a particular role. Similarly, we can consider how a particular role will contribute to a worker's success in motivating them to persist and do well in that role.

When thinking about what motivates individuals, we should consider the degree of specialization needed for the job. What are the specific skills, education, personal characteristics, and background needed to accomplish the job? Some roles require one to wear many hats and function in many roles. For example, an area pastor such as a women's or men's pastor needs to be able to teach and lead others, administrate events, work with groups and teams, troubleshoot, and deal with unexpected issues and contingencies. These roles typically provide lots of room for challenge and growth. Other roles are much more specialized and require only a limited set of skills—for example, an area coordinator, who helps administrate the affairs of a department, provides communications to members, coordinates meetings, plans hospitality, and so on. Extreme specialization means one will do a limited set of tasks and do them over and over. The degree to which a job requires specialization can greatly impact one's motivation in that role, as over time this same job provides less challenge, growth, and room for participation in bigger issues and decisions. While working in ministry means being part of the greatest endeavor God has given humanity, even the saintliest among us will tire from doing the same task over and over with little room for challenge or growth.

A few approaches to dealing with this challenge are to provide opportunities for people to work in different settings and to give them new challenges as their desire and skills increase. *Job rotation* is the practice of allowing people to work in different departments and on different tasks. *Job enlargement* is the practice of intentionally increasing workers' responsibility over time to allow for new challenges and opportunities. Job characteristics theory suggests that leaders consider several aspects of how jobs will be perceived: Is there sufficient variety in the skills and tasks required? How significant is the task? Do people have autonomy in how the task is done, and do they receive feedback on how well they are doing? If these aspects are present, people are more likely to experience meaningfulness in their work and feel responsibility for the outcomes of their work, both of which lead to higher internal motivation and higher satisfaction.

Finally, we should consider how much participation and empowerment people have in their jobs. One of the earliest findings in OB in this regard came from the Hawthorne Studies (discussed in chap. 1). These studies showed that worker productivity improved because of people's involvement in the decisions about how their work was to be conducted. This has been a consistent finding. People who are empowered to make decisions and who participate meaningfully in the affairs of their organization will be more engaged and motivated to do well. Of course, not everyone wants such empowerment and participation; for a variety of reasons, some folks are quite content to do their jobs and go home. But many are motivated by opportunities to be more involved and to make a difference in their churches. Such individuals should be recognized and put on paths that allow them to experience such involvement.

These approaches have larger organizational implications. They will require more training as people transition into new roles that require new skills, and input and support across departments will be needed too. Moreover, such approaches will require a church to think hard about its core values and responsibilities. Some leaders simply want to find qualified people, put them in their roles, and hope they are content doing that same thing forever. Approaches such as job rotation, enlargement, participation, and empowerment may require some fundamental shifts in how the organization thinks about its responsibility in developing its people. Such shifts need to come from and be supported at the highest level—in the church, this would be senior leaders and executive pastors. They need to be part of conversations about what is important and valued and what is part of the culture. But the rewards can be long-lasting, increasingly motivating staff and creating a pipeline of those who are developing as the next generation of church leadership.

Evaluations and Rewards

Considering your church's approach to evaluation and rewards is an important aspect of integrating and applying much of the previous concepts of motivation. In my experience teaching this topic over the years, I have found that the subject of evaluation and rewards has been met with the proverbial deer-in-the-headlights look from students, many of whom have rarely considered the necessity of having a well thought out and implemented approach. Perhaps this comes from our assumption that it is the Lord who rewards us for our hard work. Indeed, he will, and one day we will all receive a wonderful crown for our faithfulness (e.g., 1 Cor. 9:25–27; 1 Pet. 5:2–4). In a sense, serving the Lord is its own reward, as we see the fruit and blessings of our service in many and various ways.

Having said this, I contend that church leaders can be the instrument of blessing to those who serve faithfully in ministry, and part of the leaders' responsibility is to consider how, why, and when they reward people for their work. The idea is not to supplant the Lord's rewards but, rather, to recognize workers' contributions here and now. In addition to promising an eternal reward for service, Scripture admonishes us that elders should be compensated, a worker is worth their wage, and the church should not "muzzle an ox" while it is treading the grain (1 Tim. 5:17–18). While Paul did his fair share of secular work to earn a living, he also knew that if a church had the means, it should not expect its leaders to work for free. I believe this concept applies not just to leaders (senior pastors or elders) but to all who have made church ministry their vocation.

Why Evaluation and Rewards?

A well thought out and fair evaluation and reward system accomplishes some important things in a ministry. It can help attract and retain qualified staff members and volunteers. People generally get to choose where they will serve and are attracted to a ministry that will recognize their talent and give them opportunities to grow. Yes, most will have a sense of calling and leading to a ministry, and in the end God rewards and promotes one individual over another (Ps. 75:6–7). But the ministry should seek to recognize and reward people fairly when they choose to commit their service to the organization instead of other options. When compensated fairly, people feel valued for their contributions and can devote themselves to the job instead of looking for additional work or other opportunities. There is certainly an important place for bivo-cational ministers (those who hold a traditional job and are also lead pastors over congregations), and needing to work a secular job while pastoring is no shame; Paul did it quite successfully. Yet if you speak with many bivocational ministers, you will no doubt hear a desire to be compensated for their ministry with a full-time salary. While money alone does not motivate, a lack of it does dissatisfy (recall dual-factor theory). Moreover, we know from OB research that a good reward system helps reduce turnover, improves job performance and commitment, and reduces absenteeism.

Further, church leaders have a responsibility to help poor performers improve, and there should be consequences for not doing one's job. Recall Jesus's rebuke of those who did not do what their manager had asked them to do (Matt. 25:14–30). The more talented staff will leave if they feel there are no consequences for poor performers, as they do not want to be associated with mediocrity or be treated the same as those who do not carry their fair share of the load. Anyone who has worked on a team with a slacker can attest to this. Even in ministry these problems have costs. For that reason, an evaluation and reward system is part of the ministry's own stewardship approach, which must consider long-term costs and the ministry's success in carrying out its mission.

WHAT REWARDS?

Many think of rewards in terms of pay, benefits, bonuses, and so on. While these have a place in ministry, smaller ministries may not have the budget for them. Moreover, because volunteers make up a significant portion of a ministry's workforce, typical financial compensation does not apply. Fortunately, as we have seen from the above review of theories of motivation, there are many ways to reward people for their contributions aside from financial compensation. Recall the previous discussion on extrinsic and intrinsic rewards and consider how the following nonfinancial incentives can reward people:

Extrinsic Rewards	Examples	Intrinsic Rewards	Examples
Recognition for a job well done	A special mention, in a staff or leadership meeting, of the work someone has done recently	Achievement of personally important goals	An opportunity to investigate and begin a new outreach initiative that is on the worker's heart
Advancement to a new position with more responsibility	Promotion to a new role that builds on previous experience and achievement	Autonomy in how work is to be done	The freedom to determine how and when to run a new ministry
Accolades given either publicly or privately	Words of affirmation and appreciation in an oversight meeting	Personal growth and opportunity to learn and improve	Encouragement to take seminary classes in order to gain more Bible knowledge

These and other creative options are all ways a ministry can reward its people without having to do so financially.

LINKING REWARDS TO EVALUATION

While rewards are important and can be motivating, a ministry should consider how it is intentionally linking the distribution of rewards to people's performance. It has become a meme in our popular culture that kids receive a trophy just for showing up. While the debate over how to promote self-esteem in kids continues, OB research has shown that organizations need to be thoughtful in how they link rewards to their evaluation processes and that rewards for "just showing up" will not motivate better performance or accomplish what performance-oriented reward systems can. On the other hand, in a ministry context it is important that people are given a path forward for their ministry aspirations so they can envision their own future as being part of the ministry. While some may disagree, I contend that it is not ungodly for people to seek new or more challenging roles[12] and that the leader's role should be God's means of blessing and empowering other workers, not a means for the workers to become long-suffering or humble as they wade through an unclear or capricious system of determining which people are selected for advancement.

There is a spectrum of approaches a church or ministry can take in regard to how tightly it links evaluation and rewards. On one end is the approach that favors uniformity and equality among employees and does not closely link evaluation with rewards. There may be a set wage for paid staff based on the position alone and a series of percentage increases based on length of service. For example, all administrative assistants with no college education will start at $15 an hour and be considered for a wage increase of 3 percent annually, based on satisfactory performance of job duties. On the other end of the spectrum is an approach that is oriented heavily toward individual performance and that closely links evaluation with rewards. The ministry may consider the skills and experience a worker brings at the beginning of employment and offer raises based on certain criteria or the meeting of certain goals over time. For example, a youth pastor with a seminary degree and five years of ministry experience receives more compensation initially than one with no formal education and three years of experience. Pay increases are based on the accomplishment of goals agreed on for the youth leader, such as establishing small-group Bible studies and seeing a

10 percent increase in regular midweek service attendance. Both tenure and performance should be considered as factors linking evaluation and rewards.

Evaluation of performance can accomplish many important organizational goals for the staff and the ministry and can be instructional as well as motivational. It lets staff know that there will be regular opportunities for their hard work to be reviewed and rewarded by those over them. It gives supervisors the opportunity to give important performance feedback, perhaps identify training opportunities for high-performing staff, and establish agreed-on growth goals. It also serves as a time to let underperforming staff know of any deficiencies their supervisor is concerned about and give them specific growth goals to work toward. In this sense evaluations can establish a baseline by which to measure and evaluate subsequent work, and thus, they can be an important part of the documentation process for both fair promotion and, if necessary, discipline and/or termination.

WHAT TO EVALUATE

Christian organizations can establish regular performance-evaluation criteria. These are usually based on several categories, such as the following:

- Meeting basic expectations: personal character and spiritual commitments, observance of the organization's policies and practices (e.g., showing up on time)
- Meeting preestablished goals: completion of required or discretionary training, contributions to one's area of work, accomplishment of departmental goals
- Meeting larger organizational goals: expression of core values and other cultural values, demonstration of organizational citizenship behavior

In sum, a ministry should evaluate the type of behavior it deems important in its staff, and doing so helps the ministry accomplish its mission and promote its desired culture. While "off the shelf" evaluation forms and policies can be a good starting place, churches and

other organizations need to be sure to augment these typical evaluation criteria with their unique and missional values. An old maxim in
management says that "you get what you measure." Thus, evaluation
processes are a key part of ensuring that the high standards of the ministry are met.

When and How to Evaluate

Typically, staff are evaluated by those who most directly oversee their
daily work. This makes sense, as these supervisors are the ones most
likely to see people in action and know whether there is a deficiency

---

CURRENT ISSUES

Paying for Worship Leaders

A trend among many growing churches is to compensate people for
roles that used to be held by volunteers. The roles are not part-time or
full-time employee positions; they are what are considered contract labor
or 1099 positions (based on IRS Form 1099, which, at the time of writing, requires organizations to report to the worker and the government
amounts exceeding $650). These roles may be for people who spend a
considerable amount of time and energy at the church over the weekend.
Consider musicians, trained in their craft, who show up for a rehearsal
on Saturday at 1:00 p.m., play for a Saturday evening service, and then
return for several Sunday services, putting in a total of twelve to fifteen
hours. This commitment to the church likely prevents them from doing
much else during the weekend. Moreover, some churches feel that people
such as skilled musicians deserve compensation, and some of them free-
lance from church to church (and sometimes do local weddings or bar
mitzvahs) as part of their livelihood.

What are the pros and cons of such an approach? On the pro side, a
church, no doubt, will be able to attract and retain well-qualified musicians,
some of whom might be reluctant to give so much time over a weekend
without compensation. In today's church landscape, having high-quality
music for worship is considered a "must," and many churches are willing

in performance. While we often think of performance evaluation as a formal or annual event—and ministries should have such formal approaches—leaders may evaluate on a more regular basis and in more informal ways. While you want to avoid making every activity a "teachable moment" lest your staff encounter feedback fatigue, there are many moments in regular organizational life in which offering both affirmation and correction would be beneficial. Leaders and managers should take advantage of the natural momentum and synergy of these events. For example, team or one-on-one meetings after big events or activities, conducted while the memories are fresh, are great opportunities for evaluation and feedback. While you may be tempted to dive into

to pay to ensure their music is excellent. Further, paying musicians can be part of an equitable approach to a ministry's reward system. And of course, recruiting and retaining skilled volunteers can be a challenging task. Ask any ministry leader, and you will hear horror stories of flaky and unreliable volunteers who leave the church scrambling to find replacements at the last minute.

And the cons? Of course, this practice adds a new budget line item that, depending on how many of these roles are compensated, could be considerable. From a motivational perspective there is another important consideration. According to Deci and Ryan's theory of intrinsic motivation, when we increase extrinsic motivators, we also simultaneously decrease intrinsic motivators. In other words, if we add things like compensation to the volunteer reward system, we may also be reducing their motivation to serve from their own place of commitment. This is not to suggest that these people become mercenary: they would not be there if they did not believe in the mission and ministry of the church. Yet their work can feel more like a job than an act of service to their faith community. Church leaders can no doubt sense a tension when they introduce compensation in this manner, and they should think carefully before adopting this approach. The cost may be more than financial.

the problem areas, be sure to offer plenty of positive affirmation. If staff start to sense that you use these meetings as simply an opportunity to chew them out (no matter how much you smile), they will develop an aversion to them.

Supervisors usually offer evaluations, but another option is to take a 360-degree evaluation approach. This approach to evaluation suggests that all the people in one's work orbit should offer feedback, hence the 360-degree geometry metaphor. Evaluation and feedback are given not just by supervisors but also by peers (those at the same level in the organization) and, if applicable, subordinates (those whom the person oversees). People have differing roles and behaviors when interacting with people at different levels in an organization and thus are perceived differently. For example, a worker may come across as a terrific subordinate to their boss but a horrible supervisor to those they oversee. An organization should be concerned about how staff are perceived by all relevant members of the organization, or it may develop blind spots about the true nature of a worker's performance.

There are challenges to a 360-degree feedback approach. Subordinates may be hesitant to offer criticism of their supervisor for fear of reprisal or hurting the person's feelings. Peers may likewise be reluctant to offer feedback that is critical of their friend. Thus, like many healthy OB practices, 360-degree feedback must be part of a comprehensive approach to a ministry's people practices and must come from a work culture that encourages constructive dialogue as well as honest and sometimes difficult conversations. Further, as this sort of feedback touches on potentially sensitive areas, organizations should consider how the feedback will be given and what they will do with the information. Providing after-review coaching with someone in a mentor-mentee relationship, for example, can help such feedback be positive and actionable.

A leader's goal should be the growth and development of all their people and the acquisition of honest feedback from a variety of levels. From the newest entry-level staff members to those in key positions of leadership, including senior pastors and executives, no one should be above evaluation and accountability. Such a commitment helps the ministry continue to grow, encourages and rewards high performers, and helps low performers stay on the team.

■ Practical Leadership Application Questions ■

- How intentional have you been in considering what motivates or demotivates those you lead? What theological assumptions might impact your views?

- How can you incorporate both intrinsic and extrinsic motivational factors to make other people's jobs more rewarding?

- Which of the theories of motivation gave you fresh insight into the performance of your staff or volunteers? What action can you take to incorporate some of these insights?

- How have you intentionally focused on job design and fit to ensure workers' motivational needs are met? For example, have you considered how much empowerment or social interaction a person wants and whether the job will provide it?

- Considering equity theory in particular, how well do you think your ministry uses procedural justice and minimizes practices that can be considered unfair by some?

- How intentional have you been with rewards and evaluations? What theological assumptions might be impacting your views?

- What are some new and creative ways you can improve your approach to evaluation and rewards? Are there non-compensatory ways to offer rewards to staff and volunteers? What about compensatory ways?

CASE STUDY 1

The Gifted Campus Pastor

Campus pastor Pam was a gifted and hardworking staff member at City Church, a fast-growing multisite congregation in a sprawling and thriving metropolitan area in the United States. She had been part of the church staff since its founding twenty years before, and three years earlier she became a campus pastor at one of the older and more established campuses, located around fifteen miles from the main campus. At first Pam was very excited about this position and strongly felt the Lord's leading. She was a good administrator, and her gifts opened this door for her, as a campus pastor had many administrative responsibilities. She also loved to preach and was considered a dynamic and gifted communicator by many in the church.

As time went on, she began to wonder whether leading a campus was still the challenge and opportunity for her that it was at first. The sermons were primarily done by the senior pastor from the main campus, Andrew, so she rarely got to preach, yet she had a growing sense that using her gifting in preaching and teaching was what the Lord was calling her to. After much prayer and discussion with her husband, Pam decided to meet with the executive pastor, Raul. Pam and Raul had developed a good working relationship over the years, and she felt he would understand her. After listening to Pam's concerns, Raul said, "I hear you, my sister, and agree you are a great preacher. But you know Pastor Andrew. He feels his role in the church is to be *the* preacher, so there is little room for others to preach. But we want you to be happy here at City Church, and I think we can offer you a generous salary increase to make up for this. I know your family is putting the kids through college, and I can imagine a pay increase would help during this season." And with that Pam left, feeling heard and being excited for a salary increase. It would indeed help a lot, as they were struggling to pay for their kids' tuition.

As time went on, Pam settled back into her role, and life was a little less stressful now that she had this additional funding. But after a few months, her dissatisfaction began to creep back in. While money was no longer as tight, she still desired to preach more and did not see any opportunities to grow. In her view she was simply a church manager, making sure services and events happened smoothly and in line with the main campus's directives and policies (and budgets). While she knew that what she did was important, and while she was appreciative of her pay raise, she still felt unfulfilled in her role at City Church.

Questions for Discussion

- How can the dual-factor theory of motivation explain what is going on in this scenario? Why did the pay increase not motivate her to stay?
- Is it wrong for Pam to be discontent in her role here? Is her essential problem a lack of faith or godly contentment, or is it valid for her (and other Christians) to seek more challenge and growth in their service?
- How could the church give opportunities for Pam to find fulfillment in her work as a campus pastor—or can it? How do we help people who seemingly have more needs than there are opportunities?

CASE STUDY 2

The Unchallenged Coordinator

Gabrielle had been on staff for two years. She was a dedicated volunteer at one of the church campuses and was now working full-time in the central offices as a coordinator, serving with the children's ministry. She was always pleasant to be around and was a very conscientious and hard worker. She was a single mom, and the church took care of her and her son with decent pay and good health benefits. She had recently started taking classes at the local seminary and was really enjoying studying the Word in depth. In fact, she was even beginning to sense a call to serve in ministry full-time in more meaningful ways. While she loved serving on the children's ministry team, recently she had begun to wonder whether there was more she could do. If she were honest, she was feeling a little bored and unmotivated in her job these days and was secretly looking around at other church websites for job opportunities.

In meeting with her overseer, she began to share some of her thoughts, and she asked Pastor Tony, the lead pastor over the children's ministry, if there were other opportunities for her at the church. Tony shared, "This is great timing. We are going to be preparing the new Bible program for next year, and I am pulling together a committee to develop this. Now that you are in seminary, I think you'll be able to help us make sure the program is well grounded biblically. And as a mom, you will be able to help us ensure the program is fun and engaging for kids. In fact, I think you might be able to lead the curriculum committees. I've seen how you interact with others, and I think you'll do a great job. Don't worry; I'll still be at the committee meetings initially and will help you get established, but in time I'll let you run things. Keep in mind, we still need you to do all your current responsibilities, but I'll make sure you get enough time to do your committee work as well."

And with that, Gabrielle had a new sense of hope and was encouraged about her future at the church. While she was concerned about the additional work and the time it would take, she was excited about this opportunity. In fact, she began thinking about ideas for the curriculum right away. At night, after her son was in bed, she would think about the seminary theology course she was taking and dream about different lessons she could develop. "How can we teach a five-year-old about the eternal perichoresis of the triune God?" Well, she thought, maybe she should temper her enthusiasm just a little bit!

Questions for Discussion

- Was it predictable that someone as capable and gifted as Gabrielle would, in time, begin to tire of a routine role in the church?
- How do you think Pastor Tony's response to her enacted some of the principles of motivation theory in general and job design and fit in particular?
- How well do you think this new opportunity will motivate Gabrielle in her work at the church?

▪ Further Reading ▪

Harman, Elena. *The Great Nonprofit Evaluation Reboot: A New Approach Every Staff Member Can Understand*. Nashville: CharityChannel, 2019.

Herzberg, Frederick, Bernard Mausner, and Barbara Bloch Snyderman. *The Motivation to Work* (New Brunswick, NJ: Transaction, 2011).

Kerr, Steve. *Reward Systems: Does Yours Measure Up?* With Glenn Rifkin. Boston: Harvard Business Review Press, 2008.

McClelland, David C. *Human Motivation*. New York: Cambridge University Press, 1987.

Ryan, Richard M., and Edward L. Deci. *Self-Determination Theory: Basic Psychological Needs in Motivation, Development, and Wellness*. New York: Guilford, 2018.

Interpersonal Relationships in Organizations

Introduction

For most people, ministry involves a complex web of relationships with others. From the minute we enter a ministry role, we begin relationships with those in positions of leadership, with peers who do similar work, and perhaps with those we oversee. From church elders and board members to parishioners and volunteers to local business owners and government leaders, there is a host of other people with whom we will interact one-on-one. Life itself can be seen as a series of interpersonal relationships, beginning with our parents and siblings, proceeding to early schoolmates and friends, moving to romantic partners, and perhaps leading to a spouse and lifelong friends whom we know well and who know us well. Ironically, because relationships are so ubiquitous, we seldom stop to think about the nature of our own relationships and perhaps think about work relationships only when things go wrong—when we experience disagreements with bosses, tension with our coworkers, or a seeming lack of respect from someone we oversee. Because interpersonal relationships are at the center of so much of ministry, they are worth considering in detail.

Interestingly, a scan of many contemporary OB texts shows that they pay little attention to interpersonal relationships themselves. Even though relationships are at the heart of most organizational phenomena, they are usually understood in terms of group dynamics or as something leaders must pay attention to. Interpersonal relationships are seemingly eclipsed by the concern for large groups of people. They are taken for granted and remain invisible, even though OB is a topic focused on people! Group dynamics has some bearing on people's relationships with others, but the dynamics of just two people is much more intimate and unique, and such relationships deserve separate attention. According to a wise saying, "ministry flows through relationships."

Those with whom we establish strong relationships can become life-long ministry partners and may just end up being those who carry on our life's work. Ministry is a people-focused endeavor, and our personal relationships can determine our effectiveness or lack thereof. This chapter is an attempt to pull together a variety of organizational concepts concerning the nature of interpersonal relationships. It also moves us to the next level in our model of organizations, the interpersonal level (see fig. 5.1).

Scripture illustrates the interpersonal nature of ministry well. Think about some classic relationships seen in its pages: Moses and Joshua, his aid and successor; David's uncommonly close bond with Jonathan, of the royal family; Elijah and Elisha, his protégé, who went on to do even greater works. And of course, we must not overlook our Lord Jesus. Although Jesus was often seen ministering to large groups (e.g., Matt. 19:2; Mark 10:1; Luke 8:4) and we often look at his twelve disciples as a group (e.g., Matt. 10:2–4; Luke 6:13), we also see him spending time with individuals—Peter, John, and James in particular. He knew them personally, and they came to know and love him. In fact, the apostle John seems to relish the fact that he was the one "whom Jesus loved" (e.g., John 21:20), and this same apostle had something of a friendly rivalry with Peter (see John 20:4). Leaders in ministry, above all, should understand the nature of interpersonal relationships in order to demonstrate Christlikeness and build rapport with those God has called them to serve with and lead.

There are several ideas and concepts that can help us establish healthy interpersonal relationships in a ministry context. While some of them, such as trust, could be also seen as organizational or team phenomena

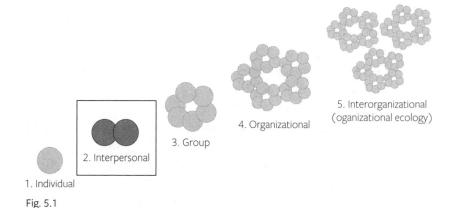

Fig. 5.1

and could be applied at multiple organizational levels, I will focus on the interpersonal nature of these concepts and will show practical ways leaders can develop better interpersonal relationships.

The Role of Trust

At the heart of all good interpersonal relationships is trust. Trust is the ability to know that others are safe for us to be around and that we can count on them when needed. Trust is the invisible social glue that holds all good relationships together. A lack of trust can create suspicion and doubt and even lead to others becoming our rivals or enemies. We know that the Lord is good and that we can "trust in the LORD with all [our] heart" (Prov. 3:5), but how do we know we can trust other people? Some people, sadly, find that they cannot trust others. They have experienced a series of disappointments when trusting others, and they are now unable to establish trust in new relationships.

I recall a ministry friend who shared with me a painful childhood experience. He was on the roof of his house, and his father stood below, watching him. He was afraid and not sure how to get back down. His father told him, "Jump down, and I'll catch you. Trust me. I'll catch you." So, he carefully sidled up to the edge of the roof, then jumped toward his father's waiting arms. But as he fell, his father stepped back, allowing him to plummet to the ground. Hurt and shocked, he staggered to his feet, and his father told him sternly, "Son, trust no one!" My friend told me this sad tale as he shared why, many years later, as an adult, he still had a hard time trusting others in life and ministry and had put up facades to keep others from knowing or trusting him. While this is an extreme example, many have been hurt emotionally by trusting someone they thought was there for them. Particularly in ministry, in which opening up to others and becoming vulnerable and transparent is part of how people minister and develop empathy, trust can be hard to develop. The pain of past disappointment leads some to be wary about trusting anyone.

The nature of trust is somewhat difficult to establish, and different approaches have been offered by people from philosophers to psychologists. Is it a set of probabilities that leads us to have confidence in others? Is it a behavior? An emotion? Paul Thagard suggests that trust is "a brain process that binds representations of self, other, situation, and emotion into a special pattern of neural firing called a *semantic pointer*."[1] While a bit technical and clinical, this approach sees trust as a combination of our regard for ourselves and others, how we feel about that relationship, and our experiences that are hardwired into our brains over time.

Trust in Organizations

Organizational psychologist Adam Grant has studied and spoken about trust as part of his work helping organizations and teams.[2] According to Grant, trust is built when we get to know people as individuals and form relationships with others around uncommon similarities, such as possessing the same unique skill or having attended the same college. Being an athlete or a "Longhorn" gives one an innate ability to trust the other person. In addition, knowing people's character and their competence helps establish trust. While we do not always need to like people to trust them, we do need to know they are people of good character who can do their job well. Taking risks together is an important way to develop trust. This is what the falling-backward trust exercise is about—taking a risk and discovering that the other is there for you. But Grant suggests a more radical approach, such as embarking on a risky expedition or project together, where individuals must learn to trust one another in order to accomplish the task. The proverbial foxhole experience can build lifelong bonds of trust between people who have gone through them together. This trust leads to high performance and innovation in an organizational context. If we do not trust others, we end up playing it safe, but if we trust, we feel confident to try new ideas and approaches. Thus, we see the importance of understanding trust and working to develop high levels of it in life and ministry.

Barriers to Trust

According to a Dutch saying, "Trust arrives on foot but leaves on horseback." In other words, trust takes time to develop but can be demolished in a single moment. As leaders, we must be aware of how our words and actions can either promote or hinder the development of trust. Here are some ways leaders can put up barriers to building trust.[3]

The first is giving inconsistent or grandiose messaging. Some leaders love to make promises and grand pronouncements. Although they sound good in the moment and no doubt come from a heart full of good intentions, they can be a mistake in the long run when it comes to developing trust. The leader tells people what they want to hear or seeks to engender excitement, hoping to win them over in the moment. The problem is that, often, the leader is not the only person involved in making or executing the decision. Different people in the organization have different perspectives and goals, and staff will hear different messages depending on whom they talk to, eventually finding out that what was said is not the whole story or perhaps even part of the story. I have encountered leaders who would make grand pronouncements from the pulpit or CEO desk without even having discussed it with staff or others who could execute the ideas. After a few of these occurrences, people learn, "There goes Steve with his big idea of the day."

Here are some ways to avoid this mistake:

- Check your priorities, and only make realistic promises you can keep.
- Save big announcements for major initiatives and things you know you can follow through on, not just your latest whim or "shiny new thing."
- If necessary, confer with others in the organization (e.g., managers and staff) before you make announcements, and make sure your

messaging is consistent with theirs before you go public, either in group settings or in one-on-one meetings.

- Learn to say, "I don't know, but I'll get back to you," rather than give a shoot-from-the-hip answer that ends up being wrong.

Another inhibitor of trust is inconsistent behavior, which is doing something for one person and not for another. Recall equity theory from chapter 4. It suggests that people have a very strong sense of justice when it comes to who gets or does what. When we treat people in ways they perceive as unfair, their trust in us is eroded. Leaders may justify this behavior, thinking it is their prerogative to decide as they wish. This may be true. But keep in mind, if this is your consistent approach—to be inconsistent—people will take note of it as a marker of untrustworthiness. Do all you can to treat people fairly, letting them know why you made certain decisions, and in the long run they will be more likely to see you as a fair and trustworthy person.

A third mistake is allowing problems to fester. People notice when things are going wrong, and they feel it is a leader's job to act. For example, when leaders allow incompetent people to remain in their jobs and everyone knows these people are in over their heads, or when leaders allow hostile or negative people to run roughshod over others and create a toxic environment, people may lose trust in the abilities or competence of the leader. Perhaps this do-nothing approach is due to the leader's desire to be liked or to avoid conflict. Whatever the reason, when a leader does not take action in situations that require it, that inaction may erode trust. Leaders must know when problems fester and must take corrective action. For example, if necessary, help reassign those who are a poor fit for their role or even the organization. By taking needed corrective action, you may make one person unhappy, but you may also make many others happy and go a long way to earn their trust.

A fourth mistake is a failure to trust others. One way to earn trust is to trust others. For a myriad of reasons, some have a hard time trusting others. Some are perfectionists or workaholics and do not give others room to do their jobs. But when we do not trust others and allow them to do their job, they will not develop professionally, and the more talented people will leave. I recall a leader who had a great knack for hiring talented people but had an utter inability to let them do their jobs, and he watched as one after another of these talented people left. Make sure your trust issues are not hindering your people from doing their jobs or causing them to look for places where they will be trusted and empowered.

A fifth mistake is not dealing with elephants in the room. Yes, every organization, even churches, has issues that everyone knows about but that the organization fails to address. In churches, which have cultures that value loyalty and submission to authority, these elephants can be big and rough skinned indeed. However, leaders need to address the things everyone is whispering about, such as the abrupt firing of someone, rumors of layoffs, or talk of a key staff person leaving. It is not enough to insist that "Christians should not gossip." While this is true, leaders can go a long way to reduce gossip and build trust by addressing issues that need to be addressed. Even Christians have a desire to know what is going on, and leaders cannot ignore this fact without losing trust. Avoid even a temporary "information vacuum," as most likely it will be the negative information and assumptions that spread, not the truth. Put yourself in others' shoes and consider how they might be interpreting a situation. With this understanding you can address their fears or concerns. I once had a boss who would say, "Run to the fire." That is to say, if there is a situation that needs to be dealt with, deal with it quickly lest it spread and get out of control. By addressing the elephants, big or small, we show people we are aware and competent, and this instills their trust in us.

The sixth mistake, and the final one discussed here, is making unequivocal statements. Leaders love to say things that sound official and certain, perhaps in order to gain confidence or sound like they are in charge. For example, some will say, "No one else will get laid off," or, "We have this handled," when in fact this is not the case. We should be hopeful and optimistic, but we should also be honest and realistic. People may become concerned if you tell them the truth, but they will trust you more than they would if you had given them false hope. Others are always watching to see whether your actions match your words. James M. Kouzes and Barry Z. Posner offer a simple suggestion for building credibility and trust: do what you say you will do.[4] The Bible has another simple term for this: honesty. Leaders can be tempted to justify little white lies or unfounded or overinflated pronouncements in the name of being a strong leader. Instead, you should offer the truth and give hope that, with the Lord's help, things will work out.

Dealing with a Breach of Trust

A sad reality is that a lot of good people are hurt or disillusioned when trust is broken, and this is more so in churches and ministries, whose foundations are built on strong relationships, loyalty, and commitment to the mission. When trust is broken in a church, serious damage is likely to occur. In extreme cases, people will leave the church en masse. Consider a church that abruptly fires its beloved youth pastor without giving a reason. First, people are disillusioned and unsure as to why he was fired. Then they learn that he was fired for acting very inappropriately with some of the girls in the group. Moreover, the senior leadership knew this was happening but waited a long time before taking action. This is a double whammy in terms of a loss of trust, and the damage can be serious and compounding. As in the Dutch proverb, trust will be lost quickly for leaders in situations like this, for which they will be deemed ultimately responsible.

Instead of going into public relations mode or spin mode—justifying, downplaying, laying blame, scapegoating, or otherwise avoiding responsibility—consider the following approach to rebuilding trust:

- *Find out the details.* We cannot address a situation until we know the extent of it. How bad is the damage? How angry are you? How angry are others, and what are they feeling and saying about the situation? Get real about what happened.
- *Own up to what happened.* Instead of downplaying or ignoring a bad situation, admit where you or the church erred. It is all right to be cautiously optimistic at times, but mere happy talk will not rebuild trust. Further, do not just say you are sorry for your action (or inaction); take responsibility for the damages. If someone was hurt by you, let them know that you know that.
- *Make changes.* Ask yourself what changes must happen before you can rebuild trust. You may need to make changes in personnel, how information is communicated, how decisions are made, and who reports to whom. In times when trust is lost, people need to see action, not just words.
- *Do not "go dark" or withdraw.* This response is understandable, and no doubt you may be hurt or scared by the situation. But do not

check out, as this can further erode trust. Get the support and encouragement you need in order to stay in the game so you can be up front with others and give them what they need. Doing so goes a long way to develop trust.

Psychological Safety

Have you ever found yourself in a setting where you did not feel safe to share your thoughts, ideas, or concerns, for fear of the consequences of being honest? Conversely, have you ever enjoyed the feeling of knowing you could be your true and honest self, being able to speak your mind and make meaningful contributions? This sense of safety is known as psychological safety and is an important concept at both the interpersonal and group levels. When people feel psychologically safe, they will share their thoughts, contribute regularly in matters in which they have expertise, and not be worried about what others say when they act as their true selves. Conversely, when people do not feel safe, they are less likely to share their opinions, make valuable contributions, and allow others to see who they truly are. This lack of safety can even lead to feelings of isolation and loneliness.[5]

There is a myriad of benefits to having high levels of psychological safety. Amy Edmondson has researched and popularized this concept as one of importance in organizations. She writes,

> Psychological safety is broadly defined as a climate in which people are comfortable expressing and being themselves. More specifically, when people have psychological safety at work, they feel comfortable sharing concerns and mistakes without fear of embarrassment or retribution. They are confident that they can speak up and won't be humiliated, ignored, or blamed. They know they can ask questions when they are unsure about something. They tend to trust and respect their colleagues. When a work environment has reasonably high psychological safety, good things happen: mistakes are reported quickly so that prompt corrective action can be taken; seamless coordination across groups or departments is enabled, and potentially game-changing ideas for innovation are shared. In short, psychological safety is a crucial source of value creation in organizations operating in a complex, changing environment.[6]

Many can relate to environments in churches and ministries where this is not the case, where there can be serious consequences for sharing an opinion that is contrary to the consensus or to the opinion of a senior leader. Out of a fear of being disloyal to a leader, "making waves," or being rejected, people will often suppress their concerns or opinions. Add to this the common misinterpretations of notions such as not touching the Lord's anointed (e.g., Ps. 105:15; 1 Sam. 24:6), submitting to a leader's authority (Heb. 13:17), and being of "one mind" (Rom. 15:6), and you get strong reasons for not always feeling safe in sharing thoughts and feelings.

At this point one might object that this goes against the authority structures established in Scripture. Please understand that I am certainly not saying workers should go against God's intended order for authority. I am suggesting that, starting with the leader, churches and ministries should reduce people's fear of open conversations about things that truly matter. It is everyone's responsibility to love, serve, and tolerate one another (e.g., Gal. 5:13; Eph. 4:2), and allowing people to be open and honest not only leads to a sense of purpose and being heard but also allows the entire ministry to benefit from the insight and diversity that is present. After all, if a staff member or volunteer is part of the ministry, they are there for a divine reason and purpose, and part of that reason may just be the unique ideas, insights, and initiatives they bring to the table. These things will never get brought to the table if people do not feel safe sharing them. Thus, providing psychological safety can be an important way a leader shows honor and respect to—and gets the most from—those the Lord has entrusted them to lead. I contend that it is a greater virtue for leaders to love and honor their people's voices than to suppress them by standing on the privilege of their authority.

Further, not providing a psychologically safe space comes with serious consequences that ministries will want to avoid: the erosion of trust and respect and the generation of backroom chatter. While we are not all prophets as such, consider how the prophet Nathan spoke truth to power when he confronted King David over his behavior (2 Sam. 12:1–10). Had Nathan avoided this confrontation out of a fear of the consequences, David would have continued in his adulterous ways and perhaps would have led himself and the kingdom into worse circumstances. And note the king of all Israel's humble response: sincere repentance. While most encounters between peers, leaders, and followers will not be this dramatic, we can see that a sense of psychological safety leads to benefits for all parties involved.

So, how can we achieve greater psychological safety in our church or ministry? If levels are currently low in the organization, attaining psychological safety may take time. People progress through stages before they feel free to make valuable contributions and challenge the status quo:

- Stage 1, inclusion safety: The basic human need to connect and belong. In this stage, people feel safe to be themselves and are accepted for who they are, including their unique and defining characteristics.
- Stage 2, learner safety: The need to learn and grow. In this stage, people feel safe to ask questions, give and receive feedback, experiment, and make mistakes.
- Stage 3, contributor safety: The need to make a difference. People feel safe to use their skills and abilities to make important contributions.
- Stage 4, challenger safety: The need to make things better. People feel safe to speak up and challenge conventional wisdom when they think there is an opportunity to improve.[7]

Consider these stages as you help develop safe spaces in your church or ministry, knowing that different people will be at different stages. As a leader, your goal is to help them progress in their sense of safety. Further, leaders can engender feelings of safety by demonstrating the following behaviors and attitudes:

- *Reduce status distinctions as much as possible.* While those in leadership love their titles, status can discourage people of lower status from feeling free and safe. Most people are somewhat intimidated by those whose status is higher than theirs (even if this is not their superiors' intention) and thus are reluctant to be honest around them. When you want candor and freedom, eschew having people call you "Pastor," "Boss," or whatever your formal title may be. "Please, call me Jennifer" can go a long way to disarm those who may be intimidated by your role and authority.

- *Be explicit, and give people permission to share openly.* While you may feel this way in your heart, do not assume people know it. Consider opening a meeting by saying, "Please, I want you all to feel free to share your ideas and opinions here. This is a safe place." Do not shut people down, cut them off, or criticize their ideas. Also, in a group situation consider calling on the quiet members and asking what they think about an issue at hand. Some people need more prompting to open up, and direct questions may give them the boost they need. If you have not been good at this in the past, people may be hesitant to open up. Be explicit. Own up to past behavior and reassure the workers that you are doing your best to change—and then stick to your word!

- *Show genuine curiosity and a learning posture.* While you may have a role of authority and expertise, showing a sense of curiosity and appreciation for others' insights can dispel a sense that you are the most important or only contributor in the room. When someone offers a seed of an idea, draw them out with good questions. "Tell me more about that" or "That is a good insight" lets people know that you are listening and that they are in a safe place where they can share. Jack Zenger and Joseph Folkman suggest that there are four distinct behaviors of good listeners:
  - They interact and make others feel supported.
  - They take a helping stance.
  - They ask questions that gently and constructively challenge assumptions.
  - They make occasional suggestions to open up creative and new paths.[8]

  By positioning yourself as a learner and not just a teacher, you make it safe for other people to give input, and in so doing you create a healthy climate where people feel respected and heard.

Work Family

In chapter 1, I introduced the idea of metaphors as a way of thinking differently about organizations, a way of looking at them with different lenses and schemas. Family is likewise a helpful metaphor for thinking about the dynamics that exist in organizations, particularly in one-on-one relationships. In the church, we are familiar with family language due to its frequent usage in the Bible. Paul refers to Abraham as the father of faith (Rom. 4:1, 11–12, 16–18) and often refers to believers as "brothers" and "sisters" and all believers as "children of God" (e.g., Rom. 8:12–14). Biblically speaking, we are all one big, happy family, with God as our heavenly Father and with multitudes of spiritual fathers, mothers, brothers, and sisters. In many church traditions people openly refer to one another as "brother" or "sister" and talk about spiritual mothers and fathers.

Because family is such a fundamental part of how each of us relates to the world and initially experiences close relationships, it can also be helpful for envisioning the way relationships work, or do not work, in an organizational context. While families are a blessing, the challenge with families, as most know, is that they are often fraught with strange tensions, dysfunctions, expectations, and a host of other, often unspoken realities that can drive behavior in odd and unhelpful ways. Thus, exploring family-like dynamics in a church or ministry can be extremely beneficial.

One tool that can help leaders see the nature of relationships is Murray Bowen's family systems theory (FST). This theory has been explored and effectively used by organizational thinkers[9] and has even been evaluated from a biblical perspective.[10] FST is "a theory of human behavior that views the family as an emotional unit and uses systems thinking to describe the unit's complex interactions."[11] It can give organizational leaders important insight into behaviors and attitudes that are often caused by below-the-surface dynamics and is a means of understanding nonrational aspects of organizational relationships. While a full exploration of FST is beyond the scope of this book, I will discuss the more relevant features and those that can help us think about the nature of interpersonal relationships in a ministry context.

As members of a family unit (or any social system), we do not act or feel in isolation. Similar to the concept of emotional contagion discussed in chapter 3, FST suggests that emotions are shared among people in the same system. If one member is feeling stressed, others in the system will feel stress in one way or another. When we feel the same emotions as others, we become fused to them emotionally and share a related emotional state. For example, if Dad comes home angry from a bad day at work, this anger is felt by others very quickly and can impact how everyone else feels and behaves. Mom may feel anxious and try to placate Dad, and the kids may feel fearful and quickly head to their rooms. When our emotions fuse with another's, we become less able to think rationally, independently, or according to guiding principles. This idea is an important aspect of FST. In organizational life, while we value and understand people as emotional beings, becoming fused and nonrational can lead to unproductive and defensive behaviors that go against the larger values of the organization and hold the organization back from operating at its highest level.

The tension people feel from the system will cause a reaction in everyone. According to FST, there are typical ways people deal with their feelings and the feelings of others, called "postures." The postures are distance, conflict, underfunctioning/overfunctioning, and triangulation.

- Distance: People distance themselves, either physically or emotionally, in order to reduce the tension. For example, they find convenient reasons to avoid a meeting where there will be emotional tension or where they would encounter someone they feel uncomfortable around. If they cannot avoid the situation, they will put up a facade of being all right but will remain emotionally detached. In the long term, distancing can be expressed by isolating oneself or "checking out" when the pressure is pervasive instead of addressing it. Extreme distancing leads to the "cutoff," which is the FST term for severed relationships. In such cases people end the relationship with the person they cannot resolve tension with. Church history is replete with cutoffs resulting from unresolved tensions over a myriad of issues both great and small.

- Conflict: This does not necessarily mean arguing or having an outburst of anger. It is any attempt to change the other person. For example, in a meeting with a subordinate, a person may deal with the other's frustration or disappointment by telling them to "look on the bright side" or by pulling the "you must submit to authority" card rather than empathizing or understanding where they are coming from. In the long term, always trying to win or attempting to change people can make leaders domineering or even turn them into bullies.

- Underfunctioning or overfunctioning: People may retaliate by not doing their job (underfunctioning) or may take responsibility for others by doing their work for them (overfunctioning). For example, if a team member is upset that she has to do a certain task she does not want to do, another member may step up and do the task for her. While this seems like a nice thing to do, it enables the other person to avoid her responsibilities and puts additional work on the nice team member.

- Triangulation: People may deal with tension by bringing a third person into the emotional mix. For example, if someone is having a problem with their supervisor, they may share what the supervisor said with a coworker, who sympathizes and in turn shares a story of a time when the boss treated them the same way. People feel comforted by others who can share their pain or frustration. These third persons need not be present or even alive. Imagine, for example, referring to the founding pastor, who passed away ten years ago but whose ghost, so to speak, still lingers in many conversations. "That's not how Pastor George would have handled that" may be the sentiment among the staff.

The above are all seemingly normal and natural ways of reducing tension, and they are not necessarily signs of dysfunction or organizational problems. We all try to escape, confront, help, accept help, or find solace by sharing with others. However, these responses become problematic when they become our go-to reactions and cause us to act irrationally and impulsively instead of doing what we know is best.

Furthermore, in an ongoing system (like a family or work group) these responses can become permanent states and part of the normal routine of the system. We all learn to adapt to an angry dad or pastor or a lazy sister or coworker and thus all move into functional roles—we placate, allow bullying, blame others, hide, and so on. These roles are not prescribed for us; rather, they become our way of dealing with the uncomfortable emotional tension we feel. Instead of dealing with a perpetually angry pastor or unmotivated coworker, we fall into line and find ways to help ourselves feel emotionally safe around them.

This leads to other important concepts in FST: the differentiated self, the desire for individuality, and the desire for closeness. The differentiated self refers to the ability to separate oneself from the stress of emotions as well as the degree to which an individual can utilize their intellectual system independently of emotions and feelings, making decisions based on their values and principles. By contrast, a person with an undifferentiated self is so fused with the emotions in a system that they no longer act independently but, rather, move into their functional role in the system. The desire for individuality refers to the need everyone has to act autonomously, according to their own wishes. It may conflict with the desire for closeness, the desire to get along with others in a system, since people feel they must do as others wish instead. In other words, people sometimes "go along to get along," and there is thus a lingering tension in their hearts and minds about a situation.

For example, imagine a church staff member who works for a self-centered or narcissistic pastor (hard to imagine, I know, but try your best!). The staff member is bright and motivated, but over time he has learned that his ideas and input are often dismissed, as the pastor is always right or must be the one to offer the solution to any given problem. Rather than be conflictual (i.e., try to reason with the pastor), the staff member lapses into distancing mode, always nodding and smiling when the pastor tells him how to do something, but in his heart he feels resentment at being dismissed or told what to do. At this point, he is not acting independently according to his own wishes. Rather, he is acting as an undifferentiated self, filling his role in this particular relationship. His desire for closeness, his desire to be accepted by the pastor, has overridden his desire for individuality. However, this staff member may be fully differentiated and speak his mind in other relationships at the church. With his own team he may feel heard and respected, and he may be able to give his own ideas. But in his relationship with the pastor, he is not.

We do not fill the same role in every relationship in a system. Each relationship is unique and has its own kind of reciprocity. In relationships we have our basic self, which is the person we would like to be as an individual, and we have our functional self, the person we are in the relationship in order to maintain closeness. FST suggests that the more we are differentiated and operating as our basic self, the more we will act as rational and healthy members of a system. In short, emotionally fused systems do not get the best from their people, as the people spend time and energy coping with emotional tension, playing emotional-support roles, and suppressing their true identities and natures in order to keep the peace.

The above survey of family systems has much to offer church and ministry leaders. While we often think we are acting as fully functional, rational, and productive team members, we may instead be filling roles required of us in order to keep the system in check. While relationships are vitally important, they can become dysfunctional and hinder us from being fully available and productive. Healthy organizations are composed of healthy relationships, from top to bottom. The challenge of an FST approach is that because we leaders are in the system ourselves, the system is largely invisible and hard to assess objectively. However, here are some practical ideas for keeping your family systems relationships healthy:

- *Seek to develop healthy emotional distance in any situation.* Using your intellect, remain detached from the emotions of the system and remain intellectually functional. Pastors in particular—who love people, feel it is their role to help them, and may have a need to feel needed or liked—must become aware of situations or relationships in which they are becoming emotionally fused. For example, do you tend to be the "savior" when people cry out for help? Are there particular people who trigger you or make you feel that you must comply with them? Become aware of how other people's emotions creep into your own emotional space so that you keep yourself from being hijacked by these feelings.

- While it may seem contrary to the previous point, *note any tendencies you have to distance yourself in relationships*, to avoid people either physically or emotionally. We all face tension in relationships, but note when this tension causes you to avoid people or situations for any length of time. Seek to identify and deal with the root causes of this tension. Similarly, avoid being habitually conflictual, always trying to win over or change others. Yes, leaders need to persuade others, but if you always need to be the winner or to get others to go along with you, you risk being seen as authoritative or overly competitive or even a bully. Choose your emotional battles wisely.

- *Avoid becoming the third party to triangles.* As a leader, people will naturally come to you with issues involving other people, and it can seem natural for you to engage in their triangulation. In fact, your work day may seem like one long series of triangle conversations. While empathy and a listening ear are good, try to display emotional neutrality and avoid taking sides. Be careful not to let the emotions of others fuse with yours and compromise your objectivity. Try to use humor to keep these conversations light, and find ways to avoid becoming the repository for other people's secrets.

If you think you may be stuck in a particular pattern of unhealthy relationships, consider finding a coach or trusted other who can help you process the situation. The more you differentiate yourself and function as an autonomous member of the system, the better you will be for the system.

Work Friends

It is natural for us to develop close relationships at work and find people who become work friends. When we spend many hours in one place with the same group of people, we will be drawn toward some people more than others. These relationships become an important and healthy part of one's work and ministry life, and work friendships are important for the healthy functioning of the organization. Elijah had one with Elisha, Paul had one with Timothy, and we, too, should have friends who are yoked with us in the service of our common cause and Lord.

Research suggests that having good work friends is not just emotionally satisfying but is also an important driver of things such as work satisfaction and engagement and a reducer of absenteeism and of loneliness, which leads to lower productivity.[12] A lack of work friends can lead to isolation, an "alone in a crowd" feeling, a sense that one does not have a soul to gravitate toward or confide in.[13] I recall one past ministry relationship that was very close, so close that when this friend left I felt a gaping hole in my work and personal life. I ended up leaving a few months later. This may sound melodramatic, but I felt much like a spouse who passes away soon after their lifelong partner passes. There was just nothing there for me once my best friend and ally was gone. Of course, I bounced back and am just fine now, and I have had a series of close work friends over the years. I thank the Lord for such people in my life.

What is the nature of these work friendships, and how can we develop, and help others develop, close and meaningful relationships at work? Do work friendships just happen in some magical way? Are they just chemistry between two people? Shasta Nelson suggests that work friendships can in fact be intentionally developed and that they are built on three pillars:

- Positivity: Positive people make us feel good and are fun to be around. Work friends are those people who like us, support us, encourage us, and make us feel all right about ourselves. Being with positive friends helps us feel satisfied.

- Consistency: Consistency means spending regular time with people. Consistency has to do with physical proximity between people—for example, having offices down the hall from each other—and spontaneity, the ability to just happen to get together. Being consistent with others makes us feel safe.

- Vulnerability: This is the ability to show our true selves to others. Recall the above discussion on family systems and the basic self. Work friends know who we are and accept us regardless. With friends, we do not usually lapse into a functional role that is emotionally draining, though this can occur. Being with friends helps us feel seen for who we truly are.[14]

As with the other relationship variables discussed, we must practice being a friend in order to receive friendship. If we want to partner with positive people, we should become positive people ourselves. Let people know about their admirable attributes and offer encouragement and recognition for who they are, not just what they do. If we want consistency, make a point of spending time with people regularly. If work schedules get busy, consider scheduling regular "hang time" with work friends so you can catch up. Working from home and hybrid work have made this dynamic more challenging, so it can require more intentionality. But it is worth the effort. To develop vulnerability, take risks with others. Vulnerability does not mean sharing all your personal secrets or home-life concerns. Rather, it means appropriately sharing your thoughts and feelings about shared life and giving others a psychologically safe place to share as well. Of all relationships, ministry friendships should be ones in which people feel safe in our presence, can confide in us, can trust us, and can be known by us. When this is the case, we model Christlikeness to others, as he is always for us, can be fully trusted, knows us truly, and wants to spend quality time with us.

CURRENT ISSUES

Leadership and Love

As Christians, we believe in the supreme virtue of love. The apostle Paul calls love "the greatest of these" when considering the virtues of faith, hope, and love (1 Cor. 13:13). Our popular culture also endlessly extols the virtues of love in novels, movies, and songs. You may already be humming "All You Need Is Love" as you read this! But what is the role of love in organizational life? Will followers respond better to leaders who show love, or is it better to be feared? Moreover, can we ensure that love is not just an ineffable sentiment but also a tangible work practice that helps us connect with others? In 2019 I developed original research to test these questions and published an article on the topic. The article demonstrated an empirical connection between a leader's expression of love and followers' perceptions of work engagement and job satisfaction, meaning that there was, in fact, a connection.[*] This idea is based on Mark and Debbie Laaser's book *Seven Desires*,[†] which I used as a guide to operationalize (i.e., to make an abstract concept explicit) the behaviors demonstrating love. According to the Laasers, love is understood to be expressed in the seven desires that must be met if someone is to feel loved:

1. To be heard and understood: our ideas, thoughts, and feelings are listened to.
2. To be affirmed: what we do well is noticed, and our accomplishments are recognized.
3. To be unconditionally accepted: we are appreciated and accepted for who we are, not what we do. This is different from affirmation, which is based on performance.

Another result of intentional friendship development is that we may develop a diverse set of friends. While most people tend to gravitate toward people who look and act like them, with intentionality we can get to know people who are not necessarily like us as we work to achieve the three pillars of work friendships. People of color report being more isolated at work,[15] and this is something that supportive work friends can address. With intentionality, ministry settings can provide ample

---

4. To be safe: we are free from fear and anxiety, knowing that others are reliable.
5. To be touched: we have (appropriate) physical contact with other human beings.
6. To be chosen: we are desired and selected by another person for a special relationship.
7. To be included: we belong to a special group or community and are thus part of something larger than ourselves.

While these seven things are not the only causes of work satisfaction or work engagement—this book itself is filled with such causes and hindrances—there is a correlation. This seven-desires approach gives leaders practical guidance on how to demonstrate love rather than just talk about it. We can, for example, practice our listening skills, help people feel accepted for who they are and not just their contributions, or choose people for special assignments. These are all tangible expressions of love that not only develop satisfaction and engagement but also express a biblical idea of supreme virtue and even the Lord's love for his people. Become a leader who shows love, and demonstrate to your people and to a watching world how leadership can express the love of Christ.

* F. A. Markow, "An Exploratory Study of Leaders' Expression of Love and Followers' Perceptions of Satisfaction and Engagement in the Workplace," in *Love and Organization: Lessons of Love for Human Dignity, Leadership and Motivation*, ed. Michael Pirson (New York: Routledge, 2022), 277–97.
† Mark Laaser and Debra Laaser, *Seven Desires: Looking Past What Separates Us to Learn What Connects Us* (Grand Rapids: Zondervan, 2013).

opportunity for the church to demonstrate a wholesome diversity and show that people with cultural differences can get along well.

While many friendships develop organically, leaders can be intentional about helping people develop good relationships at work and allow time and space for it. While the conventional management wisdom is that spending time just "hanging out" with people, talking about non-work-related issues, is a waste of time, we must remember that close relationships yield benefits that trickle into productivity and work quality. Churches, of course, are notorious for having lots of office chatter and banter, with friendships abounding. Perhaps this is a result of our genuine love for and desire to be with our brothers and sisters in Christ. A great deal of prodding is probably not necessary here. Nevertheless, leaders should give space to encourage such relationships and should not let a desire to be an efficient manager squelch the natural synergy that comes from people just enjoying being together.

What about leaders' own relationships in the workplace? Many leaders can attest, and there is research that confirms, that there is a particular loneliness for those in charge. They feel stress, alienation, and emotional turmoil that others in the organization do not.[16] They are not "one of the gang" and can be seen as a "them" to the rank and file. Some have suggested that this loneliness is a sign of good leadership, as it provides more objectivity and limits conflicts of interest.[17] Yet leaders above all need the support and encouragement that come from an understanding friend. Such friends may be professionals in other ministries, people from outside the ministry world, or mentors in whom the leader can confide. Of course, all Christian leaders have "a friend who sticks closer than a brother" (Prov. 18:24), the Lord Jesus, and they can always bring their concerns to him. Any source by which a leader can externalize ministry concerns is healthy, whether it is prayer, journaling, or conversation with a trusted confidant. Leaders should not go it alone and should find those they can be vulnerable with, receive positivity from, and spend consistent time with.

▪ Practical Leadership Application Questions ▪

- How do you intentionally develop trust in your ministry relationships?
- What barriers to trust might you or others in your organization put up?
- Have you ever had to deal with a serious breach of trust? How well do you think you handled it, and what could you do differently if it occurs again?
- How psychologically safe is your church or ministry? Has your own approach or ego gotten in the way and made others feel unsafe?
- What are some specific ways you can help create a more psychologically safe space for the people in your organization?
- What are some of the postures (distance, conflict, underfunctioning or overfunctioning, triangulation) you have observed in your ministry? In what ways might they be signs of dysfunction?
- Do you tend to become the third party in triangles? If so, do you, or could you, keep these triangles from becoming unhealthy?
- How well does your ministry encourage work friendship? Do you see relationships that offer positivity, consistency, and vulnerability?
- Have you ever sensed loneliness in yourself or others at work? How can you develop more meaningful friendships that will support and encourage you or others?

CASE STUDY

The Case of the Irate Elder

Pastor Raul was having a tough day, and it was only 10 a.m. He was just getting into the swing of things at Second Baptist Church as the newly installed senior pastor, and after a warm welcome from the congregation, things were beginning to go awry fast. In addition to facing issues with several staff members and a potential budget shortfall for the year, he learned that Elder Ed wanted to see him about "something important." Ed had been with the church since its founding twenty years ago. Raul and Ed had already gotten into some tense conversations right off the bat, and Raul was not looking forward to dealing with him that day. Nevertheless, Ed knocked on his door right at the appointment time and let himself into Raul's office.

With little fanfare he began. "Pastor, I am not happy about a recent decision you made. I just heard from Bill that you intend to shut down the food-distribution ministry. Not sure if you know this, but Bill and I started this ministry over ten years ago under the former pastor, and this has been a real blessing to us and to all the families we help feed in this community. We've been talking, and if you shut it down, we're not sure what we'll do with our time now that we're retired. In fact, I think I am going to make this a top priority in the next elders' meeting, and I'm sure I'll get lots of support from Bill and the others who have been around here a lot longer than you."

This whole conversation made Raul's stomach churn, and he could not wait for Ed to leave. Something about Ed reminded him of his overbearing father, who would always chew him out for mistakes he made. He put on a brave face and responded. "Look, Ed, I understand you are upset, and I appreciate the work you and Bill have given to this ministry all these years. It really has been a blessing to many. But you are on the finance committee, and you know the tough times we are facing right now. Something has to give, and this cut will help. It won't be permanent—just for a year or so until we get to a more stable place. Does this all make sense?" Ed looked down on Raul—he was a big man, at six-foot-five—and said, "Well, I still don't like it, and I'm going to tell all the others on the committee I don't like it. In fact, there have been a lot of decisions around here I don't like." Raul fidgeted some, then looked at his watch. "Oh, time flies. Sorry, Ed, but I need to pick up my kids from school. They are getting let out early today. I'll be in touch." Ed took his cue and left, and Raul breathed a heavy sigh of relief.

Meanwhile, Raul's wife Nancy came into the office to meet with Martina, Raul's administrative assistant, about the women's-ministry event coming up. When Nancy went to poke her head in Raul's office and say hello, Martina said, "Oh, Nancy, I wouldn't go in there just yet. Ed just left, and he really let Raul have it over his decision to cut the food-bank ministry. I think he'll be upset." On hearing this, Nancy tensed up and replied, "That Ed is such a hothead. He has given Raul grief ever since he got here. He shows no appreciation for all the good work Raul has initiated. I'm not sure how y'all have dealt with him all these years." Martina nodded and replied, "For sure. He gave grief to the last pastor as well, but we all tolerate him. He is a big tither and has a lot of influence in the church. It's just the way it is around here. But he makes me mad too." They both sighed as Raul emerged from his office, looking like he wanted to disappear.

Questions for Discussion

- How does Raul's reaction to Ed demonstrate one of the postures of FST?
- Where do we see triangulation taking place in this scenario?
- How do Ed's behavior and the responses of the church demonstrate under-performing and overperforming?
- What would be some practical ways of dealing with a situation like this?

▪ Further Reading ▪

Anwar, Mohammad F., Frank E. Danna, Jeffrey F. Ma, and Christopher J. Pitre. *Love as a Business Strategy: Resilience, Belonging and Success*. Austin: Lioncrest, 2021.

Brown, Jenny, and Lauren Errington, eds. *Bowen Family Systems Theory in Christian Ministry: Grappling with Theory and Its Application through a Biblical Lens*. Cremorne, Australia: Family Systems Practice, 2019.

Cloud, Henry. *Trust: Knowing When to Give It, When to Withhold It, How to Earn It, and How to Fix It When It Gets Broken*. New York: Worthy Books, 2023.

Creech, R. Robert. *Family Systems and Congregational Life: A Map for Ministry*. Grand Rapids: Baker Academic, 2019.

Edmondson, Amy C. *The Fearless Organization: Creating Psychological Safety in the Workplace for Learning, Innovation, and Growth*. Hoboken, NJ: Wiley & Sons, 2019.

Kouzes, James M., and Barry Z. Posner. *Credibility: How Leaders Gain and Lose It, Why People Demand It*. 2nd ed. San Francisco: Jossey-Bass, 2011.

6

Groups and Teams

Introduction

Together Each Accomplishes More—TEAM. No doubt you have heard this trite saying. You may even have the poster on your wall. In your leadership role you may think of yourself as the coach or the quarterback of the team. Because sports are so pervasive in our culture, we love to apply sports metaphors to groups of people we work with. But what are teams really, and how can we make sure ours are "winning" in our churches and ministries? Much has been written on teams by sports coaches, leadership coaches, and a host of other leaders and leadership scholars. This chapter will introduce groups and teams in an organizational setting and will discuss how leaders can get the most from the groups and teams they are called to lead. Because groups are such a central part of organizational life, leaders should have a good working knowledge of how healthy groups develop and function and how they can become dysfunctional. Further, leaders must become aware of the unique role that each individual plays as well as the special role they themselves play. I will try to avoid using tired sports metaphors and illustrations and instead offer a solid OB foundation for understanding groups and teams, relying on the concepts that have proven themselves over time and that have solid theoretical and/or empirical support. This chapter also moves us to the next level of our model: groups.

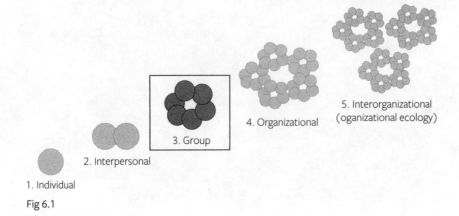

5. Interorganizational (oganizational ecology)

4. Organizational

3. Group

2. Interpersonal

1. Individual

Fig 6.1

What Are Groups?

Groups form the basic units of organizational life. When we think of an organization such as a church, we should think of it as comprising not just individuals but also distinct clusters of individuals. Most daily work in any organization is done by people working together in smaller groups. In a church the groupings may be determined by department, such as youth and children's ministries, education, local and global outreach, pastoral care, live production, accounting, and so on. Further, most churches have a board of elders or church council as well as various standing committees or ad hoc committees for matters such as special events or crisis response.

Groups versus Teams

A "group" can be defined as two or more individuals interacting with each other to accomplish a common goal. A team is a mature group with more member interdependence and more motivation to achieve a common goal. While it has become commonplace to refer to any group as a team in today's workplace (e.g., "I'd like to introduce you to our team") and the matter may seem like mere semantics, it is a mistake to think they are synonymous. Students of OB (and leaders) should note important differences. All teams are groups, but not all groups are teams. Groups and teams have unique characteristics, typically as follows:

Groups	Teams
Have leaders outside of the group (e.g., a manager or supervisor)	Have internal leaders (e.g., a team lead)
Have goals given to them	Develop their own goals
Have similar or shared roles	Have complementary and interdependent roles and skill sets
Are not considered directly responsible for success or failure, as this is attributed to the leader	Share responsibility for success or failure
Receive rewards on the individual level rather than the group level	Share in rewards as a unit

In short, a team is a group but one with much more autonomy and shared responsibility. The how and why of its functioning depend primarily on the members of the team, who share mutually in its success and allow for the contributions of uniquely skilled individuals.

Leadership functions differently for a team than it might for a group. A group can be led according to a traditional command-and-control approach—for example, the leader prescribes goals for the group, dictates how the individuals' work will be done, troubleshoots problems, manages group conflicts or decisional impasses, and evaluates performance. A team, on the other hand, needs to be more dependent on its own members for these things in order to strengthen commitment to the goals and encourage team members' sense of responsibility. A leadership role for a team is much more about getting the team to work together and take responsibility than it is about determining the nature or scope of the work.

A healthy, functioning team is one in which a single leader is either invisible or not even necessary. Many traditional organizations have a hard time transitioning to a true team approach, as doing so requires time and patience and a different leadership mindset and skill set. There may, in fact, be a short-term lull in productivity as the members learn to work together interdependently and as leaders change their role from quarterback to coach (all right, I will allow myself that sports analogy). But in the long term, teams can function at higher levels and become leadership-producing entities themselves, as members learn to take on responsibility and decision-making for themselves.

While teams can take time and effort to develop properly, there are many advantages to them:

- Diverse skills: teams provide a broader base of skills, knowledge, and resources that the team can use in reaching their goal.
- Better results: a team's outcomes may be greater than those of the individuals.
- Increased efficiency: teams can accomplish a large goal in a shorter amount of time.
- Greater motivation: sharing responsibility for the project generally increases motivation to pursue the goal.
- Leadership development: being a contributing member of a team develops the leadership skills of the members.

While there are many benefits to teams, there are some downsides:

- Uncertainty over leadership and goals: lack of clarity over who is in charge and who gets to determine the team's direction.
- Longer decision-making processes: since teams share responsibility and decision-making authority, processing through issues may take more time.
- Potential for conflict: as all members feel comfortable and share their views, there will inevitably be disagreements that take time to sort out.
- Nuanced social dynamics: teams are not just task-doing entities but are, rather, groups of human beings who need to feel connected to and get along with the others in the group if the team is to achieve optimal effectiveness.
- Potential for groupthink: the desire for harmony may suppress freedom of thought in favor of consensus.

In sum, teams offer many benefits to a church or ministry yet also create special demands and have issues that need to be attended to. These issues and others will be addressed in the sections that follow.

Group Basics

Task, Relationships, and Cohesion

With all groups there are several dimensions that are always present. The first is the task dimension, which is the relationship between group members and the work they are to perform, as well as how they will go about doing it. All groups are formed for a reason, have goals, and are expected to be productive.

The second dimension is the social dimension, the relationships between group members and how they feel about each other and their membership in the group. While they have a job to do and are expected to accomplish goals, people also need to feel connected with the others in the group, have a sense of safety, and so on.

The third and final dimension is group cohesion, which is the degree to which members get along and are committed to the group. A highly cohesive group is one in which members feel positive toward each other and the group's goals. In a cohesive group, members like each other, trust one another, and understand the contribution each member makes. Cohesion is both a cause and a result of a team's functioning well. It is usually positively related to group productivity; that is to say, the more cohesive a group is, the more productive it will be. However, cohesion has a point of diminishing returns, where too much begins to reduce productivity. This reduction can be a result of excessive socializing, an undue focus on members' feelings, or groupthink.

Social Identity and Group Identity

Social identity refers to how individuals define their self-concept through their connections and relationships with social groups.[1] Henri Tajfel defines "social identity" as the part of an individual's self-concept that derives from their knowledge of their membership in a social group (or groups) and from the value and emotional significance attached to that membership. In short, a person's social identity is the perceived overlap between their self-identity and a group's identity as well as the cognitive and emotional benefits this bestows on them as a member of the group.

The esteem in which a person holds a group is a consequential factor in social identity. For example, if someone perceives that a group has low status, they will be less likely to join or stay committed. But if they value a group, what it stands for, what it has accomplished, and so on, they will want to be part of that group and share in its collective identity. This, by the way, is the basis for the phenomenal sales of sports jerseys and memorabilia—"Go team!" (All right, there's my second corny sports reference.)

Part of the leader's role is to help groups develop cohesion and a positive sense of group identity—for example, who they think they are and what they contribute to the overall mission of the organization. By sharing history, accomplishments, and comradery and by developing stories and lore about the group, they are being deliberate about developing the group's culture. A group with strong cohesion and a positive identity will struggle and triumph together and will figure out who they are. An organization that is committed to strong groups and teams should encourage them to develop socially, become cohesive, and discover their own unique identity and culture.

If cohesion and group identity are important to group performance, what can a leader do to increase them? Consider the following actions:

- *Reach joint agreement on goals.* Rather than telling group members about decisions after the fact, consider how you can make the decision-making process one in which all group members are given an opportunity to speak. Of course, not every person's ideas or desires can be met, but procedural-justice theory suggests that simply being aware of the rules and processes helps people be content with decisions regardless of the outcome.

- *Give the members more responsibility.* Consider how each member is or is not using their primary gifts and skills and working from their passion. Group members become disconnected if the roles they have been given are not challenging or personally meaningful. Do periodic check-ins with members to see how their role is connecting their abilities with the goals of the group.

- *Increase interaction among group members.* People need to spend time with other group members in order to feel connected with them. Consider increasing the frequency of shared times, particularly in the post-pandemic Zoom era, in which many workers are completely or partially working from home.

- *Make the group smaller.* It is easy to feel insignificant in a large group, and large groups allow fewer opportunities for people's special skills to be utilized. If a group becomes too large, consider breaking it into two or more complementary subgroups, each responsible for different aspects of the group task. Doing so will help people feel seen, give them more chances to contribute, and position some workers to develop their leadership abilities.

- *Physically or socially isolate the group.* An office can be a place with distractions that pull team members in different directions. To help a group bond and to reduce these distractions, consider occasionally meeting off-site in a nice location. If this is not possible, consider a temporary "no laptop or cell phone" policy in group meetings to help keep people focused on the people and task at hand. And bring coffee and snacks!

- *Allocate rewards to the group, not individuals.* Consider how you can reward the group for its collective efforts in an equitable way so that everyone gets to share in the benefits. The rewards do not have to be financial. They can be public recognition or new and more challenging opportunities for the group that build on their previous accomplishments.

- *Finally, consider issues discussed in other chapters.* Take into account, for example, these issues:
  - Interpersonal relationships (see chap. 5): a group is a web of interpersonal relationships and is thus built on issues of trust, psychological safety, family systems dynamics, and friendships.
  - Trust and emotional intelligence (EI) issues (see chap. 3): Google did a study of their own high-performing teams and found that psychological safety and social intelligence were the most important factors in effective teamwork.[2]
  - Conflict (see chap. 7): learn to resolve differences productively.

Stages of Formation: The Tuckman Model

Try to recall a time you joined a new group, either in ministry, work, or your social life. Do you remember feeling like an outsider who did not know anyone? Do you remember perhaps having a conflict with another team member later on over how something should be done or what your role was? Do you remember having a peak experience with the group, in which everyone felt connected and glad to be part of the group? Do you remember when you had to disband the group or move on to another one, and can you recall feeling sadness over this loss of connection? If this recollection resonates with you, you are no doubt recognizing the seasons a group goes through in its shared history, the stages of its development. While there are several models and taxonomies in OB that describe this phenomenon,[3] the Tuckman model is a memorable and helpful way of thinking about it. It proposes five distinct stages in the process: the group forms, storms, norms, performs, and adjourns.[4] While not without its critics, this model persists as a simple and practical way to think about how groups develop over time.[5] It also offers leaders guidance in focusing their attention on particular matters to help the group work through the issues and concerns of the stage it is in. The following is a review of these stages:

- Stage 1, forming: This is when a group is in its infancy and members are getting to know one another. At this stage interactions are typically polite and brief as members become comfortable with the social and task dynamics of the group. They may even be considering whether or not they want to be part of the group, whether it has anything to offer them (and vice versa), and whether they like the other members.

- Stage 2, storming: Once members have decided to participate, they feel free to share their points of view and their ideas about how things ought to be done. Since the group is still relatively new and norms of trust are still being established, this sharing can lead to conflict as members vie for position and voice.

- Stage 3, norming: As the storming stage subsides and people begin to find their role and place in the group, they begin to work together more efficiently. Members become comfortable and trusting, cooperate well, and find satisfaction in how they contribute.

- Stage 4, performing: At this stage members work together well, help each other, manage conflict and decision-making efficiently, and achieve group goals. There is shared leadership, high group cohesion, and a developing group identity and culture.

- Stage 5, adjourning: This is the stage that occurs if a group disbands. Perhaps the assignment was temporary or a season in the life of the organization has concluded. Members will no longer be together as they once were. This is a bittersweet time; members feel good about the accomplishments of the group yet are sad that they will not be with the other members regularly anymore.

Leadership Roles at the Various Stages

A group has different needs as it experiences the challenges of each stage. Leadership, therefore—whether a single external leader, a single internal leader, or multiple leaders sharing the responsibilities—must be aware of the group's dynamics and needs at these various stages.

- Stage 1, forming: Help members feel comfortable with one another socially, and begin to share a vision and goals for the group. Instead of getting down to business right away, let members get to know one another personally, share the reason they joined the group, and say how they would like to contribute. These initial icebreaker sessions, which bring areas of commonality to the surface, can go a long way to help establish affinity among team members. Keep task conversations at a high level by placing the vision and aspirations front and center, instead of focusing on too many details. Get people excited about the "why" of the group rather than bogging them down with the "how" of the group. The "how" will come in time, and if you get into details or start delegating too soon, you risk inviting uncomfortable decisions the new members are not ready to tackle or commit to.
- Stage 2, storming: Conflict may emerge over a variety of ideas or needed decisions. This may be one of the more uncomfortable stages for leaders who are conflict averse or who feel the need to please others. But it is important that you allow, and not stifle, the inevitable conflict that will come when people feel safe to share and a diversity of opinions emerges. Your role as leader is to help members learn to deal with conflict; your role is not to resolve all

their issues for them. Help set ground rules for decision-making processes, whether these rules pertain to voting, consensus building, or something else. If you solve all the problems and make all the decisions, the group members will quickly learn to become dependent on you. If you squelch conflict, you risk creating a culture where conflict either is not tolerated or is the problem of the leader, neither of which is healthy. We will discuss conflict more fully in chapter 7.

- Stage 3, norming: Your role here is to help sharpen goals and ensure people are moving in the same direction. Clarify communication, remove any roadblocks, help secure needed resources, be a model of a good group contributor, and serve your people well.

- Stage 4, performing: The group is working like a well-oiled machine, and your role is to help refine processes and to rethink how and what is done. In time, the group may fall into comfortable routines, also known as ruts, and become stagnant. If this happens you need to help the group innovate, foster creative thinking, consider how circumstances may have changed, meet new or different needs, and generally do things better. The group is not at the same place it was when it started, and it should be capable of handling more complex challenges. Spur the group on to increased excellence, and motivate them to see beyond where they currently are and into the future. Additionally, you should be aware of any emerging leaders in the group. Give them the opportunity to do more and delegate more significant leadership tasks. You may even decide to let a person lead the group or another one once they have proven their readiness.

- Stage 5, adjourning: Your work should be complete, but consider having a celebration to commemorate the group's work. Encourage members to stay connected with one another and to look for opportunities to serve in the future.

Team Composition

It is important to be intentional about diversity when building a team. Our natural tendency is to surround ourselves with people with whom we are comfortable: like-minded people with whom we agree, people of a similar age, people with the same ministry background or experience, people who have a similar personality type or the same hobbies and interests. However, teams should include a diverse group of people who bring not only different skill sets and the competencies of their organizational departments but also diverse perspectives, backgrounds, personality types, and strengths. Moreover, we should consider how these differences might interact with and impact the team and its performance. While managing differences in a group may be challenging, what we initially see as a challenge may be the natural outworking of diversity in action and in the end may become the strength of the team.

For example, consider how different personalities tend to play out in team meetings. Picture a team comprising visionary thinkers, risk takers, and change agents who are convinced they can change the world with their latest ideas. These folks are typically very good at a high level of thinking but can lack the attention to detail, risk evaluation, or follow-through required for effective planning and execution. Their team meetings will be filled with excitement and passion—but who will convert all this vision and passion into action and results? Conversely, consider a group made up of highly conscientious, risk-averse folks who are good at detail and follow-through. While there will be a good plan for execution and every detail and contingency will be buttoned down, they may lack vision or the ability to get others excited about their plan. While these are extreme examples, we can easily see how different personalities impact the functioning and balance of a team. We can also see the potential for conflict, as people of differing personalities will clash over what gets done and how it gets done (see chap. 7 for more on this).

It is also important to think through different roles team members play. Models of team roles draw on theories of personality in a functional setting. For example, Meredith Belbin defines "team roles" as "one of nine clusters of behavioral attributes identified . . . as being effective to facilitate team progress."[6] These include roles such as resource investigator, social coordinator, monitor, specialist, implementer, and finisher. Social, thinking, and task roles—which are similar to different personalities and levels of EI—are complementary ways members contribute to a team in addition to fulfilling their functional or departmental role. While this model is not without its critics,[7] there is some evidence that these complementary roles can indeed improve team performance.[8]

Another role approach to team composition, one that is growing in popularity, is the working-genius model, developed by Patrick Lencioni and the Table Group. This model suggests there are six distinct roles in a group:

- Wonder: this person identifies the need for improvement or change.
- Invention: this person confirms the importance of that need and generates an idea or solution.
- Discernment: this person assesses the merit and workability of the idea or solution.
- Galvanizing: this person generates enthusiasm and action around the idea or solution.
- Enablement: this person initiates support and assists in the implementation of the idea or solution.
- Tenacity: this person commits to ensuring that the idea or solution gets completed and that results are achieved.[9]

Leaders should consider the personalities in a group and be mindful of the different role each person is playing. It is helpful to encourage the team members in their respective roles and see how they help in the overall team functioning.

Often, teams comprise people from different functional areas. For example, the directors of various departments need to collaborate and make decisions together. Thus, leaders may not be able to create a perfectly balanced team with complementary personalities or roles. Still, sometimes balance can be achieved if the leaders supplement functional-area personnel with others who are selected specially because of their gifts or personalities. The composition of a team can also be intentionally diversified so that it includes those who are not the "usual suspects." While leaders' natural tendency may be to bring in those they know or feel comfortable with or those who would benefit from being in the room, there is evidence that introducing outsiders is sometimes a great way of stimulating creative thinking and adding new dimensions to a group or team. Further, it is not just the "cool kids" who succeed. Being the underdogs can also be a way of motivating a group to overcome great challenges and of developing a distinct and innovative identity.[10]

Do you remember the movie *The Bad News Bears*? That movie featured a baseball team made up of misfit kids and rejects. Organizational psychologist Adam Grant shares a similar story of the animated film juggernaut Pixar, which brought together the misfits of the organization for a special task. These folks did not have past success and were not considered to be the insiders of the organization. But when given the chance, they shined and together went on to create one of their most successful films, *The Incredibles*.[11] Organizations may tend to exclude those who are different, unfamiliar, or odd—the outcasts—but such people may, in fact, be a wealth of potential and differing perspectives to any team. A "prophet" may be challenging but may bring in needed perspective. Leaders should step out of their comfort zones and ask, "Who is on my team, and am I intentional in bringing in a diverse set of voices, not just people chosen because of their functional area?" The leader may be able to turn their own Bad News Bears into the Incredibles!

Groupthink and Escalation of Commitment

While seeking group cohesion is typically a good thing and research shows it increases the performance of a group,[12] there can be too much cohesion, which diminishes how well a group or team performs. Overly cohesive groups can spend inordinate amounts of time on their people and relationships, to the neglect of the tasks. In a church context, a small group or ministry that starts off with gusto and achieves its goals may, in time, deteriorate into nothing more than a social group. Gone are the days of seeking to accomplish a mission. Now the members are comfortable just being together and cannot be bothered with the messiness of outreach or the other function for which the group was established. While this is an extreme example, it illustrates how overly cohesive groups get less done.

A more insidious occurrence that happens to groups is groupthink. Originally coined by Irving Janis, the term "groupthink" refers to "a mode of thinking that people engage in when they are deeply involved in a cohesive in-group, when the members' strivings for unanimity override their motivation to realistically appraise alternative courses of action."[13] Groups like this comprise proverbial "yes-men," those who will tell a leader (or themselves) only what they want to hear, despite evidence to the contrary. The characteristics of groupthink are as follows:

- Illusions of invulnerability: the belief that everything will be all right because the group is special or different
- Belief in the inherent morality of the group: the notion that the group is superior to other groups
- Collective rationalization: group justification for decisions that supports a "hear no evil, see no evil, speak no evil" mindset
- Out-group stereotypes: the practice of considering outsiders to be faceless *others* who are all the same—enemies and/or people of no consequence
- Self-censorship: the practice of biting one's lip when thinking differently, because there is an understanding that group members should not bring up anything that will rock the boat
- Illusion of unanimity: a forced, false sense of being in agreement
- Direct pressure on dissenters: the knowledge, either explicit or implicit, that members must not diverge from the consensus
- Self-appointed mind guards: those who protect a leader or the group from assault by troublesome ideas[14]

Groupthink is often the result of excessive homogeneity—for example, too much similarity in members' backgrounds, age, experience, and perspectives—and the group not changing much over time, being swayed by a charismatic leader, or otherwise becoming impervious to outside challenges and reality testing. Groups that engage in groupthink may make poor decisions, as they become an echo chamber resounding with the thoughts of a single strong member, or a few strong members, who do not consider other perspectives.

Further, these groups can engage in *escalation of commitment*, also known as commitment bias, which is the investing of additional resources into failing causes.[15] Because the group members do not want to be judged for poor decisions or be seen negatively, they collectively stick to their guns, so to speak, to prove they are right. If a group decides to go ahead with a project and things do not go well, the group will not change course or pull the plug. Rather, it will continue with the project until reality catches up with it or it sputters to a slow death.

In the worst cases, these groups engage in unethical or even illegal decisions and activities, as there is no one to challenge them or hold them accountable. Consider the fall of Mars Hills Church in Seattle, Washington, as a case in point. Mark Driscoll held sway over a group of like-minded leaders, and when someone tried to hold him or the group accountable, they were summarily dismissed from the church. While there were many reasons behind the collapse of Mars Hill, no one was able to challenge or change the mind of Driscoll or hold the group accountable. The church imploded due to poor decisions and practices, leaving many devastated people in its wake and inviting derision from a watching world.[16]

How can a leader help prevent a group from lapsing into groupthink? Consider the following ideas:

- *Change membership regularly.* This is often required per bylaws, but regardless, elders and church-council members should be rotated on a regular basis, and there should be periodic changes in the people who represent various constituencies. The basic idea here is the rationale for civic democratic elections, and this practice is useful for organizations wanting to keep groups accountable.

- *Be intentional about bringing in diverse points of view.* For example, a leader may ask those not usually represented to be part of the group in order to increase the diversity of perspectives and opinions.

- *Give members permission to dissent.* Particularly when groups are forming, leaders should let members know that no one in the group is above being challenged, even senior leaders. Leaders should also consider whether the climate is conducive to psychological safety as well as how members feel about having a voice in a group.

- *Appoint a "devil's advocate."* Churches, of course, do not want to give any room to the devil! Yet they need people who can bring contrary opinions to challenge the status quo. Leaders should let certain members know it is part of their job to bring differing perspectives and points of view, to challenge sloppy thinking or untested assumptions, to bring in outside research, and so on. This practice will force the group to think more deeply and measuredly.

- *Regularly talk about how the group makes decisions.* Make groupthink a topic of discussion and not an elephant in the room. Chris Argyris popularized the idea of making the undiscussable discussable to bring about better decisions, work through conflicts, and bring self-accountability to the group.[17]

Coaching the Team

What would any team be without a good coach? Now that we have reviewed the foundations of teams as well as team composition and major pitfalls, it is time to address how to build strong, self-directed, and high-performing teams. Since the essence of teamwork is developing the capacity of the team itself—to be autonomous, self-accountable, and fully engaged with its mission and the mission of the organization—it should be no surprise that the chief aim of team leadership is to promote and enable team functioning instead of fulfilling the traditional model of leader as hero, problem solver, blame taker, and so on. Coaching is ideally suited for this positive aim of team leadership.

Coaching has become popular among leadership consultants over the past several decades, perhaps as the logical extension and corollary of the popularity of teams. While it is beyond the scope of this book to fully explore coaching—the topic is vast—the following is an overview of how coaching can be used in an organizational and ministry setting as an effective way to lead teams. Coaching is distinct from traditional leadership in several ways. Consider the following distinctions:

Traditional Leader's Role	Coach's Role
Sets mission and goals for others	Helps team members determine their mission and goals
Provides motivation others need to keep pursuing the mission	Encourages members to find what motivates them
Sets processes for others, determines how tasks will be accomplished	Facilitates conversation about what direction and processes will look like
Aligns the organization to mission, keeps departments interconnected	Helps members connect with the organization and find their role in it, makes their function known to the organization

There are many models and approaches to coaching in an organizational setting. One such model is Peter Hawkins's systemic team-coaching approach.[18] Traditional approaches to coaching focus on one-on-one relationships, and while this approach has its place, Hawkins's approach is based on the idea that it is more optimal to coach teams rather than individuals. Recall FST, which suggests that the problems of individuals are the problems of families and that individuals inherit and embody dynamics of the social system around them. How individuals function and thrive is directly related to how well their unit or team functions and thrives. Thus, the focus of coaching should be the team, not the individuals. Hawkins's model is also a systemic approach in that each component of the model relates to the other, just as individuals are related to the team and the team is interconnected with the larger organization. In this model, the focus is on five core roles of a good coach, which pertain to the following five concerns:

1. Commission: What is the purpose of the team as determined by either the organization or the larger community of stakeholders (e.g., the denomination)?

2. Clarification: What does the commission mean to the team itself, and do the members have a sense of ownership over it? What are the team goals and key performance indicators, and do the team members have clarity about their roles within the team?

3. Cocreation: What is the process by which the team operates? For example, what are the ground rules, how are meetings run, and how does the team build cohesion?

4. Connecting: How do team members, as individuals, connect with and relate to others in the organization and to its stakeholders? For example, when a team member leaves the team space (e.g., the office), do they act as representatives of the team to other staff, partners, parishioners, and so on? When they are not with the team, do they still embody the spirit and ideals of the team?

5. Core learning: What is the team learning together, how well does it self-reflect, and what do the individual members learn by being part of the team? For example, does the team use after-action reflections to learn together and improve for future performance?

Coaching in Practice

Now that we have seen the core roles of a coach, we need to know, on a practical level, what a coach actually does with a team. Some may have an understanding of coaches that comes from sports—the coach is a fiery, usually overweight male of advancing years barking ferociously at a losing team or giving an inspiring pep talk at halftime to encourage the team to do better in the second half. Maybe you've seen movies like *Hoosiers* or *Remember the Titans*, which portray coaches who inherit losing or dysfunctional teams and turn them into champions. The victorious team hoists the now-beloved coach (or quarterback) onto their shoulders as the movie ends in triumph and vindication (cue the theatrical music and dab the tear from your eye).

Those learning how to coach should suspend the conventional ideas of what coaches do in place of more realistic and process-oriented approaches. While it is inspiring and romantic to envision the coach as the one who comes in to save the day for the team, researchers and practitioners have discovered much about what makes a coach successful in the day-to-day life of organizational teams. Coaches act more as therapists than motivational speakers.

The model of coaching developed by Hawkins includes five stages, summarized by the acronym CLEAR, which can be completed by a coach and team in about an hour.[19]

- Initial contracting: The coach does not tell the team what it will do but, rather, determines what the team needs from him or her. The coach and team together decide what the end goals are and what is to be accomplished in their time together. The coach opens the dialogue, defines the scope of the relationship, and together they determine what the results look like.

- Listening: While sports movies show coaches giving lots of speeches, organizational coaches do lots of listening, practicing active listening and empathy. They ask lots of questions, draw team members out, go beyond the stated problem to find underlying or root causes, challenge assumptions, look at body language and team dynamics, and hear what is not being said as well as what is. The coach also tries to identify any undiscussable issues that are causing roadblocks for the team.

- Exploration: The coach and team discuss their current situation and determine what they want it to be like in the future. The team is encouraged to dream and get excited about its possibilities. Research suggests that coaching that puts the coached in a positive mental state can be more effective than coaching that is problem focused.[20] If all the time is spent on discussing problems, the team will not activate the positive sentiment it needs in order to get intrinsically motivated to take on new and tough challenges.

- Action: The coach and team determine a plan for attaining their desired future. What are the skills, competencies, roles, and so on needed to get there? Specific, measurable action steps, along with individual accountability and time frames, should be established.

- Review: In time, the coach helps the team review its progress toward the goals, discuss successes and roadblocks, and identify any changes in the goals or methods that are needed to align the team with new realities.

Michael Bungay Stanier, in his practical book *The Coaching Habit*, says to ask seven questions in a coaching session.[21] These questions are designed to help individuals (or teams) get to the important issues they are facing, to open meaningful dialogue and provide a space for open reflection. These questions are the following:

- What's on your mind?
- And what else?
- What's the real challenge here?
- What do you want?
- How can I help you?
- If you're saying "yes" to this, what are you saying "no" to?
- What was most useful for you?[22]

Whichever model or approach you use to help lead a team, remember that your primary role is to facilitate team accomplishment, not provide direct leadership or supervision. If the team sees you as the boss who gives occasional pep talks or direction, no matter how subtly you do these things, you will stifle the team's capacity to engage in open and frank dialogue about what matters to them. You should be the "guide

---

CURRENT ISSUES

Social Loafing and the "(Don't) Work from Home" Movement

As a result of the COVID-19 pandemic, many organizations, including churches and ministries, either began or accelerated work-from-home (WFH) practices. Churches found many creative ways to keep their staff connected with their roles and their congregations. Everything from Zoom services and live streamed services to phone call ministries were used to keep people connected when the world was seemingly shut down and dangerous. Once the shelter-in-place orders were lifted, many organizations, including churches, continued with the practice of allowing staff to work from home. The rationales were varied: the church had spent loads of money on the technical infrastructure and wanted to leverage the investment; working from home cut out commuting time; parents could watch children whose schools were still occasionally shutting down; remote work just fit many people's lifestyles. Further, in many cases workers could easily do their job from a distance with seemingly no downside, so why not allow it?

Now that the pandemic has subsided, most churches are seeing their members return, although many have new virtual congregations due to their pandemic-era streaming efforts. Moreover, many are now wrestling with issues surrounding a workforce that has become accustomed to and happy with WFH. The success and productivity of WFH is showing to be a mixed bag. Some organizations report no change, and some even show increases in productivity. Other factors, such as stress and well-being, are also shown to be impacted by WFH.[*] Yet some leaders are wondering whether they can continue to have staff dispersed, particularly in roles that require interacting with the public. Angie Richey of Life Pacific University is one leader who is concerned and has seen drops in productivity. "No doubt, many people who have public-facing roles need to return to the office."[†] Tech guru and Tesla founder Elon Musk made headlines when he told his workforce to return to the office or find another place to "not work."[‡] At the time of this writing, there is a growing consensus that corporate leaders are wanting their workforces to return to the office for good for a variety of reasons.[**]

There are other reasons for concern from a teams and motivational perspective. First, while some roles may allow people to do tasks and be productive at a distance, groups and teams, as we learned, have an important social dimension as well as a task dimension. In other words, a job, and people's satisfaction with the job, is more than getting tasks done; it is about the support and connection with others on the team. Many people are strongly motivated by the social interactions they have within a team, and as terrific as Zoom is, working in isolation removes a key motivator for people who are so motivated. Some have low social needs and can seemingly work on their own indefinitely. Many, however, cannot. They need social interaction in order to thrive and avoid feelings of isolation.[††] Moreover, when people work in isolation, they miss out on the important synergy and serendipitous encounters that come when people gather. Meetings are more than just times to communicate or work together. They are opportunities to discover new people, ideas, events, and activities. The Allen Curve, an important contribution to communication theory from the 1970s, suggests that there is a direct correlation between physical proximity and communication that ultimately enhances innovation and creativity.[‡‡] In other words, when people from various areas gather, they collide, and good things happen. Steve Jobs famously obsessed over allowing people from different areas to meet, taking a cue from the practices of Bell Labs that preceded the Apple Computer era.[***]

Finally, organizations must think through how to make WFH options equitable for all. If some are allowed to work remotely and others are not, there may be a sense of unfairness leading to resentment or other responses equity theory would suggest.[†††]

As you consider the WFH movement and what it means for your groups and teams, be sure to consider more than productivity and the completion of tasks. Also take into account the social factor of motivation and the synergy and innovation that come when people collaborate with others face-to-face. Be equitable in determining who is and who is not allowed to work from home. The church, above all other organizations, should value community and innovation.

* See, e.g., Thomas J. George, Leanne E. Atwater, Dustin Maneethai, and Juan M. Madera, "Supporting the Productivity and Wellbeing of Remote Workers: Lessons from COVID-19," *Organizational Dynamics* 51, no. 2 (2022): 100869, https://doi.org/10.1016/j.orgdyn.2021.100869.

† Angie Richey, personal interview by the author, September 1, 2022.

‡ Here is an interesting excerpt from his communication: "If you don't show up, we will assume you have resigned. The more senior you are, the more visible must be your presence." Sam Tabahriti, "Read the Email Elon Musk Sent to Tesla Employees about Returning to the Office before Saying Headcount Will Increase," *Business Insider*, June 5, 2022, https://www.businessinsider.com/read-elon-musk-email-tesla-employees -return-office-2022-6.

** "2024: The End of Fully Remote?," Korn Ferry, accessed December 21, 2023, https://www.kornferry .com/insights/this-week-in-leadership/2024-the-end-of-fully-remote.

†† Social isolation due to WFH is a serious concern for the upcoming workforce around the world. See Gautam Kumra and Diaan-Yi Lin, "The Future of (Hybrid) Work," *McKinsey Future of Asia Podcasts*, September 2, 2022, https://www.mckinsey.com/featured-insights/future-of-asia/future-of-asia-podcasts/the-future-of -hybrid-work.

‡‡ Thomas Allen and Gunter Henn, *The Organization and Architecture of Innovation* (London: Routledge, 2006).

*** Lisa Eadicicco, "Here's Why Office Layout Was So Important to Steve Jobs," *Business Insider*, October 7, 2014, https://www.businessinsider.com/steve-jobs-office-apple-pixar-2014-10.

††† Samantha Delouya and Avery Hartmans, "Resentment Is Mounting as Some Employees Are Forced Back to the Office and Some Are Allowed to Work from Home," *Business Insider*, November 1, 2022, https:// www.businessinsider.com/hybrid-work-back-to-office-work-from-home-resentment-culture-2022-11.

on the side" and not the "sage on the stage." Find ways to come along-side the team and give members opportunities to engage in productive dialogue, keep themselves on track, commit to productivity and self-accountability, review their progress, avoid groupthink and insularity, learn together, and connect with the organization's members and its purpose. By doing so, you will multiply your own influence, building a high-capacity team that is able to lead itself and engage the ministry in dynamic and fruitful ways.

■ Practical Leadership Application Questions ■

- Consider the groups in your church or ministry. To what degree are they true teams, as described above?
- If the groups are not functioning as true teams, how has leadership, either yours or other leaders', led to that condition? What could you do to move to a true team approach? What would be the benefits and costs of doing so?
- How cohesive are the groups in your ministry, and what practical steps can be taken to increase the groups' sense of cohesion and positive group identity?
- Identify one or more groups that you oversee in your organization, and recall the stages of group or team formation. What stage is the group at right now? Are you leading them in a way that is appropriate for that stage?
- How intentional are you in promoting diversity in groups and teams? Do you seek to add members with distinct perspectives and skills, or do you tend to find only like-minded people who will support what you think and do?
- To what degree does groupthink or escalation of commitment negatively impact your core groups? Have you lapsed into potentially unhealthy patterns, and what can you do to bring self-accountability to the team?
- How well do you coach, rather than lead, your teams? What practices can you employ to do a better job of coaching?

CASE STUDY ████ ██ ██ ██ ███ ██

The Case of the Insular Lead Team

Pastor Rick was thoroughly loving his new role as executive pastor. He had been a successful executive and coach for a Fortune 500 company and was elated that the Lord had opened a door for him to serve at Friends Fellowship, of which he and his wife had been members for ten years, both of them serving as committed volunteers in a variety of ministries. This was his opportunity to use his years of management and coaching experience to impact his home church, and he had a sense of excitement each day as he arrived at the office and thought about new possibilities for the church and the ways the Lord could use him. Friends Fellowship had just arrived at the point where it could afford a full-time executive pastor. Previously, the pastor's wife, Liz, did most of the heavy administrative lifting in the church—hiring, firing, leading meetings, and spearheading the strategic-planning process. But she was now becoming more engaged in leading the women's ministry, and the church needed a full-time staff person to run the business affairs of the church. Rick was thought to be the perfect candidate by the senior pastors and the church council.

During his first week, Rick spent lots of time talking to the key leaders in the church, getting to know the leaders of the youth ministry, children's ministry, outreach ministry, live production, worship teams, and so on. His one-on-one meetings went well, and he heard a great deal of vision and passion from these leaders. Yet he could not help sensing some reservation in their voices as they spoke to him about their roles and ministries. Something was not quite right, and he was about to find out what it was.

During his first lead-team meeting, Liz opened in prayer, concluding with, "And Lord, help Rick learn his role here and all we need him to do. Amen." Pastor Gilberto then said, "Rick, I am so blessed to have you on board. I'm sure you will be a valuable member on my team." As the meeting unfolded, each leader began by giving a brief and somewhat uninspired report of things happening in their area. About ten minutes in, Pastor Gilberto interrupted, saying, "I appreciate all the information you are sharing, but I have an elders' meeting at 3, so can we all just cut to the chase here? We have some exciting news we need to share with you all." The mood in the room changed, and all eyes were on Gilberto and Liz. They began to share an "exciting new vision" the Lord had given them just the night before, which was to raise and invest three million dollars in a new building to house the children' ministry, which had been growing quickly due to the young families coming into the church. Children were the future, after all, they said, and the church needed to invest in this future. Who could argue with this logic? Moreover, Gilberto and Liz stated that their own children needed a healthy place to develop as the eventual heirs of the church.

While Gilberto and Liz were sharing, Rick was filled with confusion and cognitive dissonance. He had just finished reviewing the strategic plan, the result of months of collaboration and work among the staff, and he did not recall seeing anything about fundraising or a new building for children's ministry. What he had seen were new initiatives to bolster community outreach and missions, which had been on Gilberto's heart since last year, when his longtime friend came and inspired them to be more missions minded. It seemed to Rick that Gilberto, as a visionary leader, had a case of shiny object syndrome, something detrimental he had seen in his corporate work. Leaders had been swayed by the latest idea that came to their attention, changing directions frequently and leaving staff overworked, burned out, and heading out the door.

As Gilberto and Liz's new vision unfolded, the staff dutifully listened with deer-in-the-headlights stares, not saying much. They smiled, told Gilberto and Liz what a wonderful vision this was, and said that since they had heard from the Lord, this had to be the direction they should head in. But inside, they were all wondering about the other strategic initiatives that they had agreed to just the previous month and that they had worked hard planning for. Of concern, Gilberto had been equally as excited and sure of the Lord's direction then. As the meeting concluded, Gilberto quickly gave a few team members specific steps he wanted them to take. Rick was to "call the bank and see how good our credit is." Sonia, the director of church promotion and media, was to "work on a new promotional campaign and website." Ellen, the director of children's ministry, was to "get the children's volunteers excited about the new vision." With that, Gilberto and Liz rushed off to their elders' meeting to share this new vision.

Several people, including Rick, Sonia, and Ellen, stuck around to discuss the situation. "I can't believe this," said Sonia. "My team just spent weeks on developing new visuals and revamping the website to promote the outreach efforts we were making—and now this." Ellen chimed in, equally as puzzled. Rick took it all in and wondered what sort of leadership structure he had walked into.

Questions for Discussion

- Is this a team or a group? What are some of the indicators?
- How might groupthink be at play here? What is some evidence that groupthink is happening?

- How might Rick's own administratively minded personality be influencing how he is seeing things play out here? And how about Gilberto's visionary personality?
- What can Rick do to influence the approach the church takes to teams and decision-making processes?
- Recall the earlier discussion of FST. How are the various postures seen here (distance, conflict, underfunctioning and overfunctioning, and triangulation)?

■ Further Reading ■

Hawkins, Peter, ed. *Leadership Team Coaching in Practice: Case Studies on Creating Highly Effective Teams*, 3rd ed. (New York: Kogan Page, 2022).

Lencioni, Patrick. *The Five Dysfunctions of a Team: A Leadership Fable*. San Francisco: Jossey-Bass, 2002.

Lingenfelter, Sherwood G., and Julie A. Green. *Teamwork Cross-Culturally: Christ-Centered Solutions for Leading Multinational Teams*. Grand Rapids: Baker Academic, 2022.

Pearce, Craig L., Charles C. Manz, and Henry P. Sims Jr. *Share, Don't Take the Lead*. Charlotte: IAP, 2014.

Stanier, Michael Bungay. *The Coaching Habit: Say Less, Ask More and Change the Way You Lead Forever*. Toronto: Box of Crayons Press, 2016.

7

Conflict Management

Introduction

Conflict is an ever-present reality in organizational life, even in a church or ministry. Jesus said, "For where two or three gather in my name, there am I with them" (Matt. 18:20), and seemingly, wherever two or more are gathered, there is also potential for conflict! Most people do not like conflict, and some churches develop cultures that are averse to it, becoming unwilling to talk about the underlying causes or develop healthy ways of dealing with the conflict. These churches act as if conflict is unnatural or unbiblical or the result of an unspiritual person causing division—or maybe even the work of the enemy himself. But a close look at Scripture shows conflict is *very* biblical. Just ask Cain and Abel, Abraham and Lot, Moses and the grumbling crowd, Joshua and the kings of Canaan, David and Saul, Nehemiah and Sanballat, Jesus and the Pharisees, Paul and John Mark, and the early church in Corinth. It is also a historical reality of the church. Just consider the splits and divisions over doctrine, governance, the rights of kings, and so forth. Perhaps the greatest development in church history, the Protestant Reformation, came as the result of a conflict. All of us have been involved in conflicts in our personal lives, our work, and our ministry. Some reading this book are, no doubt, weary combat veterans, literally and figuratively. Conflict is thus not an intruder into organizational life; it is a natural part of it. The question is, How do church leaders perceive conflict, deal with it, and use it to their advantage?

The Bible admonishes us to live in harmony with one another (Rom. 12:16) and to have unity with one another (1 Pet. 3:8), and it tells us that brothers and sisters living in unity is a beautiful thing, a place where God's blessing dwells (Ps. 133). One should keep in mind, however, that unity is not uniformity or conformity, which require people to look or think the same way. The all-creative God of the universe made people unique and creative beings, and being part of his church does not mean laying down these qualities. Each of us has a distinct voice and a distinct role to play. To use a musical analogy, harmony is not everyone playing the same notes; it happens when different musical notes work together in a pleasing way, complementing and supporting one another, giving color and interest to the music, building tension and even dissonance, but always leaving the listener satisfied. Living in harmony means aligning different voices and perspectives into a pleasing and fruitful whole, not eliminating voices or insisting that everyone see things the same way. Imagine a piece of music in which a whole orchestra uses the same instrument and, all together, plays the same notes, at the same time. Sounds rather boring. Sure, Gregorian chant is beautiful, but even it has hints of harmony and different musical textures from time to time!

Conflict can be mundane and subtle, leading to hurt feelings or severed personal relationships. It can be broad and sweeping, leading to wars. And it can fall somewhere in between. While it may be the result of the enemy trying to cause division, heretics trying to lead people astray, or sincere people holding irreconcilable doctrinal positions, most organizational conflict is ordinary and understandable and can be addressed without religious tribunals or exorcisms. Adam Grant says, "In any relationship, conflict is inevitable, but it isn't unsolvable."[1] As such, church leaders need to have a good understanding of the causes of, consequences of, and cures for typical organizational conflict, seeing the negative implications of no conflict and the positive side of productive conflict. The challenge for church leaders is not to eliminate or suppress conflict but, rather, to have conflict in ways that are healthy and constructive and to manage the tension that conflict causes so that people can live in unity and harmony. This is the topic of this chapter.

What Is Conflict?

It may seem unnecessary to define conflict, since everyone has experienced it firsthand and could probably give their own definition. While there is a myriad of definitions of conflict in the OB literature, we will define "conflict" as "a process resulting in the perceptions of two parties that they are working in opposition to each other in ways that result in feelings of discomfort and/or animosity."[2] There are several important features of this definition:

- *It is a process.* Most conflicts build or unfold over time. A simple disagreement in a meeting that gets resolved quickly may be a momentary conflict, but most conflicts take time to develop and to resolve.
- *It involves perceptions.* The facts may be the same for both parties, but how they see and interpret these facts differs based on a variety of personal differences, goals, and so on. Also note that the parties involved must see it as a conflict. A spirited conversation among colleagues is not necessarily a conflict, even though to outsiders it may seem like one.
- *One or both parties must have uncomfortable feelings.* There must be something that touches a nerve and causes feelings of hurt, anger, resentment, and so forth. People can engage in a spirited conversation without it being a conflict as long as both parties play along and understand the nature of the conversation.

The Downside and Upside of Organizational Conflict

Many assume that conflict is always a bad thing and try to avoid it like the proverbial plague. While this is understandable and conflict certainly may be uncomfortable and taxing, always avoiding conflict is a misguided policy. Some Christians use verses such as those mentioned above as a reason not to speak up, confront problems, or make meaningful contributions to decisions. Or they can be overly deferential to others in authority and avoid conflict for fear of being disrespectful. Unity and respect are important virtues, to be sure, but there can also be a false harmony that indicates a lack of psychological safety and that prevents true teamwork. A lack of conflict is not necessarily a sign that all is well. In fact, a persistent lack of conflict in a group or team could indicate the following:

- *Group members do not care.* There is apathy and lack of concern over an issue, and it is not worth their emotional energy to engage. People have checked out.
- *Group members are intimidated.* There is fear about how they and their ideas will be received by others, particularly more senior people or those whom they perceive as having more status in the group. Intimidation can lead to groupthink or a lack of self-accountability.
- *Group members feel disconnected.* There is a lack of cohesion whereby members feel left out or unimportant to a group and do not have confidence that their ideas matter.
- *Group members are not trusting.* There is a lack of trust in the room, and people are reluctant to be open out of concern of being hurt or disrespected. Everyone has a strong self-preservation instinct, and few will step out when they think others may hurt them in some way.

Can conflict ever be a good thing? Healthy and open conflict does several positive things in a group or organization:

- It is an indicator that members feel safe, valued, and trusting enough to be open with ideas even when they know there may be disagreement.
- It indicates that the culture is healthy and that the health of the organization is more important than the turf of any one individual. A healthy culture is not one of uniformity but rather one that allows variety, change, and pushback when appropriate.
- It allows the groups or organization to benefit from the diversity present. Healthy organizations are diverse organizations—diverse in culture and gender, background and expertise, and perspective. As the Lord increases a group or organization's scope and size, the leader must allow the increased diversity to make a difference that is meaningful to all, not simply to keepers of the status quo.

The above is not meant to imply that there should be conflict all the time or that Christian organizations should be combative places or that every idea or perspective is valid and deserves space. These ideas are not realistic or healthy either. Rather, leaders should understand the nature of conflicts, should consider the passion and assumptions behind the diversity of ideas and perspectives they encounter, and should avoid deflecting conflict in the hopes of creating harmony. The idea is to create healthy environments where everyone, including those with dissenting points of view, can contribute in order to get the best results. This approach to conflict can also allow the leader to clarify roles, show appreciation and openness to the contributions every member makes, and lessen the ambiguity that stifles free expression.

Types of Conflict

Not all conflicts are created equal. In organizational life, conflict can take several different forms. The most typical forms of conflict are as follows:

- Task conflict: This is a disagreement of goals and priorities, direction, and so on. For example, a church elders board may disagree on budget priorities, with some wanting to invest in building needs and others wanting to devote more money to a local missions board and to outreach.
- Process conflict: This is a disagreement over how to accomplish a task or role. For example, the executive pastor may feel it is necessary for children's ministry volunteers to come to a central location to check in before service, but the children's ministry director may think this will be too inconvenient for them and may want to have check-in stations at each classroom.
- Relationship conflict: This occurs when people clash due to differences in personality, communication style, background, and a host of other individual differences. For example, Pastor Raul often gets into conflict with Elder Ed, and this conflict stems from Raul's laid-back manner and what Raul considers to be Ed's uptight and petty nature.

Causes of Conflict

There are as many specific causes of conflicts as there are people, tasks, and goals. However, conflict can often be traced back to one of several root causes, and for each cause there are a few ways of approaching a resolution.

Differences in Goals and Perspectives

As mentioned above, people often disagree over what strategic choices should be prioritized, what tasks and projects should be undertaken, and how these things should be done. In church life, there is a myriad of decisions to be made—what projects the church will engage in, how a service will be run, how the church will try to reach the community, how the board will deal with budgetary issues, how the church will recruit volunteers, and the list goes on. Even though people see the same facts, because they view these facts from the perspective of their particular office or department, they will have different goals and priorities. For example, at one church the treasurer is looking at the budget when considering which events the church should host during the coming year. Her goal is minimizing expenses and saving money, as church giving is down due to a recession. The creative-arts pastor, on the other hand, sees these events as the lifeblood of the church's community outreach, as each year they bring in hundreds of guests, many of whom make decisions to follow Christ. Saving money or saving souls—one can easily see the potential for heated conflict here. Of course, both are important; no one is disputing this. But different parties see the issue much differently due to their respective offices in the church.

This may be the most rational cause of conflict and perhaps the easiest to address, as its cause is visible. When seeking to resolve such conflict, look for ways to explore the relative merits of each perspective and solution. Typical ways to do so include the following:

- Pros and cons: Develop a list of positives and negatives for each side of a conflict, and let each party weigh in. While this may seem uncomfortable at first, it can become a good practice in team building and cohesion, as members learn to consider ideas openly, without resorting to back-channel discussions. Polarity mapping is a more sophisticated form of this approach used for long-term intractable issues that seemingly have no resolution or are paradoxical.[3] Leaders must learn to manage the tension these issues can cause over the long haul, and defining and working with polarities is important in a world of often diametrically opposed ideas.

- Negotiation: Promote open discussion and let members discuss what they are willing to concede, wait for, allow instead of, and so on. This process may lead to compromise on all sides, which is not ideal, but it can make members content until more optimal solutions are forthcoming.

- Robert's Rules of Order (or other formalized way of hearing differing perspectives and casting votes to come to a consensus):[4] Formal groups such as boards of directors often use this approach, but most organizational groups do not, often due to their size or leadership style. The approach gives members a way to build consensus and lets everyone weigh in. It can be as informal or formal as required—whatever makes sense for the group's size and culture.

- Tie breaking: We will discuss this idea more fully below, but it can be appropriate and expedient for the leader with the most formal authority in a group—but not a self-appointed authority—to decide on a matter. Allow all to share, then make a decision for the group.

Differences in Background and Personalities

While goal and perspective conflicts are relatively easy to see and predict, the conflict that arises from relational issues is more subtle and harder to see, as it stems from a host of individual differences between two parties that may be hidden or seldom discussed. They may even be undiscussable. As you may recall from chapter 2, individual differences include factors such as personality (conscientiousness, extroversion, agreeableness, emotional stability, openness to experience), culture and gender, skills and abilities, locus of control, creativity, and callings and gifts. Because of these differences, people process ideas differently from one another and may even have negative perceptions of others—"His way of seeing this is wrong," meaning "His way of seeing this is different from mine." Since a goal of any healthy church or ministry should be to bring in people from different backgrounds, with various perspectives and expertise, it is inevitable that from time to time people will have conflict with others. Sometimes two or more people will have seemingly diametrically opposed personalities, callings, and ways of processing situations.

For example, let's expand on the above example of the treasurer and the creative-arts pastor. While their goal incompatibility is one dimension of the conflict, another issue may stem from their different backgrounds and personalities. Imagine the treasurer is highly conscientious and thus focuses on a few goals at a time, has high risk aversion, is educated in finance, has little creative impulse, and feels called to make sure the church is a good steward of its resources. The creative-arts pastor, on the other hand, is low on conscientiousness and thus focuses on many goals at a time, has low risk aversion, loves new challenges and change, has a theater arts degree, and feels called to express God's creativity to reach the present generation. It is easy to see the potential for conflict when examining what makes these people tick. The treasurer perceives the creative-arts pastor as flighty, unreasonable, and unconcerned about real-world issues such as the church finances. The creative-arts pastor sees the treasurer as stodgy, unimaginative, lacking faith, and unconcerned about saving souls. Unmet expectations are at the root of this type of conflict, as one party does not act as the other expects or hopes. They both look at the other and think, "I would never do it this way."

Resolving this type of conflict can be trickier than handling differences in goals and perspectives, which can typically be discussed more openly and rationally. Conflict that comes from differing backgrounds and personalities, a lack of understanding or appreciation of others, or a lack of self-awareness or social sensitivity is much harder to manage. However, it can be healthy for groups to have open conversations about the contributions members make and the way each member is different and adds to the group dynamic. Discussing differences rather than letting them be a hidden source of frustration may turn them into a strength of the group that builds cohesion and leverages its diversity.

Some ways to deal with this type of conflict include the following:

- Team development sessions: Have times when roles and personalities are discussed. There are some good assessments of personality, strengths, and team roles that can make these types of issues more transparent. Also, doing development work on emotional and social intelligence (see chap. 3) may help some members become more aware of themselves and others on an emotional level. Develop a culture in which differences are openly celebrated, not secretly tolerated.

- Expert help: Consider bringing in an expert from outside the group to facilitate such sessions. The differences that underlie conflict may seem personal, and people sometimes become defensive, but an outside voice may lessen the discomfort and resistance. While hiring an expert may initially seem unproductive or costly, and while there may be apparently more pressing tasks to which the team needs to attend, learning to occasionally focus on personality dynamics in the group goes a long way to prevent conflict, as members become more comfortable with others and their quirks, perspectives, and so on.

- Hot buttons: Help members become aware of which issues or people set them off emotionally. For example, if someone's program is on the agenda of a meeting, that person may be inclined to get possessive, feel threatened, and be argumentative, as their "baby" is being dissected in public. As a leader, you should know your own hot buttons as well as other people's. Taking stock of the emotional potential an issue has can help you prepare for what might surface.

- Realistic expectations: One certainty in life is that you will be disappointed if you expect everyone to behave the way you think they should. Know up front what is reasonable to expect from others and what is not. Allow people to not meet your expectations without being wrong for doing so.

- Appreciation: Know the passions and perspectives each member is likely to have over a potentially conflictual issue. Be sure to show ample appreciation for these things up front. Doing so may take the sting out of criticism, as the people will know they are appreciated.

- Proper focus: Keep conflict focused on issues, not people. Sometimes this type of conflict gets personal quickly as past transgressions are brought up or assumptions about people's motives are made. Your role as leader is to help the group stay focused on the issues themselves and work through personal matters in other settings. You do not want team meetings to become group counseling or group mediation sessions.

- Understanding and forgiveness: Often a current personality conflict is a symptom of previous wounds or unforgiveness. While you may not be a team member's pastor, our faith suggests we all should be quick to forgive others. Ephesians 4:32 tells us to "be kind and compassionate to one another, forgiving each other, just as in Christ God forgave you." This applies to organizational contexts as well, and leaders can be agents of healing and reconciliation for their staff, for "blessed are the peacemakers" (Matt. 5:9). Helping make peace between team members can be a blessing to the entire team.

Differences in Status, Real or Imagined

A constant in organizational life is figuring out who is responsible for what. While we like to think a well-written job description will solve this problem—and one is needed, for certain—tasks and roles develop over time, and not every task, role, or line of authority can be articulated in job descriptions ahead of time. This is especially true in executive roles and jobs that rely more on the expertise and experience of the person than on a formal job description. Conflict will emerge when two parties disagree over who has more status—that is, who is in charge and who has the right to make decisions.[5] Moreover, some will feel that certain tasks are below their status and will deflect responsibility, leaving those tasks for people whom they perceive to be of lower status. If you have heard, uttered, or thought the phrase "That's not my job," there was probably a perceived status conflict lurking beneath the surface.

Status and roles may be clear-cut in certain cases, but in many cases they are not. This lack of clarity sometimes becomes an undiscussable issue that leads to conflict. People vie for dominance or compete to influence outcomes, and one party may feel that the other is overstepping their authority or boundaries. This can happen regardless of a person's role or title. For example, a senior staff member may think that a new staff member is assuming too much responsibility for their role or tenure. Or a paid staff member may think that a volunteer is overstepping by offering suggestions directly to the senior pastor at a private lunch. When you think or hear the phrase "He went over my head" or "She went behind my back," there is probably a perceived status conflict lurking beneath the surface.

Let's look one more time at the previous conflict example, this time through the lens of status and role. The creative-arts pastor is relatively new on staff but gained many years of experience at another prestigious church, is well liked and respected at the church, and was hired by the senior pastor specifically to develop new creative approaches to out-reach. The treasurer has been part of the church since the beginning, is personal friends with the senior pastor, and oh, did he mention his MBA degree yet? Both have a sense that they know best in this situation and that their status on the team gives them the right to assert their views. Thus, each feels the other is stepping out of bounds and on their territory. "Who is she to tell us where to spend our money?" thinks the treasurer. "Who is he to tell me how to reach the community?" thinks the creative-arts pastor. The seeds of conflict are sown. Neither person is evil or wrong here, yet both perceive they are more qualified to influence the decision.

Resolving this type of conflict can be difficult, as status is seldom if ever discussed. However, here are a few suggestions:

- *Avoid implying status differences by playing the leader card.* While pulling rank is tempting and, on occasion, effective, this is one surefire way to shut down honest communication among people.
- *Allow people to speak about unsolved problems.* Some leaders tell workers, "Don't just bring problems; bring solutions." This admonition makes sense; you do not want whiners, and you want to en-courage innovation and decision-making skills. However, if people can come to leaders only with solutions, they may not come at all. Many organizational issues are not easy to solve. Let people bring their ambiguity and uncertainty so they can process their thoughts out loud and get candid feedback from others without feeling that they must impress you with all the right answers.
- *Help team members clarify roles and expectations.* This can be done up front on a new project, when members may be unsure of who will be doing what and may bring unspoken expectations to the table due to their own status or self-perception. Provide feedback and direction in order to clarify responsibilities and correct mispercep-tions about roles.

- *Help members appreciate what others bring to the table.* Perceived status differences can come from a worker's belief that others are not as qualified or experienced as they are. Even if this belief is true, it does not mean that these other people should not be involved. An increasing appreciation for others brings with it an increasing willingness to trust others and decreases sentiments such as "I should be doing this, not them" or, conversely, "They should be doing this, not me."

Conflict Styles

People deal with conflict differently, based on a variety of factors. Given the discussion of individual differences in chapter 2, this should be no surprise. One popular way to understand conflict styles is the Thomas-Kilmann conflict model and inventory.[6] It suggests that there are five ways individuals deal with conflict:

- Competing or dominating: When adopting a competing style, people view interpersonal conflict resolution as a win-lose game. They focus narrowly on claiming as much as they can for themselves. While taking a position is important, a single-minded competitive orientation sacrifices value in the long run and perpetuates conflict.
- Avoiding: Because dealing with conflict directly can be highly uncomfortable, many prefer to avoid it. An avoidant conflict style might at first appear to be the opposite of a competitive style, but in fact, it can be similarly obstructive. It can be a passive-aggressive way of dealing with conflict, and when people consistently choose avoidance, they often allow problems to grow worse.
- Accommodating: Those who adopt an accommodating style seem agreeable and easygoing. But when people consistently put others' needs first, they may experience resentment that builds up over time. Accommodating types typically will benefit from learning to express their needs and concerns.
- Compromising: Some try to resolve conflict by proposing a seemingly equal compromise, such as meeting in the middle, or by mak-

ing significant concessions in an unequal compromise. Although a compromising conflict style can move a conversation forward, the solution is often unsatisfying and temporary because it does not address the root issues.

- Collaborating: A person using a collaborative conflict style attempts to understand the deeper needs behind other parties' demands *and* to express their own needs, seeking a win-win solution. These people see value in working through strong emotions that come up, and they propose trade-offs that will give each side more of what they want.[7]

There is some research that suggests there are correlations between Big Five personality characteristics (discussed in chap. 2) and how people handle interpersonal conflict. For example, conscientiousness, extroversion, agreeableness, and openness have a correlation with the collaborating style. Extroversion correlates with competing, while agreeableness and emotional stability do not. Extroversion, openness, and conscientiousness correlate with avoiding, while agreeableness and emotional stability do not correlate with it.[8] There is also research that suggests that men and women deal with conflict differently.[9] Men are (surprise!) more likely to use a competitive style than women, and women are more likely to use an avoiding style.

Adapting Your Style

One critique of this model, and one I have heard from students over the years, is that how one reacts to conflict may be dependent on the circumstances. For example, a worker may care about one issue more than others, and that will cause them to be more competitive when conflict concerns that issue. They are more likely to compromise on issues they care less about. Some issues may be too painful to deal with, and workers will just want to avoid them. It is true that even though people have a certain amount of predictability in how they generally feel about and respond to conflict, they can adapt their style to some degree. Conflict style, in this sense, can be situational, meaning that it depends on the context and issues. This flexibility can be useful for leaders. Consider the following applications of the five conflict styles.

- Competing or dominating: You might choose this style for important issues when you are certain you are right and when the benefit
of a resolution outweighs the negative feelings that may be created
in the dominated group or person. This style also works when there
is a crisis or sense of urgency. People are more willing to accept authoritative leadership if there is a crisis and the group needs answers
quickly. But be careful not to overuse this style or create a crisis out
of every issue. People become wary of this style before long, and they
will start to see you as authoritarian or underhanded. They may also
be less likely to engage in conflict with you (or play sports with you!).

- Avoiding: While this is typically not a good option, you can use it
to buy time if needed. Sometimes a conflict escalates or tempers
flare or people shut down or information is too limited to inform
a proper decision. A leader can temporarily table an issue—that is,
not make a decision—and revisit it when heads are cooler and more
information is available. Be sure to return to an issue as promised in
order to keep trust high, and do not simply sweep the issue under
the rug—someone will trip over that bump eventually!

- Accommodating: You might choose this style for disputes that are
of greater importance to the other group or person than they are
to you. You will often be able to tell how urgent or important a
matter feels to others, the pressure they are receiving, and so on.
You should not always acquiesce to others, particularly on matters
that are important to you—resentment will fester—but selective
use of accommodation can be effective. Argument for argument's
sake can make the conflict last longer than necessary.

- Compromising: This serves as a good backup approach when other
approaches fail to resolve the issue. The downside of the compromising style is that both parties may feel that they have lost; the
compromise may seem like a lose-lose solution. Still, it may be a
good choice till more options arise or until more time for fuller
collaboration is available.

- Collaborating: This is a style you might use when you are willing to invest time and effort to reach a resolution that maximizes
everyone's outcome. Most agree this is the optimal solution, as all
perspectives are considered and the decision quality may improve.

It also helps ward off groupthink, since it gives differing parties the opportunity to weigh in and have their voices heard.

To conclude, conflict in a church or ministry is not necessarily evil, nor should it be suppressed or treated as an unexpected intruder. The potential for conflict is always present when there is enough psychological safety for people to be candid about their thoughts, and even well-meaning Christians can come into conflict over roles, priorities, and personalities. Leaders can do a great deal to develop a healthy climate by dealing with the causes and consequences of conflict. Doing so requires the leader to help people understand and appreciate others, to demonstrate how to have honest conversations, and to know when to engage and when to table an issue. A church or ministry culture that allows people to engage in spirited and honest, though maybe difficult, conversations and allows healthy conflict is highly preferable to one where conflict is stifled, people feel their voice does not matter, and issues come up in other ways, both subtle and strident.

▣ Practical Leadership Application Questions ▣

- What has been your attitude toward conflict in the past? Do you tend to be conflict averse? If so, how has this negatively impacted issues in the long run?
- What is the conflict tolerance level in your church or ministry? Chances are it will mirror the previous question, as leaders set the tone for this. Is there any conflict-avoidant behavior, and what might the causes be?
- Do you think there are sufficient levels of psychological safety in your church or ministry for people to feel free to share their thoughts, even if they disagree? Or do people censor themselves out of fear of being seen as not submissive to authority? What can you do to help promote this?
- Which of the three conflict types (task, personality, status) have you seen in the past? In hindsight, how well was the conflict handled, and what could have been done better?

- What is your own preferred conflict style (competing/dominating, avoiding, accommodating, compromising, collaborating), and how has this helped or hindered your leadership in the past?
- How have you seen status conflicts in your own life and in your church or ministry? What can be done to work through such issues in healthier ways?

CASE STUDY

The Tense Staff Meeting

Pastor Wendy was having a great day. Things were going well at the church, and she was starting to see fruit from the new initiatives she had implemented as the new executive pastor of Hill Street Community Church. Moreover, she felt she was starting to gel with the staff, making some good relational connections. At first, some staff did not like having a female executive pastor, but most were showing appreciation for her skill and the order she was bringing to the church, which had been in disarray after a six-month vacancy. But now she was about to get a case of the Hill Street blues! Tomas, the senior pastor, was on sabbatical for three months and had put Wendy in charge of leading the church in his absence, including chairing the staff meetings. Her first all-staff meeting went something like this.

After good-natured chatter and an opening prayer, Wendy began the meeting. "Thanks to all of those who contributed their time this past Saturday for our special community outreach event. I know this was a day off for many of you, and Tomas would be proud to know so many were there and making a difference right here in our own backyard. Over one thousand people showed up, and we gave away five hundred backpacks filled with school supplies and forty boxes of new kids' clothes. So many people were blessed. We plan to do this again each month for the rest of the year. It's going to be great." A round of hearty "amens" was heard around the room. But not everyone joined in.

Pete, the church's financial director, chimed in. "Wendy, while we all appreciate this ministry and your zeal to find new ways for the church to connect, I am not sure you had the right to authorize this spending. This event cost us over $20,000 at a time when giving is down and money is tight. Usually, Pastor Tomas makes this sort of spending decision. When he returns, I'm sure he will have something to say about all this going on without his approval." Wendy responded, "Pete, I discussed this with him before he left on his sabbatical, and he seemed very supportive. Further, your office approved all the check requests. Besides, how can you argue with all the fruit that we saw, the lives that were touched on Saturday?"

Then Martha, the outreach pastor, spoke up. "There goes Pete again, counting every nickel. Of course, we all know giving is down—you remind us at every meeting—but why do you have to discount the good work Wendy is trying to establish here? It's been years since we've done anything special for the people right here in town. I think this outreach should be a priority. If we let the ministry be led by financial statements, we'd all be huddled in the corner, not spending anything. In fact, I think I recall that one of the twelve disciples had this same attitude toward Jesus! Where is your faith at, anyhow? The Lord will provide. He always does."

Pete replied, "Of course he does, Martha, but Pastor Tomas has appointed me to oversee the finances, and we can't just implement every new idea someone has. At this rate we will indeed be meeting in the dark—we won't be able to pay our electric bill! I'm confident Tomas will side with me here, and I am going to press this issue with him. We can't let the Wendys of the church take over. There is too much at stake." It was getting personal for Wendy as she felt the sting of Pete's comments, and she began to feel uncertain and to check out emotionally.

Bill, the new head of church operations, chimed in next. "I think we all can see both sides here. The outreach was good but too expensive. Here's an idea for next time, Pete. What if the outreach event costs only, say, $5,000. And Wendy, what if we did the events once a quarter instead of every month?" Some quietly dismissed this suggestion, thinking, "Bill just got here. What does he know?" More ideas and numbers were tossed around, but matters became complex quickly as everyone threw in their two cents on how to solve the problem.

Feeling the tension in the room, Mark, the head of pastoral care, said, "I don't think we are getting anywhere here. I think we should just stop, pray, and let the Lord direct us here." With that, the discussion ended abruptly before the issue could be resolved. Mark offered a brief prayer, asking the Lord to "help us overcome our differences and be in unity." Other church matters were then discussed, but Wendy could not help reflecting on what had happened and feeling unsettled over the issues—her decision, Pete's authoritarian response, the tension between Pete and Martha, Bill's ideas, Mark's avoidance of the issue, and her own sense of hurt. It had become too much for her, and she couldn't wait for Pastor Tomas to return.

Questions for Discussion

- How do you see the three different causes of conflict (goals, personality, status) coming into play in this scenario? Which pairing of personalities exemplifies each cause?

- How do we see the different conflict styles at play here (competing/dominating, avoiding, accommodating, compromising, collaborating)? Was Pete right in asserting so much authority? What was the cost of his actions?

- If you had to give this group some advice on how to manage the conflict, what would you tell them, based on the information in this chapter?

▪ Further Reading ▪

Barthel, Tara Klena, and David V. Edling. *Redeeming Church Conflicts: Turning Crisis into Compassion and Care*. Grand Rapids: Baker Books, 2012.

Hakim, Amy C., and Muriel Solomon. *Working with Difficult People: Handling the Ten Types of Problem People without Losing Your Mind*. 2nd ed. New York: TarcherPerigee, 2016.

Oetzel, John G., and Stella Ting-Toomey, eds. *The Sage Handbook of Conflict Communication: Integrating Theory, Research, and Practice*. Thousand Oaks, CA: Sage, 2006.

Susek, Ron. *Firestorm: Preventing and Overcoming Church Conflicts*. Grand Rapids: Baker, 1999.

Woolverton, David E. *Mission Rift: Leading through Church Conflict*. Minneapolis: Fortress, 2021.

8

Leadership, Part 1

Foundations and Traditional Approaches

Introduction

Leadership is the crown jewel of organizational behavior. Much has been said on the topic over the past fifty years, perhaps too much. Leadership has become a multibillion-dollar business and has spawned countless books, academic resources, seminars, educational programs, gurus, and academic societies, perhaps in a way that no other field has in recent memory. It is hard to walk through an airport terminal without tripping over a stack of freshly printed leadership books by politicians, coaches, business executives, and even pastors, all vying to contribute to the conversation based on their experiences and philosophies. No doubt you have read some of these books—maybe you have even written your own book! And yet with all this discussion, study, and writing, leadership is still seemingly elusive, challenging to define, and notoriously difficult to do well. Warren Bennis famously said that leadership is like beauty—it's hard to define, but we all know it when we see it![1] And yet OB scholars and practitioners continue to define it, conceptualize it, and, more importantly, do their best to practice it well.

In this chapter and the next one, I will highlight what I believe are the more essential and worthwhile ideas that have emanated from the field, giving you a way to think about leadership historically and holistically. I will look at its development as a topic of interest among scholars and practitioners, define it, review different approaches and theories, and suggest practical ways to develop your own leadership and the leadership of others in your church or ministry. Chapter 8 will focus on the background and development of earlier and more foundational leadership theories, and chapter 9 will look at newer and emerging areas in the field.

Many believe that the modern era of leadership studies was inaugurated in 1978 with the seminal book by James MacGregor Burns entitled *Transforming Leadership*.[2] In the church world, authors such as George Barna and John C. Maxwell popularized leadership with their books published in the 1980s and 1990s.[3] Of course, interest in leaders and leadership began long before this. Ancient Greek writers examined the virtues and vices of warriors and kings in search of lessons. The Bible is a book about great (and not so great) leaders who redemptively impacted the world. Consider the lives of biblical figures such as Abraham, Joseph, Moses, Joshua, Saul, David, Solomon, Nehemiah, and, of course, our Lord Jesus, the ultimate picture of leadership, God himself serving as the model for what leadership can and should look like. Christians tend to focus on Jesus's "servant leadership," which involved taking the form of a servant and letting others become great. Yet there is much more we can learn about leadership in the Gospels; valuable lessons include having a bold and sweeping vision (it doesn't get much bolder or sweeping than making "disciples of all nations," Matt. 28:19), investing in quality relational time with followers, speaking candidly and not backing down from opponents or challenges, and making sacrifices. Books have been written on the subject and, no doubt, will continue to be written.[4] Of course, no leader is as flawless as our Lord. Biblical scholar John Goldingay writes of the triumphs and foibles of some of Israel's more notable leaders in 1 and 2 Samuel, highlighting that leadership is not all success and glory. It is done by fallible humans who have character flaws, are subject to temptation, and make mistakes that may lead many others astray—and yet God works with them and redeems it all.[5] Scripture offers a wealth of ideas and principles for Christian leaders, inviting them to learn from the best and the worst.

Perhaps part of what makes the topic of leadership so fascinating to us is that it allows us to envision ourselves, frail and fallible, as able to rise to new heights and make a difference in the world. This romance of leadership has been noted in the leadership literature as something that comes from our (largely Western) notion of success, which includes pulling up our bootstraps, making something of ourselves, and a host of other popular ideas derived from the self-help and positivistic psychology culture we are part of.[6] We tend to glamorize leaders and hold them ultimately responsible for success or failure, be it of sports teams, businesses, churches, or nations. If things are going well we say, "Give that leader some praise—and a raise!" If things are going poorly, we cry, "Fire them!" Yet we know that failure or success is determined by much more than the actions of an individual, no matter how talented or experienced. Organizations are webs of interrelated actions, ideas, systems, and cultures, all contributing to the organization's performance. Any discussion of leadership should be prefaced with some cautions about what it can and cannot accomplish. John C. Maxwell's general law that "everything rises and falls on leadership" is a good example of the tendency to overemphasize and overvalue leadership, and it is not necessarily, as the book title suggests, irrefutable.[7] Yes, leadership is important, but as this book has hopefully demonstrated thus far, there is much more to an organization's health than what any one person (or any series or group of leaders) can do for it.

At this point there should be a sign:

LEADERSHIP AHEAD. PROCEED WITH CAUTION!

Defining Leadership

There are perhaps as many definitions of leadership as there are people who have attempted to define it. Definitions of leadership have evolved over time and reflect not only a particular author's point of view and theoretical lens but also the societal norms and values of the day. Consider several definitions from the past as well as more current ones:

- The creative and directive force of morale.[8]
- The process by which an agent induces a subordinate to behave in a desired manner.[9]
- Directing and coordinating the work of group members.[10]

- An interpersonal relation in which others comply because they want to, not because they have to.[11]
- Transforming followers, creating visions of the goals that may be attained, and articulating for the followers the ways to attain those goals.[12]
- Actions that focus resources to create desirable opportunities.[13]
- A process where individuals with shared work establish direction, alignment, and commitment.[14]
- A process whereby an individual influences a group of individuals to achieve a common goal.[15]
- A formal or informal, contextually rooted and goal-influencing process that occurs between a leader and a follower, groups of followers, or institutions.[16]

Early definitions reflect a clear delineation of power in which the leader has it and must get others to follow. "Force," "persuasion," and "inducement" are terms associated with this post-industrial, scientific-management approach to leadership, developed when leaders were "large and in charge" and followers knew their place and were obligated to obey.

Fortunately, this authoritative understanding of leadership is largely passé, though authoritarian leaders themselves still roam the earth in various forms. Later definitions began to revolve around terms like "vision," "transformation," "goals," and "teams." The idea that leaders were there not merely to enforce policy or extract compliance but rather to develop healthy cultures and inspire others to a shared and worthy vision became the central feature of leadership. More recently, definitions of leadership have become even less centered on the "leader as hero" idea and more focused on ideas such as the right conditions for success, ongoing processes and iterations, and the importance of context. We will dig deeper into these post-heroic approaches later in this chapter and in the next one. The thing to notice at this point is that *how people envision and define leadership is dependent on a host of factors and perhaps says as much about the people's culture and ethos as it does about leadership itself.*

Therefore, notions of leadership are, in many ways, social constructs, and what is considered effective leadership is determined by the qualities and behaviors that the culture affirms elsewhere.[17] For example, around

1900, when the Industrial Revolution had finished and scientific advancement was giving society amazing machines and ideas such as standardization and division of labor, followers were seen merely as cogs in the great machinery of the world, and a leader's job was to make sure people knew their proper role and functioned well in the machine. A classic example is Henry Ford and the assembly line. A good leader was efficient and made sure everything worked well together. In the knowledge work era, which began in the 1920s, and then in the era of civil rights social upheaval and generational transition, which started in the 1960s, the public demanded they have a say in the world. Leadership reflected this desire for justice and fairness, and leaders began to see followers not merely as doers of tasks but as partners who worked with them for a common cause. Classic examples are Martin Luther King Jr. and social movements. A good leader was passionate about their people and their cause, giving voice to all groups.

Today, in an era of rapid change and flux, beginning around the year 2000, norms have been defined by instability and the diffusion of responsibility and voice. Technology has greatly increased the ability of people around the world to produce and publicize whatever they want without partnering with a middleman. Affordable, powerful computers and the ubiquitous internet have spawned a host of innovations such as digital media creation and distribution, exemplified by YouTube and SoundCloud. Social media has given virtually everyone the ability to gain a platform. While many people like to poke fun at them, "influencers" are, in a sense, the reflection of leadership in the modern era. Those with ambition and the ability to attract followers gain a voice. Prime examples of the contemporary approach to leadership are Steve Jobs, Elon Musk, and the technology revolution. Leaders are networked together, keep up with rapid change, innovate, and have a global reach.

Paradoxically, this change and splintering has allowed organizations to grow through technologically mediated networking. Churches and ministries have seen the impact of this development as leaders have expanded their reach and attracted people from around the world to their ministry. Some Christian organizations have members and ministries that are more regional than just local. This change is reflected in innovations such as the multisite church, church networks like Acts 29, and the strictly virtual church, which has no physical location. Denominations are in decline, and independent networks of like-minded ministries are emerging, largely as a reflection of the fact that our technologically mediated world has cut the cord, so to speak, and allowed leaders of organizations to work with whomever they like.

Now that we have defined leadership, let's look at some other foundational ideas about leadership from the field of OB. The previous overview put notions of leadership in their larger context and showed the trajectory of these notions, and the following will move from rather abstract ideas to more concrete realities, looking at leadership in its organizational context.

Leadership versus Management

An important distinction can be made between leadership and management. Scholars like A. Zaleznik[18] and J. P. Kotter[19] first articulated this distinction, and it has been helpful ever since. In some sense, the term "management" has been somewhat superseded by "leadership." Everyone wants to be seen as a strong leader, not merely as an efficient manager. The term "manager" may suggest a small-minded bureaucrat, someone who enforces policies and punishes others when there are violations. While this may be the case on occasion, it is important to jettison this preconception and see the value that both leadership and management offer. The following table shows how these two interrelated concepts are distinct:

Leader	Manager
Innovates, developing new ideas and solutions	Administrates, implementing ideas and solutions
Takes a long-term perspective and thinks about legacy	Takes a short-term perspective and considers how action will impact the near future
Inspires others to take action by exerting positive influence and being a role model	Ensures others take action by enforcing policy and compliance
Challenges the status quo and inspires change, the result being that people think and act differently	Keeps the status quo and ensures stability, the result being that people act predictably
Asks the "what" and "why" questions, focusing on purpose and meaning	Asks the "how" and "when" questions, focusing on the projects and the means

As this table suggests, leadership is about creating change, inspiring others to a larger vision, and rallying the troops to engage in meaningful action, whereas management is more about the particulars and getting things done. Management expert Peter Drucker famously said, "Management is doing things right, leadership is doing the right things," and, "There is nothing worse than doing the wrong thing well."[20] Leadership inspires others to join an organization or movement or project, whereas management ensures that the job gets done. This description may seem to give leadership a more positive appeal—after all, we would much rather be inspired than held accountable—but from a practical perspective we can see that both are equally necessary in effectively running an organization, whether it be a business, school, or church. Inspirational motivation and vision are important, but they require execution, which includes a plan of attack, stewardship of resources, and accountability for success.

Thus, the issue is not which is more important. Both are equally important. The issue is how an individual or group can balance them both well. For example, a pastor may inspire others and keep them focused on the big picture of kingdom work but lack the ability to help the church follow through and execute its ministries well. Some leaders are inspirational idea factories. Every meeting with them features a breathtaking array of exciting and inspiring ideas that set the room on fire with possibility. Yet these ideas never materialize, as the leader is not able to develop a workable plan for getting things done or is so enamored of the latest shiny thing that they quickly forget about last week's grand idea. Some individuals excel in being creative and connecting with others, while some think more concretely and stay focused. As we think about leadership on an organizational level, we should consider how people's personalities support necessary leadership and/or management functions. We need both inspiration and execution. They are not mutually exclusive; they are inextricably linked as part of organizational leadership.

So far I have discussed leadership and management as distinct kinds of work, and it would be natural to envision the prototypical leader or manager, as if people in positions of authority embodied strictly one or the other. However, the fact is, leadership and management are embodied in the same person. Typically, one cannot choose either to lead or to manage; both come with the territory of a position of authority. Most leadership roles are, in fact, management roles, with varying degrees of managerial responsibilities and opportunities for leadership. Typically, the higher up in an organization one is, the more opportunity one has to exercise typical leadership functions, such as innovating, contributing to strategic decisions that impact the whole organization, and inspiring large groups of people. The term "middle management" applies to those who are neither at the top nor at the bottom but, instead, oversee departments or areas. This is sometimes the "sour spot" for leadership, as opposed to the "sweet spot," because the role typically comes with much responsibility and a high degree of accountability to the executive level, which is more involved in strategy and decisions. Yet some people excel and remain at this level due to their personal makeup and ambitions and truly serve as the backbone of the organization.

Regardless of the level in the organization, one can exercise leadership and, by the grace of God, advance to greater levels of influence and authority while proving oneself to be called and capable. As Jesus said, "Whoever can be trusted with very little can also be trusted with much" (Luke 16:10). Transitioning from management tasks to leadership tasks does not necessarily come with a formal promotion but is nevertheless an advancement, one that occurs when the manager acquires experience, maturity, wisdom, and a whole host of qualities and competencies, which will be discussed later in this chapter as part of the process of leadership development.

Theories of and Approaches to Leadership

Since the early part of the twentieth century, leadership has been viewed by OB scholars and practitioners through a variety of lenses produced by a variety of schools of thought. These theories of leadership reflect years of study and research and constitute the bulk of what we truly know about effective leadership. Initially considered part of the field of management studies, leadership began to be studied in its own right in the late 1970s after the publication of Burns's aforementioned book *Transforming Leadership*[21] and the articulation of a distinction between leadership and management.[22] The flourishing of the leadership consultancy trend of the 1980s and 1990s drove further study on leadership as its own discipline. In the following section we will review the theories that have proven enduring and should be included in any OB student's toolbox.

Before we dive into the particular theories and approaches, a few things should be noted about the ways leadership has been approached:

- "Leadership theory" refers to the body of knowledge about leadership that has researchable and causal theories behind it. That is to say, there is a cause-and-effect relationship between an action and a result, and there is a body of empirical research to back it up. Different theories have more or less of these elements. The ones discussed below are of this variety. Such theories are part of the social-science tradition of studying human behavior.
- There is an important distinction between leadership theory and pop leadership. The latter is seen in the myriad of books by celebrity leaders who have success in their own contexts and great stories to illustrate their ideas. These books have their place but often lack empirical support, being based instead on anecdotal evidence and the leader's own experience.
- There are many helpful biblical and theological approaches to leadership offered by notable authors. The spiritual leadership literature, primarily for pastors and other church leaders, has been helping people for quite a while, and you are no doubt familiar with it and have been blessed by it.[23] These approaches focus largely on the character and spiritual formation of the leader and should be considered essential reading for all church and ministry leaders.
- There are Christian authors who have attempted what I would call Christianized leadership, taking a larger, sometimes popular leadership idea and giving it spiritual support.[24] For example, the concept of vision became popular in the 1980s, with the advent of transformational leadership, and some have written on vision as an important concern for church leaders that has some biblical support.
- Other Christian authors seek to rigorously integrate the field of leadership studies with Scripture and Christian practices, and they make an important contribution in helping church leaders appropriate mainstream leadership concepts.[25] This current book might also be a good example of this approach.

- We all have implicit theories of leadership[26] and have heard folk wisdom about leadership.[27] We internalize the ideas we develop with experience, along with things we hear other people say about leadership, to help us lead. We see leaders all around us—pastors, politicians, business leaders—and glean from them what we perceive is part of their leadership. For example, perhaps someone had a coach in high school who would often raise his voice and point out every mistake the person made. This may have become an unconscious part of what this person thinks leaders should do. Or perhaps a person hears someone say, "Leaders are readers," and decides to pick up a leadership book.

- These implicit theories of leadership tell us whether someone is a good leader. For example, if a pastor is an excellent preacher and is humorous, we will likely assign them the label of "good leader" because that is what we think pastors should do well. These latent, unreflective ideas may or may not be accurate, and thus, we should challenge some of the assumptions we have about what constitutes good leadership. My intention is that this chapter will help you do just that as you glean from many foundational ideas and make your understanding of leadership more adept and thoughtful.

The following are reviews and summaries of the past one hundred years of thinking and writing on various leadership theories and approaches.[28]

Trait Approaches

The earliest attempts to conceptualize leadership were done through the lens of trying to ascertain and describe the observable traits of a leader.[29] Originally called the "great man" theories, these studies looked at how leaders differed from non-leaders. The key research question was, What defining characteristics make leaders different from others? Those who took this approach looked at such variables as physical attributes, family of origin, birth order, moral characteristics, and mental abilities. Examining outstanding leaders like Abraham Lincoln, Mohandas Gandhi, and Napoleon, these researchers sought to find commonalities between great leaders. While from a commonsense point of view this would seem to be a reasonable approach, there was an inability to attribute the success of the leaders to any specific trait. Some great leaders were born first, some last. Some were tall, some short. Some were highly intelligent, some not. Alas, there were no traits universally associated with effective leadership.

But the trait approach was not a complete failure or dead end. In fact, there are still trait-like approaches used today. For example, the Myers-Briggs temperament sorter, which is based on Jungian archetypes, can be seen as a neo-trait approach, seeking to demonstrate personality characteristics, such as extroversion or openness, that lend themselves to a successful leadership profile. Further, many still feel that certain traits separate leaders from non-leaders, such as extroversion, intelligence, drive, and courage.[30] Though they are not the determining factor for leadership, some traits are consistently demonstrated by effective leaders:

- Intelligence: strong verbal, perceptual, and reasoning abilities
- Self-confidence: certainty about one's competencies and skills, having self-efficacy
- Determination: a desire to get the job done complemented by initiative, persistence, dominance, drive, and proactivity in the face of obstacles
- Integrity: honesty, trustworthiness, taking responsibility for actions, loyalty, dependability, forthrightness
- Sociability: an inclination to seek out pleasant social relationships and a tendency to show high EQ and be friendly, outgoing, courteous, tactful, diplomatic, and demonstrably concerned for the needs of others.[31]

In addition, leadership researchers have noted, as we all have, that not all leadership traits are positive and healthy. There are "dark side" traits, such as narcissism, overconfidence, hubris, manipulation, even psychopathological behavior, that can accompany even successful leaders.[32] Particularly in larger-than-life charismatic leaders,[33] the dark side is sometimes extreme and in certain cases eventually undermines the leader. Consider history's most notorious figures, such as Adolf Hitler and Joseph Stalin. Or consider church leaders who possess unusual charisma yet devastated their ministries. Traits such as tremendous oratory skills, charisma, and so on have led many a leader and organization—even in the church—to plummet from great heights.

In view of what has been said, perhaps we could develop a trait-oriented definition of leadership: leaders are those who possess certain attributes that are necessary and desirable in the role of a leader.

Behavioral and Situational Approaches

The behavioral view of leadership emerged out of the ashes of the trait movement and sought to find something that could be attained and refined—and, more importantly, observed, since many of the leadership-related traits such as determination were abstract constructs and, as such, were hard to develop in others. If there were no specific enduring traits that distinguished leaders from others, then perhaps examining how leaders behaved was the key to understanding leadership.

Studies, particularly those of Elton Mayo and of Ohio State University, began to examine two distinct foci: the leader's task-oriented behavior and the leader's relationship-oriented behavior. Terms such as "consideration" and "initiating structure" entered the leadership lexicon. In task behaviors, the leader facilitates goal accomplishment and determines what a person or group should be accomplishing. In relationship behaviors, the leader focuses on helping followers feel comfortable with themselves, each other, and the situation.

This distinction has become foundational in thinking about and practicing leadership. There is inherent tension in what leaders do, and they must always seek to balance and integrate these two aspects. A "high task" leader shows more concern for the task than the people and may alienate people and fail to make the personal connections that are vital to successful leadership. On the other hand, a "high people" leader may know what needs to be accomplished but may be hindered by excessive concern for people and their feelings. For example, consider a church whose leader feels that their primary function is to promote social connection among parishioners and who neglects outreach and mission. The church can feel more like a social club than a congregation charged with making "disciples of all nations" (Matt. 28:19). Jesus himself is a good example of a leader who knew his task yet made time for his people.

We can see that this is not an either-or situation; it is not the case that a leader is either about the task or about the people. Clearly both are important. The question is, How do we know when to focus on which? To address this tension, Paul Hersey, along with Ken Blanchard, developed a now-classic theory of situational leadership.[34] Though challenged by some,[35] situational leadership suggests that a leader consider the maturity level of followers in order to determine the degree to which the leader should focus on task behavior and relationship behavior. "Follower maturity" is how ready followers are to perform their job. It includes their *capability* of doing a task, which has to do with job skills, experience, and so on, and their *confidence* to do the task, which has to do with such factors as motivation and self-efficacy. Within situational leadership there are four different leadership styles, each of which applies to a particular combination of capability and confidence. The four leadership styles are as follows:[36]

- Directing: This style is to be used with followers who are unable and unwilling—that is, those who have low capability and low confidence. Followers who have the lowest amount of readiness need the highest amount of attention, and the focus should be on task behavior more than relationship behavior. This leadership style can be used when someone is new to their role, lacks confidence, or fails to meet expectations. When someone lacks basic job knowledge or cannot make decisions for themselves, a leader can be more direct and task oriented about how a job should be done. They may set clearly defined goals and deadlines and regularly check in on progress.
- Coaching: This style is used with followers who are willing but unable—that is, those who have high confidence but low capability. The leader can serve as an influential, supportive figure for those who show interest in learning how to do the job. This style is high on both task behavior and relationship behavior and is used to help motivated followers learn to do a job well.
- Supporting: This style is to be used with followers who are able and unwilling—that is, those who have high capability and low confidence. Followers may have the necessary skills without the

motivation, or they may have become discouraged. When practicing this style, leaders let the worker do the decision-making but
provide encouragement and support along the way.

- Delegating: This style is to be used with followers who are able
  and willing—that is, those who have high capability and high confidence. Such workers are experienced, competent, and motivated.
  Much hand-holding or cheerleading is not required, and the leader
  should let the workers do their jobs with little interference, simply
  helping them align with the larger organizational goals and culture.

A major benefit of the situational leadership approach is that it helps
leaders engage followers at the level that is appropriate for them instead
of acting on the leaders' own ideas of what a leader should do or mis-
matching their approach. For example, some Christian leaders feel that
creating good relationships is paramount—and of course, it is. But when
someone is new to a role, they need to learn how to do the job more than
they need a new friend. On the other hand, some leaders have a hard
time delegating and empowering others. These leaders err if they treat
mature, ready-and-able followers in the same way they treat newbies. The
mature followers will quickly become frustrated as the leader microman-
ages them, constantly watching over their shoulder or second-guessing
their decisions. Learning to discern followers' maturity levels and leading appropriately constitute an important skill for effective leadership.

How could we define leadership from a behavioral and situational
point of view? This school of thought would say that leaders are those
who successfully navigate their responsibility to accomplish their task
and their responsibility to develop relationships with their followers and
that a leader will be most effective if their style and approach are aligned
with the contextual needs of a particular situation.

Charismatic Leadership

Following the early work of Max Weber, Robert House, Jay Conger,
and other "neo-charismatic" scholars, leadership thinkers began to
look at a particular style of leadership, that of the charismatic leader.[37]
Charismatic leaders are seen as larger than life, have unique and often
charming personalities, and can light up any room they enter in order

to demand attention. In some sense, this is the general understanding of leadership that many people have. One can intuit that the leader is in charge and going places. A charismatic leader is characterized by the following attributes:

- They offer a vision and articulate a promise of a future that is better than the status quo.
- They are able to articulate vision using colorful and symbolic imagery that connects with people on a deep level, and they often take personal risk and are self-sacrificial.
- They often display unconventional behavior; they may be flamboyant, flashy, loud, and unconcerned with pleasantries, political correctness, or diplomatic conduct.
- They are sensitive to environment, know what is going on, and can use resources to bring about change.
- Crisis often leads to their ascent, and they promise answers to people's deep felt needs.
- They are sensitive to followers' needs, respond to and capitalize on these needs, appeal to their inner motives, and inspire emulation and emotional adoration.[38]
- They are concerned with impression management; their image is always maintained via dress, status symbols, and so on. They dress the part and are rarely seen out of costume.[39]

Charismatic leadership theory differs from the others discussed thus far in that it is considered attributional in nature. That is, followers ascribe these attributes to the leader, whether or not they truly exist. Researchers in this area began to look at the needs and desires of the followers as a key element in the success of the leader. Followers desire this leader, and power and influence can be held by the leader only if the followers attribute it to them.

Consider some of the better-known leaders who are often considered charismatic in this sense: Martin Luther King Jr., Malcolm X, Bill Clinton, Donald Trump, Richard Branson, and Joel Osteen. And of course, no list of charismatic leaders would be complete without despicable figures like Adolf Hitler and David Koresh. This is what perhaps makes understanding or appreciating this charismatic approach to leadership so challenging. On the one hand, we all admire leaders who are inspiring and commanding and who promise to do great things. On the other hand, we know what this type of power can do in the wrong hands. With these leaders, beauty is truly in the eye of the beholder, and charismatic leaders are often very divisive. People either love them or hate them; there is no middle ground. One man's hero is another man's devil. Perhaps you cringed a little when you read the list that included very different people such as Trump, Clinton, Malcolm X, and Osteen all together. Depending on where you stand on the political or religious spectrum, you no doubt either love or despise at least some of these men. Such is the nature of charismatic leadership.

While these leaders are inspiring and sometimes accomplish amazing things, they may also produce devastating results. History attests to a host of charismatic leaders who have led organizations, nations, and churches over the proverbial cliff. Weber called charismatic leadership the most unstable form of legitimate authority.[40] This is due in part to the changing nature of followers, who may desire what the leader represents one day and despise it the next day. It is also due in part to the person of the leader. Therefore, it is important to make a distinction between positive and negative charismatics. Positive charismatics have a socialized power orientation, emphasizing an internalization of the ideals of the organization by the followers. Negative charismatics, on the other hand, have a personalized power orientation and tend to emphasize personal identification between followers and themselves. Simply put, negative charismatics instill devotion to themselves, and positive charismatics instill devotion to the ideals. Negative charismatics are often excessively narcissistic, become paranoid, and insulate themselves from criticism.

Further, in an organization, charisma may create an achievement-oriented culture that has an intensity that is hard to sustain. If it is sustained, the culture may create stress and psychological disorders. Other negative effects of charismatic leadership include a tendency toward groupthink, delusions of infallibility, blindness to potential threats, excessive risk taking, and failure to develop successors.

While not all churches are led by charismatic leaders, some indeed are. Founders of megachurches or church movements are often charismatic.

For example, Aimee Semple McPherson, founder of the International Church of the Foursquare Gospel, was a classic charismatic in every sense.[41] She seemed larger than life to her followers, used flamboyant methods, and instilled devotion in her followers, many of whom were women and would dress in a similar manner to "Sister Aimee."[42] She started her own radio station, built the largest church in Los Angeles in the 1920s, and left a legacy of churches across the globe as well as a denomination that still thrives today. As a female, she led courageously at a time when men dominated leadership in the emerging Pentecostal scene. She also had downsides (some might say downfall), some of which have been present in other charismatics. She had marital problems and saw her family fall apart, squandered church resources, disappeared and then reappeared with a fanciful and unfounded story that was the subject of a highly publicized yearslong scandal, and suffered from burnout and depression, eventually dying from an overdose of sleeping pills at a relatively young age. While she is perhaps an extreme example of a charismatic church leader, you no doubt can envision other contemporary church leaders who have larger-than-life kingdom-building appeal and yet burn up and burn out. There seems to be an intoxicating blend of real spiritual power and public adulation that leads to the meteoric rise and fall of such leaders.

Although these leaders are often the beginning and end of an organization, it is possible for success to continue, albeit in a different fashion. For example, after McPherson's passing, her denomination was led by her son Rolf K. McPherson. Rolf was decidedly less flamboyant than his mother, and he stabilized the movement. Aimee was a visionary, but Rolf was a builder, and he led it into much greater national and international growth than his mother did in her day.[43]

How does an organization continue after the charismatic leader leaves the scene? To keep the flame burning, an organization should consider the following:

- *Find a successor.* Often, a child or close insider is ideally suited to take the reins of power. In the case of Aimee Semple McPherson, her son was a capable leader who understood and embodied the church culture and was able to take the torch and fan the flame in new and important ways.

- *Institutionalize the vision.* The organization can no longer be the personality cult of its leader. It must shift its focus to what that leader stands for. The organization must find ways to articulate the leader's passion and vision and make its values explicit outside of the person and presence of the leader.
- *Embed the leader's ideals into the culture of the organization.* When a vision is articulated, it must be "owned" by the organization. The organization must keep the founder's vision and purpose alive. It should celebrate its history, tell its stories, and appoint people who embody and practice its ideals to be leaders, role models, and bearers of the torch (see chap. 10 on changing organizational culture).
- *Prepare for new horizons.* While keeping the founder's vision and memory alive, the organization must give room for new leaders and new vision to emerge. Honor the legacy of the charismatic founder, but do not hinder the next generation from serving the Lord in their way and in their day.

Transformational Approaches

A similar though more easily replicable approach to leadership is that of transformational leadership, originally espoused by James MacGregor Burns[44] and later by Bernard M. Bass and Bruce J. Avolio,[45] Warren Bennis,[46] and others.[47] Transformational leaders are seen as those who are inspirational and visionary and who have the ability to engender genuine motivation and support in their followers to achieve a common vision. While transformational leaders are similar to charismatic leaders and do have the appeal of charisma, there is a much greater focus on empowering others, giving away the vision, and making others' growth the leader's goal. The two kinds of leadership can be contrasted as follows:

Transformational Leaders	Charismatic Leaders
Empower others	Keep power for themselves
Build others	Are built by others

While there have been various models and approaches to transformational leadership, a seminal and still useful approach to conceptualizing it is the Four I's model. To be transformational, leadership must include the following four dimensions:

- Idealized influence
  - Leaders act as strong role models who stand for the values of the organization.
  - They set high standards of moral and ethical conduct. While some transformational leaders, like some charismatic leaders, can lead followers astray, true transformational leaders help the church or ministry keep to the highest ethical and moral standards, helping guard against the sort of excesses that can bring down an organization.
  - They influence others to follow the vision by making it appealing and attractive and connecting it with larger kingdom vision and purpose.
- Inspirational motivation
  - Leaders communicate high expectations to followers. Because people live up to, or down to, others' expectations, transformational leaders must set a high bar, letting people know that much is expected of them but also expressing the confidence that they can meet the challenge successfully.
  - They inspire commitment to and engagement in a shared vision, encouraging followers to make the vision their own.
  - They use symbols and emotional appeals to focus group members so that they achieve more than self-interest. This is a great appeal of the charismatic and transformational leader—the ability to make ideals understandable through vivid imagery, word pictures, and stories.
- Intellectual stimulation
  - Leaders stimulate followers to be informed and innovative. A transformational leader does not propose to be the first and last word on creativity and innovation in an organization. Rather, the leader intentionally empowers others to think for themselves. They share information with others and do not hold on to power by keeping important information in their own back pocket.

- o They challenge their own beliefs and support followers in trying new approaches and developing innovative ways of dealing with organizational issues. They foster an environment where people are safe and encouraged to innovate, think outside the box, and bring new and fresh ideas to the table.
- Individualized consideration
  - o Leaders listen carefully to the needs of followers, communicating that they, the leaders, are concerned about the followers as people, not just as workers fulfilling their role or title (see the Current Issues sidebar "Leadership and Love" in chap. 5).
  - o They act as coaches to assist followers in becoming fully actualized. The goal is to empower people to serve in ways that are meaningful and important to them, not just the organization. Leaders should get to know their people to find out what drives them so that they can help them fulfill their potential.
  - o They help followers grow through personal challenges. Life can be tough, and transformational leaders show high levels of emotional intelligence and are supportive and encouraging when followers are going through difficult times.

Transformational leadership can be contrasted with transactional leadership. The latter is based largely on a "this for that" approach. For example, someone works hard in order to receive a bonus or reward or to avoid punishment. A transactional leader is one who can get others to follow not out of a commitment to or connection with the vision but, rather, out of compliance with rules and roles. Transactional leaders may be those who passively manage, meaning they avoid involvement and put out fires, or those who actively manage, meaning they monitor for mistakes or reward achievement. Of course, there is a place in leadership for monitoring and rewarding, and they should both be part of a leader's "full range" style of leadership.[48] However, if this is the only approach a leader takes, they are most likely engaged in transactional and not transformational leadership.

One final note on transformational leadership is that the transformation is not a one-way street. The leader's job is not merely to transform followers but also to be open to the input and influence of others. These leaders recognize that they, like the followers, are in process. They do not pretend to have already "arrived," and they model an unpretentious humility that invites others to contribute to their growth and insight. This is a challenging posture for some leaders to take. Some feel it is their job as the leader to have all the right answers or never show any sign of lack or weakness. This may be what is expected of the leader based on cultural norms (see chap. 9 for more information on cross-cultural leadership). Transformational leadership can be challenging, but those who learn to practice it will see phenomenal results at both the individual level and the group level.[49] Important outcomes such as commitment, work satisfaction, trust and motivation, organizational citizenship behavior, and commitment to the organization's culture are all positively impacted by transformational leaders, and this kind of leadership should be something church leaders work on developing.[50]

Looking at leadership from this perspective, we can see that a charismatic and transformational definition of leadership would be this: leadership is about inspiring loyalty and admiration in others, and the leader not only has the ability to communicate to others that they possess desirable characteristics and abilities but also takes into account the needs and motivations of the followers in an open and mutually influential relationship.

Psychodynamic Approaches

This next approach to understanding leadership comes from the fields of human personality and psychological development. Chapter 5 discussed family systems theory and the idea that work relationships may be impacted by and reflect people's personal family dynamics. This, perhaps, is nowhere seen more clearly than in leader-follower relationships.

The psychodynamic approach to leadership does not look at the qualities a leader possesses (traits), the things they do (behaviors), or their own personal magnetism (charisma). Rather, it looks at leadership in terms of intrapsychic processes that are related to proposed structures of personality, those developed by Sigmund Freud and others.[51] The work of Manfred F. R. Kets de Vries is an example of this type of leadership scholarship.[52] In this view, leadership behavior has to do with the relationship between a leader and follower, which includes underlying and unconscious needs and desires. The leader-follower interaction is, in this sense, a reenactment of unconscious family dynamics. These psychodramas impact more than just a single leader-follower interaction. They can impact the whole of the organization. Further, leaders who lead from a place of hurt or past trauma can negatively impact the whole culture of their organization, which in turn reflects and embodies these same issues. Here are some ways this dynamic might play out in a church or ministry:

- A pastor who subconsciously feels threatened may compensate by threatening their subordinates, and this pattern of threatening others becomes the norm in the culture or causes others to have an unhealthy avoidance of the pastor.
- A pastor who needs to be in control will likely attract followers who need to be controlled. The result will be unhealthy organizational dynamics; for example, there will be passive followers who simply react to the pastor's demands and/or who are unmotivated to innovate.
- Groupthink might emerge as an outworking of one's unconscious desire to be in control or, conversely, of followers' acceptance of being controlled.
- A follower with an overbearing and controlling mother may resist a pastor's authority, seeing her in this situation as a substitute for her mother. This antiauthoritarian attitude can emerge in relationships far beyond the person's family of origin.

These family psychodramas and outdated scripts are replayed repeatedly and can be the source of tension and conflict in leader-follower relationships. Kets de Vries and others suggest that until leaders recognize these patterns and see the way they themselves are transferring feelings from past situations to current ones, they cannot change. These patterns can, in ways small and large, derail effective leadership yet fly under the leader's radar, like a saboteur waiting for a victim. In particular, executive leaders may plateau in their leadership due to these unhealthy patterns and find breakthroughs only by doing deep, reflective work with a competent coach or counselor.

Transactional analysis is another approach that can be used to understand the dynamics of the leader-follower relationship.[53] This approach focuses on the background and psyche of the leader and follower to determine the dynamic that takes place when they encounter one another. It suggests that there are three main modes, or ego states, people have in relationships: parent, child, and adult:

- Parent: a person thinks, feels, and behaves in ways copied from their parents. They are "in charge" and demand that others listen to them.
- Child: a person thinks, feels, and behaves as they did as a child. They are either compliant and submissive or petulant and resistant to authority figures.
- Adult: a person has thoughts, feelings, or behaviors that are a direct result of current happenings, and they do not seek to inordinately control, resist, or submit to others.

According to this theory no one permanently remains in any one of the ego states but, rather, shifts in and out of each depending on the dynamic of a particular interpersonal relationship. For example, a pastor may be a parent when in a meeting with a junior staff member (who thus assumes a child role), but this same pastor may become the child when interacting with a church elder or domineering parishioner (who assumes a parent role). This approach suggests that effective leadership and followership depend on two or more people operating in the adult ego state. It is important to recognize that a person's relationships with a follower (or leader) may be based on transactional analysis issues and not issues at hand.

Using this paradigm, we could define leadership as something that happens when the psychological attributes in individuals encounter one another and thus form a leader-follower relationship that is healthy and fulfills the needs of both individuals.

Spiritual Approaches

While the approaches discussed above seek to determine certain explicit and observable characteristics and behaviors of leaders and the leader-follower relationship, the spiritual approach focuses on the personal dimension of the leader's spirituality. For Christians, spirituality has always been foundational to leadership. Our sense of connection with God's plan and calling on our lives, and our character and spiritual health, are of utmost importance for Christian leaders. As mentioned in the introductory section of this chapter, numerous authors have written on this topic, and I encourage you to dig into this wonderful literature.

In the past decade, the idea of spirituality in leadership has become a topic of interest for leadership and OB scholars. While not explicitly rooted in Judeo-Christian spirituality,[54] these approaches nevertheless recognize that there is something transcendent, meaningful, and purposeful to the act of leadership that goes beyond notions of productivity, satisfaction, and profit. They see the necessity of leadership being rooted in values and embodying strong morals and ethics.

An example of this approach includes L. W. Fry's model of spiritual leadership.[55] In this model there are several key areas of importance:

- There is a sense of transcendence of self. Leaders see leadership as their calling or destiny. They lead from a commitment to something or someone outside themselves.
- The leadership has meaning beyond earning profit or self-satisfaction. Leadership is stewardship and a virtue that serves others.
- The leadership must develop the following:
  o Vision, which is a definition of destination, reflection of high ideals, and encouragement of others to have hope and faith
  o Altruistic love as expressed in virtues such as forgiveness, kindness, integrity, empathy, honesty, patience, trust, and humility
  o Hope and faith, which promote a sense of calling and higher meaning

This is perhaps the most difficult approach to leadership to define from an OB perspective, for several reasons. First, while these are thoughtful and interesting models, measuring one's sense of spirituality is difficult, as it is subjective and the evidence of it is not uniformly agreed on. Models such as Fry's seek to operationalize[56] the key variables, yet they can still be hard to articulate or quantify. Second, views of spirituality have shifted over the past decades. Initially, people typically used a Judeo-Christian view of spirituality, which was centered on a biblical and theistic worldview. More recently, this theistic view has shifted, and spirituality in the postmodern sense can mean any inner processes deriving from any religious or nonreligious orientation. "Spiritualities" would be a better term for describing this pluralistic worldview. Finally, since it is a newer construct, there are few theoretical or empirical research models to support this view, though there is evidence from the leadership literature that it is becoming an emerging topic for consideration.[57]

As believers, we, of course, do not need to wait for empirical evidence before we practice such leadership, and most will practice it because it is rooted in our faith and in many biblical concepts. Hopefully we will see more scholarship devoted to spiritual leadership in the coming years, particularly from a Judeo-Christian worldview, and I believe this is a way in which we can interact with the OB community and bring our faith values to the table.

Using a spiritual paradigm, we can create a spiritual definition of leadership: leadership is an internally motivated phenomenon that is a direct result of the leader's sense of relationship with the spiritual realm and is informed by the morals and precepts that are consistent with the leader's sense of spirituality.

▪ Practical Leadership Application Questions ▪

- How do you define leadership, and what does your definition say about what is important to you in this season?
- Do you lead well or manage well? How can you develop more balance between these two elements?
- What traits do you possess that help you to lead well? What are the flip sides to your traits that can hinder your leadership?
- Do you tend to be more task focused or relationship focused in your leadership? How can you become more intentional in focusing these behaviors on the needs of your followers?
- How does your church or ministry deal with charismatic leaders? Are there any glaring potential issues, such as groupthink or leadership succession, that you need to face now or in the future?
- How transformational or transactional is your leadership? How well do you empower others to do their jobs well?

- What below-the-surface psychodynamic issues are taking place in your leadership relationships? What outdated scripts might you be enacting, and how do you see parent-child-adult relationships taking place in your leadership relationships?
- How do your own spiritual values and sense of calling impact your leadership? Where is God in your understanding of your leadership?

▪ Further Reading ▪

Conger, Jay A., and Rabindra N. Kanungo. *Charismatic Leadership in Organizations*. Thousand Oaks, CA: Sage, 1998.

Cormode, Scott. *The Innovative Church: How Leaders and Their Congregations Can Adapt in an Ever-Changing World*. Grand Rapids: Baker Academic, 2020.

Day, David V., and John Antonakis, eds. *The Nature of Leadership*. 3rd ed. Thousand Oaks, CA: Sage, 2017.

Kets de Vries, Manfred F. R. *The Leader on the Couch: A Clinical Approach to Changing People and Organizations*. San Francisco: Jossey-Bass, 2006.

Kouzes, James M., and Barry Z. Posner. *The Leadership Challenge: How to Make Extraordinary Things Happen in Organizations*. 6th ed. Hoboken, NJ: Wiley & Sons, 2017.

Ledbetter, Bernice M., Robert J. Banks, and David C. Greenhalgh. *Reviewing Leadership*. 2nd ed. Grand Rapids: Baker Academic, 2016.

Northouse, Peter G. *Leadership: Theory and Practice*. 9th ed. Thousand Oaks, CA: Sage, 2021.

Segal, Morley. *Points of Influence: A Guide to Using Personality Theory at Work*. San Francisco: Jossey-Bass, 1996.

9

Leadership, Part 2

Emerging Approaches

Introduction

The previous chapter introduced contemporary leadership theory and gave an overview of several important mainstream theories. Hopefully it gave you a sense of some of the trends in leadership studies that scholars have developed over the past century. Of course, much more has been and could be written about each of these theories, and I encourage you to look at any of them in greater depth. The endnotes are a good place to start when looking for references, as I have listed many seminal works there.

In addition to these theories, there are other notable areas of interest developing in the field of leadership studies. Many have arisen due to changes in society and new ways of thinking about who can lead and what roles leaders have in organizations. The increasing role of women in the workplace and in leadership, as well as the increasingly diverse social and cultural landscape, have impacted leadership studies. These factors were not at the forefront of early leadership scholarship, which was primarily developed in an era when most leaders were white men. This is not a criticism or dismissal of the historical canon of leadership studies. Everyone—men and women, white people and people of color— can glean much that is of value from historical leadership studies. But a shift in this area, as with many fields of contemporary scholarship, is notable in OB.

Leadership studies have also continued to address the development of leadership in individuals and the role of organizational culture in facilitating this development. While the person of the leader continues to be a focus, we can see a shift from the *leader* to *leadership*. Attention is turning away from the heroic leader and toward approaches that treat leadership as a phenomenon that happens at a time and place, not simply as an extension of an individual. The important role of the follower is also considered in the leadership equation. Finally, the ideals and practices of servant leadership have moved beyond the good intentions of the super-spiritual to become an actionable approach that is effective both in and outside church contexts.

Gender and Leadership

Since more women are now in roles traditionally held by men, leadership and OB scholars have been keenly interested in women and leadership. In particular, they have focused on the unique challenges women face when leading and the differences between the way men lead and the way women lead.

This is a topic fraught with theological implications, as different traditions view women in leadership roles differently. This book will not open that can of worms but will merely review some of the key issues and ideas raised by OB thinkers in this area.

Early discussions of women in leadership used the metaphor of the glass ceiling to describe the barriers that women faced when trying to attain roles of leadership.[1] These barriers were largely seen as resulting from the prejudice of male managers and the sexist ways women were treated in the workplace. But there is more to the story of why women do not advance into roles of leadership in the same way men do. Through their research, Alice H. Eagly and Linda L. Carli later introduced a more nuanced metaphor to the conversation, that of the labyrinth, a maze of impermeable walls that are confusing and difficult for women to navigate.[2] This idea proposes that it is not just male prejudice or stereotypes that hinder women from advancing in roles of leadership, though there are still vestiges of these problems. In addition, marriage and parenthood tasks, such as having and raising children, fall to women more than men. Working women are thus expected to be "superwomen" and juggle competing priorities. Moreover, these other responsibilities can take women out of the workforce as they tend to family matters and slow down their career advancement.

There is, furthermore, a unique challenge known as the "double bind." Women are expected to be communal—to be kind, friendly, sympathetic, to help people get along, and so on. By contrast, men are expected to be agentic—assertive, forceful, ambitious, self-confident, and so on. If women are highly communal, they may be criticized for not being agentic enough and for lacking the qualities typically possessed by leaders. But if they are highly agentic, they may be criticized for lacking communal qualities and not acting the way women are "supposed" to act. Either way, critics may leave the impression that a woman doesn't meet the requirements for important roles.[3] What can help women navigate this maze? Women must learn to face these unfair expectations and network with other women leaders for support and mentorship. For their part, male leaders need to help champion the female leaders in their organizations, who may be less likely to self-promote and who face challenges to their leadership.

As for the question of whether men and women lead differently, re-search suggests that, yes, they do. Women tend to be more naturally transformational than men.[4] As discussed earlier, transformational lead-ers are generally concerned about individuals and promote the welfare of the group over individual ambition—the communal side of leadership. In this sense, women have an advantage over men, who may be more task driven, overlook individuals, be overly agentic, or lack natural emotional intelligence and other soft skills necessary for effective leadership. Some even argue that there is a "feminine advantage" of women leaders and that they should embrace the differences their gender provides.[5] In ad-dition to having these soft skills, women are often persistent in the face of adversity and may be equally tough as, or tougher than, men when needed. In sum, the research on this topic suggests the following:

- Men and women are equally effective overall as leaders.
- Men and women are more effective in roles congruent with their gender.

- Women are less effective than men when the role is masculinized (e.g., military), the role involves supervising large numbers of men, or the leader's performance is rated by men.
- Women are somewhat more effective in education, government, and social service and are substantially more effective in middle management.
- Women are less likely to self-promote for leadership positions.
- Women are less likely to emerge as group leaders but more likely to serve as social facilitators.
- Men are more likely to ask for what they want. Women are less likely to negotiate or self-promote, and they receive more backlash when they do.[6]

While the research in this area is growing, those who have worked with competent female leaders know that some women are as effective or even more so than some male leaders. Churches should be inclusive and recognize the gifts and callings God has granted to some women. "Male and female he created them" (Gen. 1:27).

Culture and Leadership

When I was a kid growing up in Southern California, we would visit the wondrous place called Disneyland in nearby Anaheim. Back in the day, one of the cheesiest rides was the Small World ride. Perhaps you remember this song from your childhood: "It's a small world after all. It's a small world after all. It's a small, small world." On this ride the tune would play in a variety of languages as diminutive puppets dressed in exotic garb danced around a tiny boat, which floated along at a snail's pace as all the passengers waited anxiously to get out and move on to the fun rides like the Matterhorn—which, ironically, also depicted an exotic locale but at least had a roller coaster and a monster!

This was Disney's vision in the 1960s, and it is our reality in the twenty-first century. Our world is indeed a small one—an interconnected place that requires leaders to understand the cultural contexts in which they lead. Churches, of course, have experienced this reality as they have ministered across the globe via missions activity, both supporting and sending missionaries, and as they have served locally in churches becoming more diverse and inclusive. No longer can one assume a homogeneous church or workforce and presume that one's own background and culture is right and all others are wrong. This is precisely the definition of ethnocentrism, the tendency to think the world revolves, or should revolve, around one culture's way of seeing and doing things. Cross-cultural leadership has perhaps become the quintessential twenty-first-century competency as leaders have sought to understand and reach a globally interconnected world. It is indeed a small world, but perhaps this ride will prove to be fun as we find ways to accomplish Jesus's mandate to "make disciples of all nations," not just the ones that are like ours (Matt. 28:19).

In the past forty years there has been a surge of interest in and research on the topic of leading cross-culturally. For example, N. J. Adler and S. Bartholomew have articulated cross-cultural competencies for leaders. To lead cross-culturally, leaders must be able to do the following:

- Understand business, political, and cultural environments worldwide
- Learn the perspectives, tastes, trends, and technologies of many cultures
- Work simultaneously with people from many cultures
- Adapt to living and communicating in other cultures
- Learn to relate to people of other cultures from a position of equality rather than superiority[7]

In a seminal study of international scope, Geert Hofstede developed a model of cultural dimensions that impact how management and leadership are perceived among different national cultures.[8] What is seen as good leadership in one culture may be seen as ineffective in another. This model has developed over the years and currently considers the following dimensions of culture:

- Power distance: This dimension expresses the degree to which the less powerful members of a society accept and expect that power is distributed unequally. The fundamental issue here is how a society handles inequalities among people.
- Individualism versus collectivism: This is the degree to which a culture tends to have a preference for loosely knit social connections,

called individualism, or for its opposite, collectivism, which is a
tightly knit framework in society in which individuals can expect
their relatives or members of a particular in-group to look after
them in exchange for unquestioning loyalty.

- Masculinity versus femininity: The masculinity side of this dimension represents a preference in society for achievement, heroism,
  assertiveness, and material rewards of success. Society at large is
  competitive. Its opposite, femininity, stands for a preference for
  cooperation, modesty, care for the weak, and quality of life. This
  dimension is similar to the contrast between communal and agentic
  behavior.

- Uncertainty avoidance: This is the degree to which the members of
  a society feel uncomfortable with uncertainty and ambiguity. The
  fundamental issue here is how a society deals with the fact that the
  future can never be known. "Should we try to control the future or
  just let it happen?" This could be seen as a social locus of control.

- Long-term versus short-term orientation: A long-term orientation
  is a preference to maintain time-honored traditions and norms
  while viewing societal change with suspicion. A short-term orientation, by contrast, takes a more pragmatic approach and is open
  to change and adaptive. This dimension could be seen as social
  risk tolerance.

- Indulgence versus restraint: Indulgence means allowing a relatively
  free gratification of basic and natural human drives related to enjoying life and having fun. Restraint means suppressing the gratification of needs and regulating it by means of strict social norms.[9]

Building on this research in perhaps the most sweeping management
research project with an international scope are the GLOBE studies.[10]
Based on Hofstede's dimensions, this research identifies nine cultural
(national) clusters and suggests a typical effective leadership profile for
each. Leaders are deemed to be effective if they fit certain profiles:

- Anglo (e.g., US, Britain): Leaders are competitive and results
  oriented.
- Confucian Asia (e.g., China, Japan, Taiwan): Leaders are results
  driven and encourage cooperation over individual goals.

- Eastern Europe (e.g., Russia, Poland): Leaders are forceful and supportive of coworkers, and they treat women with equality.
- Germanic Europe (e.g., Germany, Netherlands): Leaders value competition and aggressiveness and are highly results oriented.
- Latin America (e.g., Mexico, Brazil): Leaders are loyal and devoted to their families and similar groups.
- Latin Europe (e.g., Italy, Spain): Leaders value individual autonomy.
- Middle East (e.g., Turkey, Egypt): Leaders are devoted and loyal to their own people, and women are afforded less status.
- Nordic Europe (e.g., Denmark, Sweden): Leaders make long-term success a high priority, and women are treated with greater equality.
- Southern Asia (e.g., Philippines, Thailand): Leaders value the strong family and have a deep concern for their communities.
- Sub-Saharan Africa (e.g., Nigeria, Zimbabwe): Leaders are concerned about and sensitive to others, and they demonstrate strong family loyalty.[11]

These profiles can help people match their leadership to cultural norms in ways that are more effective. For example, Anglo countries, and the United States in particular, are considered to be low in power distance and high in individualism. A leader is just "one of the gang" who often seeks to reduce status distinctions and promote individualistic ideals such as personal initiative. Eastern European countries, on the other hand, are shown to have a high power distance and a collective orientation, as do Latin and Asian clusters. Leaders are thus expected to be in charge and to look out for the well-being of the group. Imagine a typical US leader who travels to Russia, sits down with their Russian subordinates for a decision-making meeting, and takes a typical consensus-building approach: "Look, I am just one of the team along with you all. What do you all think we should do here?" The team members would be reluctant to speak up. In this culture, it is the leader's job to provide answers and direction, and followers are in no position to question them. Further, this leader would be seen as weak for lacking decisive authority in the group. One can see in this example the potential for leadership mishaps and ineffectiveness as well as the need to understand cultural norms when trying to lead cross-culturally. It can be challenging when one's ideas of leadership are based on one's own culture, and admittedly, the vast majority of leadership and OB research is Anglocentric. To modify the old saying, "When in Rome, lead like Caesar would lead," and learn to temper your enthusiasm for the practices that may not work in that context.

This GLOBE study also identified the leadership traits that are universally desirable. People want leaders to be trustworthy, positive, intelligent, decisive, just, dependable, and informed, as well as be skilled in problem solving, administration, and team building. Universally undesirable traits include being unsociable, irritable, egocentric, and dictatorial. It is interesting to note that, even though some national clusters such as Latin America have a high power-distance orientation, being dictatorial is still undesirable there. Being cooperative and sociable is a trait that is desirable universally, regardless of national attitudes or norms.

There is much that can be helpful here for leadership. The findings about culture can help leaders identify their cultural biases and preferences. This same awareness can assist them in adapting their styles in order to become more effective in different cultural settings and with different groups of people, and it can equip them to communicate more effectively across cultural and geographic boundaries. Further, insight on culture and leadership can be used to build culturally sensitive websites and communications, design new staff and volunteer orientation programs, conduct training programs in relocation transition, and improve global team effectiveness.

Servant Leadership

No doubt, readers of this book are familiar with the concept of servant leadership. We recall Jesus's admonition, "You know that the rulers of the Gentiles lord it over them, and their high officials exercise authority over them. Not so with you. Instead, whoever wants to become great among you *must be your servant*, and whoever wants to be first must be your slave" (Matt. 20:25–27). Several theories of servant leadership have emerged that seek to put feet to this admonition—besides the ones that Jesus washed! These approaches address the practical question, How can leaders in organizations demonstrate servanthood and not just talk about it as an aspiration? In my experience, church leaders do a great job of talking about servant leadership but in practice demonstrate little service of others, instead having others serve them while justifying it by their status or position (ouch!). While occasionally picking up trash or stacking chairs is servant-like, we need to develop practices that are people focused and give life to others, not ones that just demonstrate we are willing to roll up our sleeves once in a while.

In 1977 Robert Greenleaf, in his seminal book *Servant Leadership: A Journey into the Nature of Legitimate Power and Greatness*, articulated an understanding of the nature of servant leadership.[12] Later on, Larry Spears, building on Greenleaf's work, introduced ten practices that exemplify servant leadership:

1. Listening: The servant leader will listen intently to others. They seek to listen receptively to what is being said and not said. "Be quick to listen, slow to speak" (James 1:19).

2. Empathy: People need to be accepted and recognized for their special and unique spirit, and servant leaders should seek to understand the perspectives of others.

3. Healing: Servant leaders recognize that they have an opportunity to help make whole—spiritually, emotionally, and even physically— those with whom they come into contact.

4. Awareness: This is the recognition of circumstances and contexts and, in particular, an understanding of issues involving ethics, power, and values. Nothing is less servant-like than a leader with a proverbial tin ear who is insensitive to the nuances or attitudes of others around them.

5. Persuasion: The servant leader seeks to convince others rather than coerce compliance. Think transformational, not transactional.

6. Conceptualization: This is giving the big picture that inspires others to dream great dreams and think beyond day-to-day realities.

7. Foresight: This is learning lessons from the past and knowing the realities of the present as well as the future consequences of a decision.

8. Stewardship: Servant leaders know that they are holding something in trust for another. Their organization and its assets do not belong to them, so they are careful not to take advantage of their position.

9. Commitment to the growth of people: Knowing that people have intrinsic value and are made in the image of God, servant leaders invest in the development of others.

10. Building community: Servant leaders ensure that others connect in meaningful ways, developing strong and healthy relationships across the organization.[13]

Spears writes, "These ten characteristics of servant-leadership are by no means exhaustive. However, I believe that the ones listed serve to communicate the power and promise that this concept offers to those who are open to its invitation and challenge."[14] They also give us a good starting point by offering tangible practices that will impact people's lives in meaningful ways.

In the early 2000s, Regent University instituted a series of research roundtables led by Bruce Winston and Kathleen Patterson to continue the work of understanding servant leadership in church and other organizational contexts. There is now a considerable body of research on the topic, and I encourage you to investigate it more thoroughly.[15] Some of the research suggests that servant leadership works in a variety of contexts, including some of the top businesses in the world. For example, Southwest Airlines has been known to practice servant leadership and has achieved extraordinary success over the years, with legendary stories of its founding CEO, Herb Kelleher, visiting staff in the hospital.[16] As Augustine wisely stated, "All truth is God's truth," so it should be no surprise that those who practice leadership in a biblical manner will flourish regardless of their context.

Followership and Leadership as an Emergent Property

There is an old Afghan proverb that says, "If you think you are leading and no one is following, you're only taking a walk." The last approaches to be considered are those that do not seek to see what a leader does or what the leader's personal characteristics are. Rather, these approaches seek to discover when leadership is happening as a real-time or emergent property and to determine the role of followers in the leadership transaction.[17] As we have seen, traditional approaches look, for the most part, at behavior, personal characteristics, and so forth. These other leadership approaches, however, seek to define leadership as something that happens irrespective of the person of the leader, and they seek to determine the role followers play as leadership is co-constructed in a time and place. Such approaches are a bit abstract, to be sure, but they are still an important way to think about leadership and how it happens.

Consider this illustration. There are people who have formal titles or positions of leadership yet do not actually provide much leadership. Conversely, there are people without a formal title who nevertheless actually provide leadership. There are also times when there is no formal leader in a group and yet a decision or other usual leadership function takes place. Imagine that a group of peers on a team gathers to discuss an issue, with no formal leader present that day. The meeting ends with new ideas or decisions even though no one was "in charge." We may chalk that up to high levels of trust and cooperation, which were no doubt present. But because of the outcome of the meeting, we also know that leadership did, in fact, take place, regardless of titles or roles. This is the focus of these approaches—to see when and how leadership actually happens.

One of the earliest approaches in this vein was leader substitution theory, developed by S. Kerr and J. M. Jermier.[18] This approach posits that certain situational factors can enhance, neutralize, or substitute for leader behaviors. Consider the above example of the successful leaderless meeting. These members were surely competent, knew the group's vision and goals, and were able to function without a designated leader. They brought to the table the necessary ingredients for leadership, and thus, a leadership substitute was present.

Another approach along these lines is leadership ontology, developed by Wilfred H. Drath and colleagues at the Center for Leadership Studies.[19] This model suggests that leadership occurs when three particular elements are present. If a group can bring them to the table, the role of a single or formal leader is lessened, as leadership is occurring through other means. The three elements are as follows:

- Direction: agreement on the vision and goals
- Alignment: coordination of various stakeholders
- Commitment: motivation to do the work

This theory opens up many interesting ways to envision leadership more as an activity and less as a person. Craig Pearce and colleagues describe shared leadership and suggest that leadership acts can be brought forth by different members of a group and that leadership can be fluid and shift to a member with the most insight or competence in a certain area, irrespective of role or title.[20] Charles C. Manz and Henry P. Sims Jr. discuss self-leadership, which is having the intrinsic ability to do what needs to be done without a leader, and superleadership, which takes place when leaders empower followers to be self-led.[21]

Finally, there is Joe Raelin's concepts of leadership-as-practice and the leaderful moment.[22] These concepts suggest that to find leadership we should look to the practices within which it is occurring and ask, What exactly are the specific situational dynamics that allow leadership to occur? Leadership is a result of these practices, these microprocesses. Typically, leadership is occurring when there is a change in a trajectory, a turning point, or a change in a pattern. Leadership-as-practice looks for the space in which leadership happens, the moment when it is cocreated in a group, and seeks to discover the practices that bring energy and release the group to cocreate. This can happen irrespective of the person with formal authority. This approach also has implications for leadership development, as organizations can become intentional in creating learning spaces in groups that allow participants to collectively gain the capacity to examine, in real time, their leadership practices that bring benefit to the group. In this sense, followers engage in leadership metacognition—thinking about thinking—so as to understand the dynamic they need in order to lead effectively in their own context. This, of course, may take time away from the task but can deliver a wealth of important insights about how the group or team does leadership at its best and how it can improve its eventual outcomes.

Leadership Development

The above review of theories and concepts is foundational for understanding what leadership is and does and for comparing the various approaches and theories developed over the years. And yet we are still left to wonder, How does a person actually grow in their ability to lead effectively? This is the final topic of this chapter: leadership development (LD).[23]

Unfortunately, some leaders give little attention to how leadership is developed in their own lives and ministries. Church and ministry leaders typically study the skills that are, more or less, specific to their professions—for example, preaching, counseling, church administration, cross-cultural ministry. Every profession has its set of skills and concepts that are necessary for being a competent practitioner, and ministry is no exception. By contrast, when OB thinkers and writers discuss LD, the focus is on the types of skills and competencies that are transferable from one role or profession to another. Preaching and counseling are necessary skills for a pastor, but learning to be a transformational leader who can inspire vision in a team is helpful for pastors, business executives, and all who are responsible for leading others in an organizational setting. Thus, LD focuses on acquiring the universal competencies that can help people regardless of the context. This is an important distinction. Many churches hold "leadership training" of some sort that, in fact, is focused on personal development or spiritual inspiration. This is, of course, good and helpful, but it is not necessarily LD proper. Moreover, as we will see, training events and seminars are only a piece of the LD puzzle.

There are some common myths about LD. There are some people who feel that leadership is all common sense or that the only school where one can learn leadership is the "school of hard knocks"—that is, experience and adversity. Others feel that leaders are "born, not made"; one either has leadership ability or doesn't. While these ideas may seem intuitive, they are, for the most part, false. To be sure, common sense helps leaders (and the rest of us), tough experiences can help people develop grit, and some naturally have traits that lend themselves to effective leadership. Nevertheless, there is much people can do to accelerate their growth and expand their leadership capacity. Leadership does not have to be something people stumble into and figure out. Imagine that a surgeon was asked, "How did you learn to do surgery?," and she replied, "Well, I just sort of figured it out, made a few mistakes along the way. Surgery is just common sense, and I was born to be a surgeon." That would be preposterous. But some leaders take a similar attitude toward their own development and assume they'll just figure it out as they go. Those whose vocation is dealing with matters of eternal significance and whom people trust with their lives should be more serious about their development as leaders.

Defining Leadership Development

LD involves "expanding the capacity of members to engage effectively in leadership roles and processes" and "building the capacity for groups of people to learn their way out of problems that could not have been predicted."[24] Notice that this definition works regardless of one's role, vocation, status, or title. Also note that it is about both individuals and groups. On the one hand, we can focus on how individuals can develop as leaders. On the other hand, we can think about LD as something that is embedded in the organization itself as a place where leadership is developed with intentionality. Finally, note that LD happens in a particular role or setting. While a church or ministry may encourage learning about leadership, it may not make room for such training with any regularity. Assigning a book for staff to read or hosting a seminar with a noted leadership expert is one thing. It is quite another thing to be purposeful in everyday life about allowing people to practice leadership or be reflective about and advance in their leadership skills. Thus, LD is more than offering seminars or classes; it is something that needs to be a part of the culture. Churches must provide opportunities for people to learn about leadership and give opportunity for them to lead, having an expectation that its people will advance in ever-increasing roles of leadership.

LD can be seen as a reflective cycle:

- Learning about new ideas and practices of leadership
- Having real-world experiences
- Intentionally reflecting on those experiences
- Refining one's practices as a result of the reflection (we can see this cycle in fig. 9.1)

Some may note the similarity between this model and the stages of David Kolb's learning theory, which similarly suggests that for learning to take place from experience, people must actively reflect on that experience and draw conclusions from it.[25] For example, imagine a leader who repeatedly encounters resistance from a new staff member. He can

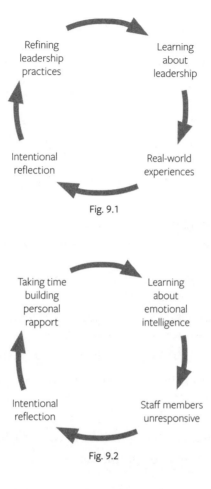

Fig. 9.1

Fig. 9.2

blame the new staff member and assume this person does not have what it takes to succeed in ministry, or he can add some new ideas into his repertoire of explanations—maybe the staff are not being sufficiently motivated (theories of motivation), or perhaps the leader has not taken enough time to get to know this new staff member well, along with her unique personality (emotional intelligence, individual differences). We can see this cycle in figure 9.2.

LD is the process by which we learn ideas that can help us lead, incorporate these ideas into practice, and intentionally reflect on their impact. We make these new leadership habits part of our repertoire of leadership skills and thus increase our leadership capacity.

We can also infer from this cycle the necessity of the entire organization being involved. Of course, individuals can always reflect on their practice of leadership, but organizations with a leadership development culture make room for experiences and reflection. The idea is not just that people will fulfill their responsibilities but also that they will ask, What did we learn about leadership in the process, and how can we leverage the experiences we are having to intentionally accelerate our growth as leaders?

Leadership Development in Practice

How do people develop as leaders? The research suggests that there are several areas of focus in intentional LD. In order to develop full leadership potential, leaders must grow in the following five areas:[26]

1. Individual cognitive complexity and critical thinking: Leadership involves facing unique and vexing challenges, ones that defy easy or quick solutions. Leaders must nurture the ability to think critically about issues, asking questions such as:
   o What are the *real* issues, not just the surface issues?
   o How did they get to this state, and what is their background and history?
   o What are different approaches to dealing with the issues, and what are the pros and cons for each approach?
   o What are some likely unintended consequences for different solutions?

2. Social intelligence: How do people relate to one another and to the leader? Leadership is largely the ability to relate to and work with a wide variety of people, some of whom the leader will like and some of whom the leader will find challenging.
   o Who is "in the room," and what are their expectations?
   o What makes certain individuals thrive? What motivates them?
   o Are there various groups that cluster together?
   o Have I invested in developing enough social capital to support certain expectations of others? How large is my "trust bank account"?

3. Openness to creativity, challenge, and exploration: Because leadership is about change and moving an organization forward, leaders

must learn to develop new and fresh approaches. "We have never done it that way before" should be banished from the lips of all leaders; instead, they should ask, "What are new ways of approaching this matter?"

- ○ Brainstorming, both alone and in a group, is useful for getting lots of ideas on the table.
- ○ Working with a diverse range of creative people can help the leader and the organization stay fresh.
- ○ Leaders should ask what the user experience will be like for those who will be affected by any change or decision.
- ○ Leaders should learn to make adjustments along the way.

4. Tolerance for ambiguity yet a sustained focus on goals and mission: The way forward is rarely straightforward, and leaders will face times when outcomes are unclear. Some have a hard time with this and make decisions prematurely and poorly.

- ○ Leaders should temper an attitude that insists on having things done "right" or done immediately. Things will be done more correctly as the leader learns to take time to process.
- ○ Few decisions are permanent, and leaders should learn to accept process over perfection.
- ○ There is an important difference between "must" issues and "could" issues. Not all decisions require the same sense of urgency, and few have only one "right" solution. There is wisdom in standing on principle when *necessary* and on tolerance when *possible*.
- ○ Leaders should ask whether any codependent or control issues tend to force them to seize control when they are confronted with ambiguity.

5. Self-discipline, doing what is right without being told to do so: Leadership requires initiative in the following areas:

- ○ Knowing whether an issue is within the leader's purview, knowing when to act and when not to act, and actually acting when appropriate
- ○ Dealing with, rather than putting off, issues that are important to others or the organization

- ○ Cultivating habits that enable the leader to perform at their best at all times
- ○ Developing the spiritual, emotional, and physical disciplines that help one stay fresh and engaged over the long term

Further, effective LD practices should include the following elements:

- Valid ideas about leadership: Leaders should imbibe correct notions about leadership, such as those in the current chapter (and the rest of the book). While there is a plethora of ideas and approaches, leaders should focus on the ones that have been proven valid in a variety of situations. Learn to question outdated assumptions as well as folk leadership wisdom that may not look deep enough beneath the surface.
- Feedback from multiple sources: Leaders are not always the best judge of their own development, and they sometimes have blind spots. Other people, those who can see them in action, can provide insight about their leadership that the leaders may not see themselves. Leaders should become comfortable with receiving feedback from a variety of perspectives.
- A concrete and focused development plan: Focusing on a few key areas at a time, rather than generically saying, "I want to become a better leader," will yield better results. It is helpful to ask, What areas of leadership, what particular approaches or competencies, do I want to improve in? Leaders should operationalize their thinking about leadership to specific and measurable areas.
- Repeated interventions: Leaders must practice and practice and practice in order to improve. A common LD myth is that attending a workshop or reading the latest hot book on leadership will make someone a better leader. Such resources may inspire or inform, but there is no substitute for having real-world experiences and working until one has mastered a particular competency.

Finally, understand that LD requires activities that provide feedback, are challenging, and give support. Usual areas of practice focus on:[27]

- 360-degree feedback: While feedback can be painful, everyone needs it in order to grow. No one likes to hear about their flaws, yet feedback that is only positive can be mere flattery. Typical organizational performance reviews are top-down, from a supervisor to a subordinate. But LD performance evaluation must come from people at different levels in the organization, as everyone sees the leader in a different light and each perspective may be an important source of feedback. There has been some valid criticism of bureaucratizing 360-degree feedback,[28] and it can be unduly complex for a smaller church or ministry. Regardless of how formal or sophisticated the approach is, leaders need not only official reviews and top-down input but also feedback from peers with whom the leaders often can be more open and candid. Further, those whom leaders oversee can give important insight. It is wise to identify people whom the leader can trust and who are likely to give good, objective feedback without feeling threatened. Subordinates may be reluctant to say how they think the leader is doing, especially if they think the leader is doing a poor job. But a leader who cultivates transparency and candor may find people more willing to give the feedback that is needed for improvement.

- Mentoring or coaching relationships: This is a hot topic, and leadership coaches abound, with good reason. A mentor or coach can give the type of feedback and support that other LD methods cannot. While 360-degree feedback is good, it can be impersonal and lack a developmental aspect. A good coach also provides the support and encouragement needed to help the medicine go down. Keep in mind that, as mentioned in chapter 6, coaching is not simply giving a good pep talk or sharing one's own experience. A good coach knows how to listen and ask the questions that help the learner come to the right conclusions on their own. Those engaging in LD should seek out the people who can do this for them, perhaps even a paid coach or consultant.

- Role rotation or "stretch" assignments that are appropriately and intentionally challenging: Everyone can get stuck in ruts, and what was once new and challenging can become old and routine in time. As possible, leaders should move into new areas that will help them acquire new skills, make new relationships, and stretch out. They should also consider how the organization enables people to pursue this kind of growth. Often, people get pigeonholed into certain roles they are good at and are left there. But organizations ought to be intentional in providing new challenges for those with leadership potential lest they crave, and find, opportunities elsewhere. While it is sometimes risky to put new or less experienced people in charge of areas, people may step up and flourish if they are given opportunities. Many a leader has found their calling when given the opportunity to do something new and challenging—including this author! Leaders can become leader makers when they step out of their own comfort zone and allow others the opportunity to step out of theirs.

▪ Practical Leadership Application Questions ▪

- How well do you, or how well does your church or ministry, empower women and people of color to move into and excel in roles of leadership? What might be some barriers?
- What challenges do you foresee in practicing servant leadership in the "real world"? Which of Spears's ten skills could you work on to help you become a better servant leader?
- What is your own cross-cultural leadership intelligence? How can you develop to better serve diverse groups both in and outside your church or ministry?
- Where in your organization do you see leadership happening and emerging? What are those leaderful moments, those places where leadership takes place in real time, and how can you make these into learning occasions?
- How intentional are you in your own leadership development? How intentional is your church or ministry in developing a leadership-development culture?

CASE STUDY

The Case of Leadership Succession

RISE Church was a twenty-year-old dynamic and fast-growing church, founded by Pastor Rick and his wife Tina. RISE stands for "reach, inspire, serve, and engage," which are the core values of the church. Rick and Tina began the church in their living room with a handful of friends, and it grew to over three thousand people, outpacing all other churches in their movement and becoming a resource church for their region. Rick was a dynamic, charismatic leader who delivered upbeat and relevant Bible teaching in a style that the average Joe could understand. His theology was a little unorthodox for some, and his critics even accused him of being irreverent. But most in the congregation saw him as a spiritual leader who heard from God and trusted him implicitly, and his approach to faith was widely appreciated. Sadly, Rick was tragically killed in a hunting accident.

Over the years he had his share of acolytes on staff and on the board of elders, many of whom were his longtime friends or others he trusted. While he micromanaged some of the staff, he gave free rein to others—as long as that rein served his growing public image. He began his own podcast, wrote several books, and did outside speaking engagements regularly. It seemed to some that Rick was becoming bigger than RISE church, and such people saw a gap in church leadership, as various staff members seemingly felt in charge when Rick was away.

Rick did not like to appoint any particular staff member to lead the church in his absence, for fear that they might take over. Predictably, there was a certain amount of ambiguity over who was in charge, and this ambiguity led to chaos at times. Some breathed a sigh of relief when Rick was gone on his frequent trips, as he often would throw out new ideas randomly, causing existing plans and programs to be shuffled or sidelined as staff figured out how to do the next new thing. With him gone, the workers could focus on their tasks. Others felt that there was a void when he was gone, as they were overly dependent on him and his leadership and they did not know what they should be focusing on. They were not being prepared to run things, were rarely given decision-making authority, and felt stifled in their growth as leaders. Now that he was gone permanently, this sentiment became permanent for some.

All of this came to a head at one particular elders' meeting. After a time of prayer, Elder Kevin started off, "Brothers and sisters, the time has come for us to consider a successor for Pastor Rick. While no one will ever replace him, the church cannot continue in its current leaderless state. We have all been praying and fasting, and

I believe we have come up with several good candidates to be Rick's successor, so let us consider them now." And with that they began to discuss the candidates.

The first was Madelyn, a senior staff member who had been with Rick and Tina since the beginning. She had left a lucrative career in marketing to join RISE and had led the large events and social-media teams. She was also a vocal advocate for women in ministry leadership and was a role model to many of the younger female staff members and volunteers. While she was not a highly organized person, she had gone to seminary, was likable and charismatic in her own way, and was a very gifted preacher. Some of the elders had theological reservations about putting a female in charge, but they knew they could trust Madelyn as a leader.

Next was Ted, another longtime staff member. Ted, too, had left a good career as a businessperson and used his corporate experience to help streamline the affairs of the church. While Ted was a good administrator, some felt his people skills were lacking. He could be abrupt with other staff, would interrupt junior staff members during staff meetings, and was often too busy with his own ministry, the Business Leaders' Fellowship, which was growing as a resource to those in the region. Many of the elders liked Ted; some were old friends, and they played golf together each week.

Finally, there was Elijah, a new but very competent staff member. Elijah had just completed his Doctor of Ministry degree and was an excellent Bible and theology teacher. Elijah oversaw the educational ministries of the church, did fill-in preaching when Rick was away, and had very good administrative and people skills. Many of the younger staff liked to hang out in his office and have meandering conversations about theology and life, and he was becoming a mentor to many of them. The elders admired Elijah, but some were a bit dismissive of his "book learning" and felt he had a lot to learn about the "real world."

After all the candidates were reviewed, Elder Tom stood up. "These are all great candidates, and each brings something unique and important to their leadership that could help the church during this season of transition. Do we have to choose just one? What if we used a team leadership approach? I have read that shared leadership can be very effective." Some nodded in agreement and thought this was a great idea. But others balked and pushed back, saying, "We don't think this approach will work here. Because Pastor Rick was such a commanding and charismatic figure, our church needs to find someone who can have that same presence and vision. Everyone knows 'too many cooks spoil the broth.' The church will become a mess if we don't appoint someone to be in charge. And besides, one leader is biblical!" Then Elder Juan spoke up. "We would not be in this situation if the church had done a better job at developing leaders in the first place. If any changes are made, I think the first one should be to improve our leadership-development pipeline." Someone else suggested that Tina, Rick's widow, should take over the church. But others pushed back on this, stating that while everyone loved Tina as the pastor's wife, they were not confident she could run the affairs of such a big church. She had little experience, and many felt she lacked the right stuff of a leader—she was too nice and could not stand up under pressure. Besides, she still had younger children to look after and was coping with the shock of losing her husband. It would be too much to throw this responsibility on her now.

Others chimed in with various opinions and ideas, opening up other cans of worms that had been ignored in the past. Rick had left not only a gaping hole but also a few skeletons and some piles of dirt swept under rugs, and now was the time for the elders to sort things out. Everyone settled in; it was going to be a long elders' meeting this week.

Questions for Discussion

- Which of these candidates do you think would be the best fit for this role, and why?
- Do you think the elders' concerns about these leaders are valid? Why or why not?
- Do you think a shared leadership approach would work here? Why or why not?
- What could RISE do to develop its leadership pipeline so that it would help the younger staff grow?

▩ Further Reading ▩

Avolio, Bruce. *Full Range Leadership Development*. 2nd ed. Thousand Oaks, CA: Sage, 2010.

Eagly, Alice H., and Linda L. Carli. *Through the Labyrinth: The Truth about How Women Become Leaders*. Boston: Harvard Business Review Press, 2007.

Greenleaf, Robert K. *Servant Leadership: A Journey into the Nature of Legitimate Power and Greatness*. New York: Paulist Press, 2002.

Herrington, Jim, Trisha Taylor, and R. Robert Creech. *The Leader's Journey: Accepting the Call to Personal and Congregational Transformation*. 2nd ed. Grand Rapids: Baker Academic, 2020.

House, Robert J., Paul J. Hanges, Mansour Javidan, Peter W. Dorfman, and Vipin Gupta, eds. *Culture, Leadership, and Organizations: The GLOBE Study of 62 Societies*. Thousand Oaks, CA: Sage, 2004.

Livermore, David A. *Cultural Intelligence: Improving Your CQ to Engage Our Multicultural World*. Grand Rapids: Baker Academic, 2009.

10

Organizational Culture

Introduction

Culture is like the air we breathe. Rarely seen but always there, culture is ubiquitous and influences almost everything about an organization. Much of our culture is invisible because we are part and partakers of the culture, like a fish that is oblivious to water. Further, while there has been much discussion about culture, much of it is superficial at best, and people often invoke "culture" when they want to say positive things about themselves, like "We have a great culture around here" or "This is an important part of our culture." Some ministries add a set of values to their website or have them displayed nicely on a wall, thinking the list somehow represents their culture. Yet that is only the top layer of culture and is often more aspirational than real. Culture is so deep and entrenched that people often struggle to realize what their true culture is or to describe it objectively. There is much more to a church's culture than meets the eye, and leaders must recognize the true nature of their culture and their role in it. This is the focus of this final chapter and the fourth level of analysis (see fig. 10.1).[1] In some sense, the culture of a church is an aggregation of many of the topics and practices discussed so far in this book. So, if you have been paying attention, you are well on your way to having a positive impact on your organizational culture!

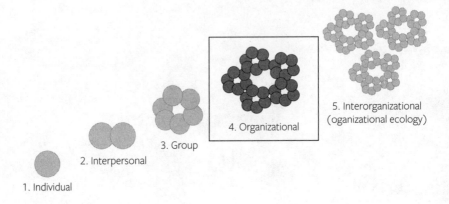

5. Interorganizational
(oganizational ecology)

4. Organizational

3. Group

2. Interpersonal

1. Individual

Fig. 10.1

Organizational culture (OC) is, as discussed in chapter 1, a metaphor for describing an organization. It is not a reality exactly, but it is an important frame of reference and a means of analysis and discussion for those who lead. OC is an OB application of cultural anthropology, a discipline that seeks to understand how human societies operate. Interestingly, Christian missionaries were the first cultural anthropologists, as they sought a better understanding of other cultures in their attempts to spread the gospel to people who were very different from them. In the 1980s, management practitioners and consultants adapted these ideas of culture and applied them to businesses, seeing them as unique entities with cultures all their own.[2] Thus, OC became an important way to think about and describe what an organization is. It can be contrasted with the classic bureaucratic view of organizations as static and impersonal structures, a perspective that focuses on the formal hierarchy, departments, job descriptions, reporting relationships, and so on and overlooks the assumptions, values, or history on which these things are built. This culture approach has been adopted by church consultants and authors as well.[3]

It is important to recognize the distinction between an outside perspective and an inside perspective, respectively called the "etic" and "emic" descriptions of culture.[4] Those inside a culture can understand and describe how things work with great detail. And yet as insiders they may become immune to how it impacts them. It thus takes an outsider's eye to make sense of it, compare it to other cultures, see how well it supports stated objectives and aspirations, and make recommendations for change. Understanding culture requires both the proximity to see it and the objectivity and bravery to face what it really is, warts and all.

Defining Culture

While different definitions of OC abound, we will start with Edgar Schein's: culture is a pattern of shared basic assumptions learned by a group as it solves its problems of external adaptation and internal integration. It is a product of joint learning.[5] Note the following from this definition:

- *Culture involves patterns.* Patterns are developed over time through repetition and habit. Things we do once or twice are not part of culture. Culture includes only those things that are habitual and part of regular and ongoing behavior.
- *Culture is built on assumptions.* Assumptions are taken for granted and rarely examined. They are just there, and they are true to us. This is why examining culture is difficult; we rarely consider or challenge our assumptions.
- *These assumptions are shared.* Everyone in our group believes them to be true. This point hints at a challenge for building culture: keeping everyone aligned to the culture. Some share the assumptions more than others. There are true believers, and then there are the deviants.
- *Culture has developed over time to help us deal with both the outside world (our larger social environment) and our internal world (the organization itself).* In this sense, culture keeps us bound together and helps us relate to the outside world and position ourselves within it in a distinct way.
- *It comes as a result of learning over time.* Through many experiences, patterns of assumptions emerge and become solidified as part of our reality. This point provides another hint as to why changing culture is hard: it has taken time for the culture to become what it is, and thus it takes time for it to become something different.

Built on our assumptions are shared values. Values can be seen in our cultural norms—that is, our behavior and the expectation to act accordingly. Sometimes values are articulated and written down, but more often they are the unwritten rules implied and well known by insiders. Consider the following example:

> The staff handbook requires staff to arrive at work at 9 a.m. This is the written policy, built on the value of punctuality. Yet Bob trickles in anywhere between 9 and 10. The reason is that he must help his kids get to school, and everyone knows that his wife, Pam, began her new job and that Bob is now doing "kid duty" in the morning. Because the church loves and supports Pam and values parents being involved in their kids' lives, and because the senior pastor also trickles in at an inconsistent time in the morning, this has become an acceptable practice and is now a norm. No one really minds, even though it is not what the handbook requires.

This illustration shows how cultural norms can trump the formal structure and bureaucracy. There are rules, and then there is "how we really do things around here." This is one of the key challenges of and goals for working with culture—aligning norms and behaviors with stated policies, practices, and objectives. This is also an important way to think about whether a culture is good or healthy. The culture can be assessed according to the degree to which it supports the agreed-on and stated objectives and leads to members being productive and engaged in their work. In reading the above example, you may have thought Bob was a slacker who needed to get his act together. Or you may have thought that the church needed to change what the handbook said about when the workday started. Either would be fine, but which solution best aligns with greater goals and objectives? If structure and policy compliance are pressing objectives, then Bob needs to figure out how to arrive on time. But if helping staff achieve work-life balance is more pressing, then the rules should be changed.

One way to visualize the complexity and levels of culture is to view culture as the proverbial iceberg. We can see artifacts and behaviors above the water, but the vast majority of culture is hidden and below the surface. This iceberg model of OC can help us understand how culture exists at different levels of visibility (see fig. 10.2).

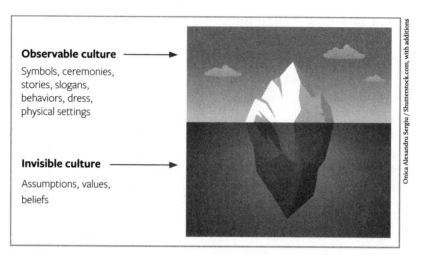

Observable culture ⟶
Symbols, ceremonies, stories, slogans, behaviors, dress, physical settings

Invisible culture ⟶
Assumptions, values, beliefs

Onica Alexandru Sergiu / Shutterstock.com, with additions

Fig. 10.2

Culture also involves an organization's history, heroes, stories and myths, and symbols. Every church or ministry has its history or story arc. It began with some person or event; went through a series of victories and challenges, successes and setbacks; and is now in its current chapter. It has developed a repertoire of stories that have been retold over time and that help it define what it is and what is important. Certain figures, often a founder, are larger than life and have a strong influence on how the organization tells its story and what it stands for. Some of these stories take on mythical proportions—not in the sense that they did not really happen but in the sense that they are now succinct and contain a "moral" at the end. Symbols are the visual elements that stand for "us." Flags, logos, icons, even fonts and webpage banners all say something about who we are and what we stand for.

In a way, culture is what gives people a sense of belonging to something different and special, something that is unlike any other church or ministry. It is the organization's unique personality, what sets them apart from others. Yet as part of the universal church, Christians have shared assumptions and values, a shared history and story, and shared heroes and symbols, all of which contribute to the church's unique identity and make it different from the businesses and the other institutions of the world. Christians are grounded in the eternal story of God's redemption found in Scripture, take their values from its pages, and worship Jesus not just as another founder but as the Creator and Savior. Every church is rooted in this culture and yet finds its own unique and local expression based on, perhaps, a denomination, movement, or founder.

This is also a challenge for a local church: to forge its own unique culture and identity, relating to its local environment and culture, while being faithful to the biblical story. If a church becomes too engrossed in its local culture, it may fall into syncretism, merging various and perhaps incompatible belief systems, and risk becoming no different from a so- cial club or movement. On the other hand, if a church becomes insular and out of touch with the larger culture, it risks being marginalized or irrelevant. While a full exploration of this point is beyond the scope of this work, consider the current cultural debate over the acceptance of transgenderism and the LGBTQ+ community. Conservative churches will reject them outright, whereas liberal churches may adopt the "love is love" mantra and fly a rainbow flag on their front lawn. Both churches would claim to love Jesus and follow his teachings, but a variety of dif- ferent assumptions, values, and historical developments have led them down two very different paths. This is the force of culture clearly shaping distinct church identities.

Types of Cultures

There is a variety of ways to think about culture types. One helpful way is to use Schein's distinction between dominant cultures and subcultures:[6]

- Dominant culture: This is the culture that most would recognize, and ideally, it is a reflection of the values and the story of top leader- ship, the organization's founding, and so on. The dominant culture is perhaps an aggregation of much of the organization's history, values, and behaviors and is the culture that most readily captures what the organization stands for. It may be represented by the hierarchical leadership, those who make the decisions and are the face of the orga- nization. The dominant culture is the organization's mainstream.

- Subcultures: These are the microcultures that exist within the larger organization. For example, in a church there may be distinct cultures in groups such as:

- ○ Worship ministry: the creative praise artists and musicians
- ○ Missions or outreach: the brave adventurers on mission to reach the world
- ○ Educational ministry: the educated, intellectual teachers of the church
- ○ Youth ministry: those who "have fun and disciple the young"
- ○ Pastoral care and counseling: the caring and compassionate helpers

While of course subcultures will reflect the larger values and ideals of the dominant culture, they will also develop their own unique sense of identity based on their area of expertise. A meeting of the educational ministry group might feel like a college colloquium, whereas a meeting of the youth ministry team might feel like a music festival. Each has, in the interest of reaching those it serves, developed a culture that reflects its own area of ministry.

The above example includes subcultures that are specific to *departments* of an organization. Schein suggests another way of thinking about subcultures in an organization; he proposes three classes—the executive, the operator, and the engineer—which can transcend formal departments. The executive class includes those who hold formal authority in the hierarchy, typify the official "party line," and represent the power structures. The operators are those in the organization who work together, develop their own identities and sense of being a team, and exhibit high levels of trust. The engineers are those who solve technical problems via technology or other professional skills. Both the operator and engineer classes can, at times, be in opposition to the executive class, as they stick together and learn to negotiate with the executive class. The dichotomies of brains versus brawn, brass versus rank and file, and the people versus "the man" all come to mind here.

A major challenge of working with culture is keeping all these classes aligned. Subcultures can become islands unto themselves, as each one feels that its area is the most important. For example, in a church the missions folks might feel that they are the ones doing God's work, heeding the Great Commission, and that the church does not support or fund them as well as it should. The worship folks feel that the church is about offering worship to the King. What can be more important than that, and why should the songs be cut down to a total of twelve minutes each Sunday service? Those in roles of formal authority have the prerogative to make decisions, but if they do so without considering what is important to others, such as those who execute the work, they may create tension and a culture where people are not pulling together. Such problems can lead to a culture being unhealthy or toxic. There is a certain tone deafness of one subculture or class to another.

In addition to considering dominant cultures and subcultures, we can think of culture in terms of strong ones and weak ones.

- Strong culture: This is not necessarily a good or positive culture. A strong culture is a culture that is deeply felt and reflected by most in the organization, one that is "deep and wide." It is a result of history and years of cultivation by strong leadership, with all perspectives pulling together. The tension between the various classes and departments is minimal.
- Weak culture: A weak culture is not adhered to by most and/or is not held deeply. This lack of buy-in can be due to a variety of factors, such as weak or dissipating leadership, values that are not seen as genuine and are imposed from the top, the strength of splintering subcultures, or the above tensions between executive, operator, and engineer classes.

The challenge for leadership is to create strong cultures, where the important values are not just known but believed and acted on at all levels of the organization, from senior leadership to brand-new staff and volunteers.

The Competing Values Framework

Another way to think about culture types is Kim Cameron and Robert Quinn's competing values framework.[7] This model describes culture in terms of flexibility versus stability and internal versus external focus, and it portrays four different culture prototypes:

- Clan culture (flexible and internally focused): A clan culture is based on values such as loyalty, trust, and commitment to the orga-

nization. There is a collaboration orientation, and people's participation and development are highly valued. As the name implies, this
type of culture feels like a family, and leaders can seem like father or
mother figures as they mentor others and develop team cohesion.

- Hierarchy culture (stable and internally focused): This is a culture
  where rules and policy control behavior. There is a level of for-
  mality in operations and in reporting relationships. Efficiency and
  coordination are supreme values, and leaders are those who can
  bring about smooth and efficient control processes that keep the
  organization aligned.

- Ad-hocracy culture (flexible and externally focused): This is a culture that values creativity and innovation. Understanding problems and creating novel solutions are important, and leaders are
  entrepreneurial and create energy and vision around a new brand
  or approach.

- Market culture (stable and externally focused): This culture has a
  competitive and hard-driving orientation, seeking to meet goals
  and expand the organization's reach. Growth is the supreme virtue,
  over and above people, and leaders can be hard drivers who push
  the organization to produce and to accomplish its goals.

One can, of course, see different aspects of these four types in any
one organization. An organization's culture does not fit squarely in one
box or another; it can overlap and blend. However, a culture will often
feel like one type more than another. The value of this model is in helping leaders bring their organizational culture into alignment with the
stated values and vision and recognize that there is often tension in an
organization around these culture types, hence the phrase "competing
values" in this model's name. Some in the organization will feel the tension acutely, depending on their perspective.

For example, imagine a church with a strong clan culture feel—not
hard to do. Most of my students over the years have expressed that this
best reflects their church's culture. There is a premium on relationships, and the leaders are highly pastoral and caring. No problem there.
However, imagine that this church also has a mission and has goals for
reaching the community. Year after year the church experiences warm

pastoral care and fellowship yet fails to grow or accomplish its goals. It has, in effect, become a social gathering for current members. There are some members who recognize this tension and want everyone to stop "singing kumbaya" and get out there on the streets, where the people really need Jesus. In this example, there is a misalignment between the culture and its stated mission and goals. Using this model, we could say that the church is neither healthy nor sick but is misaligned and needs to refocus on creating a culture that is more creative (ad-hocracy) and/or goal-oriented (market) in order to better support its stated mission.

Of course, the tension in this example might be a microcosm of the tension in the universal church at large. There will always be competition between "in-reach" and "outreach," and there will always be a need for leaders to integrate both aspects of the mission. Another perennial tension in church culture is between its high value on people and relationships (clan) and the need to develop stability and efficiency to better steward its growth (hierarchy). As a church grows, it generates a need for systems and processes that will bring stability and a sense of organization. "Mom and pop" management will not work in a growing church. Thus, keeping the church people-oriented and bringing efficiency commensurate with its size is a point of OC tension.

Characteristics of Culture

While each organizational culture is unique, there are characteristics that can help us describe a culture. For example, Stephen Robbins and Timothy Judge describe various characteristics of culture:[8]

- Risk tolerance: the degree to which members are encouraged to be innovative and risk taking
- Conflict tolerance: the degree to which people are willing to engage in open dialogue over contentious issues
- Individual initiative: the degree of responsibility, freedom, and independence that individuals have
- Integration: the degree to which units within the organization are encouraged to operate in a coordinated manner

- Management support: the degree to which managers provide clear communication, assistance, and support to their subordinates
- Control: the number of rules and regulations and the amount of direct supervision that is used to oversee and control employee behavior
- Identity: the degree to which members identify with the organization as a whole rather than with their particular work group or field of professional expertise
- Reward systems: the degree to which reward allocations are based on members' performance criteria in contrast to seniority, favoritism, nepotism, and so on.

Other characteristics could be used to describe aspects of a contemporary organization, such as:

- Spirituality: the degree to which transcendent and eternal values are considered in the mission and operation of the organization
- Ethics: the degree to which ethical values drive the behavior of the organizational members, rewarding good behavior and not tolerating bad behavior
- Diversity and inclusivity: the degree to which the organization intentionally includes and empowers women and people of color
- Leadership development orientation: the degree to which the organization is intentional in identifying its leadership pool and preparing those people for ever-expanding roles of leadership

A church, as part of the larger Christian community, could also be described along the lines of historical and contemporary importance:

- Denominational orientation: This is the degree to which the church identifies with its historic founding or movement. Some churches experience tension in their relationship with their denomination and choose to eschew traditional names and rebrand themselves. For example, a church may change its name from First Baptist Church of Jollyville to First Jollyville or another contemporary-sounding name with no reference to a denomination. Other churches may avoid traditional denominations altogether and be part of a loose network of churches such as the New Apostolic Reformation[9] or the Association of Related Churches.[10]

- Traditional orientation: This is the degree to which the church adheres to the historic doctrine and liturgical practices of the church at large. This can include the following:
  - Attitudes toward the Bible and its interpretation and authority
  - Attitudes toward women in roles of leadership
  - The feel of the sanctuary and church service (e.g., type of seats and decor, musical style, preaching style)
  - The adoption and use of technology (e.g., social media, video announcements, live stream service)

Changing Culture: A Tricky Proposition

A popular discussion about culture concerns the degree to which it can or should be intentionally changed and the degree to which leaders can engineer culture change from the top down. Consider the following examples.

An elder in the church makes a comment: "We have a toxic culture around here. No one trusts anyone, and we all seem to be pulling in different directions." The senior pastor and his team agree—trust and morale are low, and there is a lack of clarity on goals and priorities. They set out to reestablish trust and morale and to clarify goals and priorities through a series of town-hall meetings and strategic-planning initiatives. There is some renewed enthusiasm for a season, but after about a year, there is the same sense of low morale, mistrust, and confusion over goals and priorities.

Or consider another common scenario—when two churches merge.

Small Church has dwindled in size over the years yet still has many faithful members and physical assets. The board of elders decides to take up the friendly offer of Big Church to merge into their church and become a satellite congregation. All their assets are transferred, the building gets a makeover and a new sign, and a new pastor, who was on staff at Big Church, comes aboard. At first everyone is excited and grateful, as the people have averted being scattered and the new pastor is an excellent communicator. But after the honeymoon is over, leaders from both sides begin to realize that there are serious cultural differences. Small Church has been traditional in its worship style, whereas Big Church is very contemporary; Small Church is invested in diversity and inclusion, whereas Big Church is primarily white and conservative; and Small Church has little risk tolerance and is conflict averse, whereas Big Church likes to take risks and invite dialogue.

It may be tempting in this scenario to insist that Small Church adopt the culture and values of Big Church wholesale—after all, Big Church rescued them from death and is successful, and they are footing the bill! But to dismiss the heritage and values of Small Church seems wrong, and the purpose of the merger was not to acquire their building but to honor and build their people, many of whom have been faithful for decades.

These two examples show the difficulties that attempts at culture change can bring, and they highlight the need to understand how to approach culture change.

There is, of course, evidence that in the corporate world healthy cultures lead to better performance than unhealthy ones,[11] and this is no doubt true in the church and ministry world as well. Hopefully, by this point in the book you will have understood what leaders should focus on when developing healthy cultures in the first place. People-oriented practices, trust and empowerment, motivation, conflict resolution, team building, and transformational leadership, for example, are all ways an organization can become healthy. But sometimes the realities of toxic, parochial, or stagnant cultures confront newly installed leaders, and thus, a challenge is presented to them, as in the above scenarios.

One of the most substantial findings in the research on OC is how impermeable and resistant to change it really is despite the promises of consultants and leadership gurus. A founding leader or pastor can have long-term influence on a church ministry's culture even after they have left the scene. A promise to change or fix culture can end up producing just another top-down initiative that fails to deliver and thus adds to the cynicism and lack of trust between the executive and operator classes. This is not to say leaders should take a fatalistic view of culture or throw their hands up and say, "Oh well, there is nothing we can do about this." But leaders must recognize the depths of culture and realistically assess their role in shaping and managing it.

So, what can a leader do to address a culture that they have inherited or that, over time, has atrophied and become unhealthy? The following are best practices for intentionally addressing culture.

Begin at the beginning. The best time to implement the "right" culture is when staff and volunteers are new, as part of a socialization process into the organization. All new personnel should receive an orientation not just to human resources practices and policies but to the history and values of the organization, including what it stands for and what it wants its people to stand for. Of course, another way to address this issue is to hire the right people, considering those who are a good culture fit. But as discussed in chapter 2, you need to be intentional about achieving a diversity of skills, experiences, and backgrounds in your organization. Hiring only people who are just like you can produce an insular and un-creative culture. Further, these culture orientations must be more than organizational window dressing and should align with reality.

Once people enter, there is an implicit socialization process in which they discover things on their own by seeing the values, attitudes, and behaviors of others. If people spend a couple of days getting the "party line" from senior personnel but quickly discover, when they begin their regular work, that the unwritten rules and norms are vastly different, they can become puzzled or cynical. Give a realistic preview, and be hon-est about what currently exists rather than give a sugar-coated version of the truth. People will appreciate your aspirations and may even see themselves as change agents and part of the "new guard" that brings the ministry into the future.

Know the leader's job. I discussed leadership proper in chapters 8 and 9 and will not recount what effective leadership looks like here. In terms of change, leadership should keep in mind the following directives:

- *Remember that leaders are role models for what culture will look like.* "Do what I say and not what I do" will not work in leading culture change. Leadership, from the top on down, must exemplify what the culture should look like, because culture becomes a corporate embodiment of what leaders value and practice. Much of culture is rooted in values, and values are "caught" and not "taught." People are smart and catch on quickly to what is really important. Do you want to be a church that is involved in evangelism? Make sure you yourself are involved in evangelism. Do you want your people to study the Bible more? Make sure you yourself are studying the Bible more, and begin carrying one around! Who you are and what you do become the key drivers of true culture.

- *Watch how you respond to critical incidents.* When someone is "squeezed," others see what is really in them. Christian leaders, above all, should be men and women who practice what they preach, avoid hypocrisy, and model healthy values for their people, even when times are tough. What the leader pays attention to and rewards indicates what is truly important.

- *Find and keep leaders who can also model what the culture should look like.* Doing so might mean letting go of some current leaders and finding new ones. This is a challenge in churches that value loyalty and are reluctant to fire anyone or that are used to working with well-intentioned but misguided volunteers. But if Joe is an obstacle to change, then Joe has to go! Perhaps you can see, at this point, why culture change is so difficult; it often requires tough decisions about people that many pastors are unwilling to make. But you cannot truly change your culture unless you have a leadership team that is 100 percent committed to the change.

- *Be honest about how your own emotional and spiritual health impacts your church, for better or worse.* While we all are works in progress, it is critical to understand that healthy leaders lead healthy churches and unhealthy leaders lead unhealthy churches. While this is tough to admit—and I write this in love and concern—*you* may be part of the problem. There is no shame here, and pastors must recognize their own sense of being "wounded healers" in need of ongoing help themselves.[12] If you need encouragement, counseling, coaching, a sabbatical, or even psychotherapy, find it, and let the Lord bring a season of health and renewal to your life so that you can better lead others.

- *Have a clear vision of the new culture.* Leaders must be able to articulate what the culture will look like. Take time to write and refine, along with key personnel, your vision for the church and how the church might look different than it does now. Communicate this in words, but mostly deeds—often. Clarity of vision and purpose can set you on a path to practices and accomplishments that make others feel better about the culture itself. Keep in mind here that setting a new goal, such as growing by 10 percent a year, is good but not a culture change. Rather, a goal of growing in size by developing healthy leaders focuses on a culture issue (i.e., attitudes toward leadership development) and will still lead to numerical growth. Culture change focuses on root causes more than outcomes, so your vision for culture must address those roots, not simply the outcomes.

- *Adopt the language of the culture you want.* Harness the power of the human language to instill values, and speak in ways that represent what your values are. For example, if you want your organization to be a place that empowers women, don't refer to leaders in general as "him." Also, develop simple catchphrases that are memorable and capture important values. My first church, Hope Chapel in Hermosa Beach, had a great one: "Give 'em heaven." It represented the church's evangelistic zeal.

- *Create new titles, symbols, and ceremonies.* For example, if you seek to build a culture that honors its volunteers, come up with a better name for them. "Volunteer" is dull. How about "chief servants" or "staff assistants"? Create a new ceremony in which incoming staff assistants are recognized and outgoing ones are honored and celebrated (without any begrudging of their exit). The possibilities are endless.

Learn how to study your culture. You may be so steeped in your own culture (the etic view discussed above) that you have a hard time seeing it objectively and thus identifying the problems therein. If your goal is to change the culture, you need to be able to articulate it well. Here are some practical ideas:

- *Visit other churches or ministries.* Do this not just to get ideas but to put your own organization into stark relief. If you have not been outside for a while, make some field trips to other places you admire, and note how they do things differently. Seek to understand their assumptions and values.

- *Question the assumptions behind your culture.* Listing corporate values is easy; articulating assumptions behind them is more challenging because people rarely think about them. The better you can articulate your assumptions, the better you will be able to get to root causes of issues in your culture.

- *Make a distinction between espoused values and enacted values.* Espoused values are the things we *say* we believe, and enacted values are the things we truly believe, as seen in our behavior. While we all like to believe these two are the same, they usually are not. I often ask my students to consider this question: What are the values of your church that are based on what leaders actually do, not what they say? Try that exercise. It may be eye-opening.

- *Learn to make the undiscussable discussable.* Be honest about what your values are, even if they do not align with your stated values, and become comfortable with having honest conversations about this rather than glossing over issues.[13]

- *Consult an expert.* If the above points seem impossible (and they very well might be), you may need to bring in someone from the outside to help. Consider contracting with a qualified organizational development consultant who can help bring some objectivity to your discussions.[14]

Be patient. Your culture did not become what it is overnight, and it will not change overnight. Culture change is a long-term proposition and may even outlast your tenure. If you expect things to change overnight, you may push too hard on the wrong levers and become disappointed. It may be tempting to start new programs, adopt new slogans or value statements, and then expect these things to change the culture as soon as people see the exciting new things. Programs and slogans are good, but people will believe there has been a change only when they see the values lived out by those they respect who persist in them over time. In fact, because culture is so pervasive, they might not even realize there is a change. The altered culture will just be the way it is around here now.

Finally, remember this:

People do not change their values, for example, by simply being told that they should. Rather, norms, beliefs, values and assumptions are usually the product of repeated experiences extended over a lengthy period of time in combination with implicit or explicit reflections on both the

nature of those experiences and the extent to which they were personally satisfying.[15]

The best sermon or pep talk in the world will not make a dent in an
entrenched culture. People will smile and nod but in the end will return
to business as usual. By attending to the best practices of OB, and by
the grace and wisdom of God, over time you can reestablish health in
your culture. When you do so, people will *see* your commitment and not
simply hear about it. Then they will genuinely make the new changes
part of their experience and reality.

■ Practical Leadership Application Questions ■

- How might your insider perspective help you understand your organization's culture? How might it also present blind spots and be
  a challenge to objectively understanding it?
- What are some of the more distinct points of your culture, such as
  heroes, stories, myths, symbols, and lingo? How do these connect
  to and/or support some of your values, both stated and implicit?
- Where might there be points of disconnect between the stated values and expectations and the unwritten rules and norms of your
  culture? What has been the impact of these points of disconnect,
  and what are some steps you can take to address them?
- How would you make a distinction between the dominant culture
  and the subcultures of your church or ministry? Can you identify
  the executive, operator, and engineer classes? Do you have a strong
  culture or weak culture, as defined in this chapter?
- Which of Cameron and Quinn's four culture types (clan, hierarchy,
  ad-hocracy, market) best captures your culture? What points of tension (competing values) might there be among various perspectives?
- How would you describe some of the characteristics of your culture (e.g., risk tolerance, management support, diversity, leadership
  development, denominational orientation)?
- In terms of culture change, which of the leader's jobs can you begin
  to address in this next season? What can you do to help keep yourself

accountable to new practices (e.g., being a role model, rewarding the right thing)?

CASE STUDY

The Case of the Entrenched but Changing Culture

Alex knew he was in over his head. He was excited about his new role as executive pastor at Saint Thomas Unified Church (STUC). But as he began to work behind the scenes, he was finding more than the excitement of a Sunday morning service or his initial elation over being selected for this role. It was indeed his dream ministry role and was right in line with his sense of calling, gifts, skills, and education, and he knew the Lord had opened this door for him. Having recently completed a master of divinity with an emphasis on church administration, he was eager to use all his knowledge to serve the congregation he loved. But reality was a lot tougher than he expected, and he began to see roadblocks that could hinder his task, which was to bring a better sense of organization and fulfillment of the church's mission, in concert with the senior pastor and elders.

The first problem was living under the shadow of the founding pastor, Thomas, known as "Saint Thomas." Of course, that was a playful inside name for him; to the congregation he was just Pastor Tom. But the staff lovingly paid tribute to him, and he was in many ways a saint who poured his life out before he sadly passed away after a yearlong battle with cancer. His passion was to serve the poor in the community through innovative outreach initiatives, to fundraise for the local mission, and to preach on matters of social justice and change. Of course, this latter issue made some in the church uncomfortable, as "social justice" was code for "liberal" in their minds and many were very conservative politically. But Thomas was an entrepreneur and an enigma who did not fit squarely into any one political box, and this was what attracted many people to him and the church.

Now that Thomas was gone, the current senior pastor, Pedro, who was now lovingly referred to as "Saint Pete," was being held to the same standards and expectations, but he clearly was a different type of leader. Pedro was more of a methodical builder than the visionary Thomas, and he wanted to help the church stabilize after ten years of tremendous growth. There was administrative chaos in many corners of the church, and this was why he hired Alex in the first place. All the past growth had been made possible by a frantic pace of relentless work, set by the energetic Thomas, but that pace had taken its toll. Staff burnout and a lack of clear processes had become serious issues, and many talented staff members had left. The staff were now in a season of rebuilding and were trying to get better organized. Pastor Pedro was identifying which workers were in line with his slow-and-steady approach to church growth. Alex saw the need to bring a sense of predictability and pacing to the staff and help them all flourish and develop their own leadership capacity. This led to tensions with some of the long-timers, who were used to rapid change and growth, who liked to "go with the flow," and who chafed at all the new policies and procedures. These folks began to wonder whether Pedro was the best fit for STUC. He shared Thomas's heart and vision but wanted to go about fulfilling that vision in a much different way.

Another major challenge was the recent combining of a smaller local church with theirs. In the past, Thomas had developed a strong relationship with other local pastors and one church in particular, the Church of the United Transfer Students (CUTS—go with me here!). Although Pedro was not as well connected outside the church as Thomas had been, he still felt obligated to continue this endeavor and to honor Thomas's legacy as a community builder. CUTS had been founded around the same time as STUC by a group of college students. CUTS was attended primarily by single, energetic, college-age world changers living on a shoestring. They could not be more different from STUC members, who were largely older, affluent tithers with children who were of college age. The reason Thomas loved the CUTS people might have been their zeal to share the gospel, engage in mission, and give their lives.

Of course, the demographic differences provided another point of tension when the merger happened. The STUC folks appreciated the zeal of the CUTS people but seemed to look at them as aliens from another planet. The CUTS people arrived one Sunday morning after the merger was announced, gobbling down all the free donuts and bringing a sort of rowdy energy as they talked about Jesus and craft beer in the same sentence. The CUTS folks also had qualms about their new "parent church," as they called it. To them, STUC members were too comfortable and out of touch. One of their leaders exclaimed, "They still sing Bill Gaither hymns, for goodness' sake, and there was not a single electric guitar on the platform. What is wrong with these people!" Many of their volunteers and a couple of staff were now serving at STUC, but they often felt out of place and did not know how things worked. They inadvertently created their own subculture of "Cutters," as they began to refer to themselves. They felt that they were called by the Lord to bring new life and "cut through" the stodgy and old-fashioned attitudes (in Jesus's name, of course) of the "Stuckers."

Alex knew that these issues were serious and systemic and would not be resolved by a sermon or two or through church rebranding. The church had tried these things, but the attempts all had failed after an initial burst of enthusiasm. In fact, they had left many people a bit jaded and disillusioned—one more idea that went nowhere, as often happened when Pastor Thomas was in charge. As he pondered all these culture shifts and clashes, he prayed, "Lord, help me make sense of all this!"

Questions for Discussion

- What are some of the culture clashes seen in this case?
- What are some of the attitudes and values that lie beneath the surface of these situations? How could you articulate these into stated values that might be a rallying point for everyone?
- Based on our discussion of culture change, what are some ways the leadership could establish new norms, and what behaviors would help them develop a strong culture around a unified vision?

■ Further Reading ■

Cameron, Kim S., and Robert E. Quinn. *Diagnosing and Changing Organizational Culture: Based on the Competing Values Framework*. 3rd ed. San Francisco: Jossey-Bass, 2011.

Chand, Samuel R. *Culture Catalyst: Seven Strategies to Bring Positive Change to Your Organization*. New Kensington, PA: Whitaker House, 2018.

Coyle, Daniel. *The Culture Code: The Secrets of Highly Successful Groups*. New York: Bantam, 2018.

Gibbons, Paul. *The Science of Successful Organizational Change: How Leaders Set Strategy, Change Behavior, and Create an Agile Culture*. New York: Pearson Education, 2015.

Malphurs, Aubrey. *Look Before You Lead: How to Discern and Shape Your Church Culture*. Grand Rapids: Baker Books, 2013.

Schein, Edgar H. *Organizational Culture and Leadership*. Hoboken, NJ: Wiley & Sons, 2010.

Notes

Chapter 1 Introduction to Organizational Behavior

1. Barbara Kellerman, "The Leadership Industry," BarbaraKellerman.com, November 15, 2014, https://barbarakellerman.com/the-leadership-industry.
2. Gareth Morgan, *Images of Organization*, rev. ed. (Thousand Oaks, CA: Sage, 2006).
3. Lee G. Bolman and Terrence E. Deal, *Reframing Organizations: Artistry, Choice, and Leadership*, 7th ed. (San Francisco: Jossey-Bass, 2021).
4. This group also publishes the *Journal of Management, Spirituality and Religion*.
5. Margaret Benefiel, *Soul at Work: Spiritual Leadership in Organizations* (New York: Seabury, 2005).

Chapter 2 Individual Differences

1. John C. Turner, Michael A. Hogg, Penelope J. Oakes, Stephen D. Reicher, and Margaret S. Wetherell, *Rediscovering the Social Group: A Self-Categorization Theory* (New York: Basil Blackwell, 1987), x, 239.
2. Peter O'Hanrahan, "The Enneagram at Work," The Enneagram at Work, https://theenneagramatwork.com/the-enneagram-at-work.
3. Reggie McNeal, *A Work of Heart: Understanding How God Shapes Spiritual Leaders*, 2nd ed. (San Francisco: Jossey-Bass, 2011).

Chapter 3 Emotions, Attitudes, and Perceptions

1. John M. Ivancevich, Robert Konopaske, and Michael T. Matteson, *Organizational Behavior and Management*, 11th ed. (New York: McGraw-Hill Education, 2018), chap. 3.
2. Daniel Goleman, *Emotional Intelligence: Why It Can Matter More Than IQ*, rev. ed. (New York: Bantam, 2006); and Goleman, *Working with Emotional Intelligence* (New York: Bantam, 1998).
3. Daniel Goleman, Richard Boyatzis, and Annie McKee, *Primal Leadership: Unleashing the Power of Emotional Intelligence*, 10th anniv. ed. (Boston: Harvard Business Review Press, 2013).
4. For an interesting review of this phenomenon, see Gardiner Morse, "Executive Psychopaths," *Harvard Business Review*, October 2004, https://hbr.org/2004/10/executive-psychopaths.

5. Arlie Russell Hochschild, *The Managed Heart: Commercialization of Human Feeling* (Berkeley: University of California Press, 2003).

6. Archibald D. Hart, *The Anxiety Cure: You Can Find Emotional Tranquility and Wholeness* (Nashville: Word, 1999).

7. Archibald Hart, "The Purpose of Burnout: An Interview with Dr. Archibald Hart," interview by Jerry Ritskes, Clergy Care, 2013, https://clergycare.ca/2019/05/23/the-purpose -of-burnout-an-interview-with-dr-archibald-hart.

8. John M. Ivancevich, Robert Konopaske, and Michael T. Matteson, *Organizational Behavior and Management*, 11th ed. (New York: McGraw-Hill Education, 2018), chap. 9.

9. Adapted from Peter G. Northouse, *Leadership: Theory and Practice*, 9th ed. (Thousand Oaks, CA: Sage, 2021).

10. Adapted from David D. Burns, *The Feeling Good Handbook* (New York: William Morrow, 1989).

11. For good research on this point, see Jack Zenger and Joseph Folkman, "Quiet Quitting Is about Bad Bosses, Not Bad Employees," *Harvard Business Review*, August 31, 2022, https://hbr.org/2022/08/quiet-quitting-is-about-bad-bosses-not-bad-employees.

12. Adapted from Jack Kelly, "People Don't Leave Bad Jobs, They Leave Bad Bosses: Here's How to Be a Better Manager to Maintain and Motivate Your Team," *Forbes*, November 22, 2019, https://www.forbes.com/sites/jackkelly/2019/11/22/people-dont-leave -bad-jobs-they-leave-bad-bosses-heres-how-to-be-a-better-manager-to-maintain-and -motivate-your-team.

13. See C. A. Smith, D. W. Organ, and J. P. Near, "Organizational Citizenship Behavior: Its Nature and Antecedents," *Journal of Applied Psychology* 68, no. 4 (1983): 653–63, https://doi.org/10.1037/0021-9010.68.4.653.

14. L. Rhoades and R. Eisenberger, "Perceived Organizational Support: A Review of the Literature," *Journal of Applied Psychology* 87, no. 4 (2002): 698–714, https://doi.org /10.1037/0021-9010.87.4.698.

Chapter 4 Motivation, Evaluation, and Rewards

1. For a seminal work and a definition of "motivation," see M. R. Jones, ed., *Nebraska Symposium on Motivation, 1954* (Lincoln: University of Nebraska Press, 1954), x, 322.

2. V. H. Vroom, *Work and Motivation* (New York: Wiley & Sons, 1964).

3. Edward L. Deci and Richard M. Ryan, *Intrinsic Motivation and Self-Determination in Human Behavior* (New York: Plenum, 1987).

4. A. H. Maslow, "A Theory of Human Motivation," *Psychological Review* 50, no. 4 (1943): 370–96, https://doi.org/10.1037/h0054346.

5. J. A. McCleskey and L. Ruddell, "Taking a Step Back—Maslow's Theory of Motivation: A Christian Critical Perspective," *Journal of Biblical Integration in Business* 23, no. 1 (2020): 6–16, https://cbfa-cbar.org/index.php/jbib/article/view/548.

6. Frederick Herzberg, Bernard Mausner, and Barbara Bloch Snyderman, *The Motivation to Work* (New Brunswick, NJ: Transaction, 2011).

7. C. P. Alderfer, *Existence, Relatedness, and Growth: Human Needs in Organizational Settings* (New York: Free Press, 1972).

8. David C. McClelland, *Human Motivation* (New York: Cambridge University Press, 1987).

9. E. A. Locke, "Toward a Theory of Task Motivation and Incentives," *Organizational Behavior and Human Performance* 3, no. 2 (1968): 157–89, https://doi.org/10.1016/0030 -5073(68)90004-4.

10. J. S. Adams, "Towards an Understanding of Inequity," *Journal of Abnormal and Social Psychology* 67 (1963): 422–36, https://doi.org/10.1037/h0040968.

11. For an overview of business ethics and the role of justice, see Alec Hill, *Just Business: Christian Ethics for the Marketplace* (Downers Grove, IL: InterVarsity, 2017).

12. See Paul's comment on taking advantage of an "open door" of opportunity for ministry service in 1 Cor. 16:9.

Chapter 5 Interpersonal Relationships in Organizations

1. Paul Thagard, *Brain-Mind: From Neurons to Consciousness and Creativity* (Oxford: Oxford University Press, 2019).

2. Adam Grant, "How to Trust People You Don't Like," *WorkLife with Adam Grant* (podcast), March 2018, TED, https://www.ted.com/talks/worklife_with_adam_grant_how_to_trust_people_you_don_t_like.

3. Adapted from Robert M. Galford and Anne Seibold Drapeau, "The Enemies of Trust," *Harvard Business Review*, February 2003, https://hbr.org/2003/02/the-enemies-of-trust.

4. James M. Kouzes and Barry Z. Posner, *The Leadership Challenge: How to Make Extraordinary Things Happen in Organizations*, 6th ed. (Hoboken, NJ: Wiley & Sons, 2017).

5. Gianpiero Petriglieri, "Why Work Is Lonely," *Harvard Business Review*, March 5, 2014, https://hbr.org/2014/03/why-work-is-lonely.

6. Amy C. Edmondson, *The Fearless Organization: Creating Psychological Safety in the Workplace for Learning, Innovation, and Growth* (Hoboken, NJ: Wiley & Sons, 2019), introduction, Kindle.

7. Adapted from Timothy R. Clark, *The Four Stages of Psychological Safety: Defining the Path to Inclusion and Innovation* (Oakland: Berrett-Koehler, 2020).

8. Jack Zenger and Joseph Folkman, "What Great Listeners Actually Do," *Harvard Business Review*, July 14, 2016, https://hbr.org/2016/07/what-great-listeners-actually-do.

9. See, e.g., Morley Segal, *Points of Influence: A Guide to Using Personality Theory at Work* (San Francisco: Jossey-Bass, 1996).

10. See, e.g., Jenny Brown and Lauren Errington, eds., *Bowen Family Systems Theory in Christian Ministry: Grappling with Theory and Its Application through a Biblical Lens* (Cremorne, Australia: Family Systems Practice, 2019).

11. "Introduction to the Eight Concepts," Bowen Center for the Study of the Family, accessed October 5, 2023, https://www.thebowencenter.org/introduction-eight-concepts.

12. Hakan Ozcelik and Sigal G. Barsade, "No Employee an Island: Workplace Loneliness and Job Performance," *Academy of Management Journal* 61, no. 6 (2018): 2343–66, https://doi.org/10.5465/amj.2015.1066.

13. For a good review of this research, see Shasta Nelson, *The Business of Friendship: Making the Most of Our Relationships Where We Spend Most of Our Time* (New York: HarperCollins Leadership, 2020).

14. Nelson, *Business of Friendship*, 39–42.

15. Leslie Hunter-Gadsden, "Why People of Color Feel the Loneliest at Work," *Forbes*, May 19, 2020, https://www.forbes.com/sites/nextavenue/2020/05/19/why-people-of-color-feel-the-loneliest-at-work.

16. Ami Rokach, "Leadership and Loneliness," *International Journal of Leadership and Change* 2, no. 1 (2014): 48–58, https://digitalcommons.wku.edu/ijlc/vol2/iss1/6.

17. Mandy Gilbert, "Feeling Lonely? That Means You're Actually a Good Leader," Inc.com, April 19, 2017, https://www.inc.com/mandy-gilbert/feeling-lonely-that-means-youre-actually-a-good-leader.html.

Chapter 6 Groups and Teams

1. For a review of seminal theories of social identity theory, see Henri Tajfel, "Social Categorization, Social Identity and Social Comparison," in *Differentiation between Social Groups: Studies in the Social Psychology of Intergroup Relations*, ed. Henri Tajfel (London: Academic Press, 1978), 61–76; and John C. Turner, Michael A. Hogg, Penelope J. Oakes, Stephen D. Reicher, and Margaret S. Wetherell, *Rediscovering the Social Group: A Self-Categorization Theory* (New York: Basil Blackwell, 1987).

2. Julia Rozovsky, "The Five Keys to a Successful Google Team," Re:Work, November 17, 2015, https://rework.withgoogle.com/blog/five-keys-to-a-successful-google-team.

3. For a thorough scholarly overview, see Janis A. Cannon-Bowers and Clint Bowers, "Team Development and Functioning," in *APA Handbook of Industrial and Organizational Psychology*, ed. Sheldon Zedeck, vol. 1, *Building and Developing the Organization* (Washington, DC: American Psychological Association, 2011), 597–650, https://doi.org/10.1037/12169-019.

4. B. W. Tuckman, "Developmental Sequence in Small Groups," *Psychological Bulletin* 63, no. 6 (1965): 384–99, https://doi.org/10.1037/h0022100.

5. Kate Cassidy, "Tuckman Revisited: Proposing a New Model of Group Development for Practitioners," *Journal of Experiential Education* 29, no. 3 (2007): 413–17, https://doi.org/10.1177/105382590702900318.

6. "The Nine Belbin Team Roles," Belbin.com, accessed October 5, 2023, https://www.belbin.com/about/belbin-team-roles.

7. See, e.g., Adrian Furnham, Howard Steele, and David Pendleton, "A Psychometric Assessment of the Belbin Team-Role Self-Perception Inventory," *Journal of Occupational and Organizational Psychology* 66, no. 3 (1993): 245–57, https://doi.org/10.1111/j.2044-8325.1993.tb00535.x; and Simona Lupuleac, Zenica-Livia Lupuleac, and Costache Rusu, "Problems of Assessing Team Roles Balance—Team Design," *Procedia Economics and Finance* 3 (2012): 935–40, https://doi.org/10.1016/S2212-5671(12)00253-5.

8. See, e.g., Barbara Senior, "Team Roles and Team Performance: Is There 'Really' a Link?" *Journal of Occupational and Organizational Psychology* 70, no. 3 (1997): 241–58, https://doi.org/10.1111/j.2044-8325.1997.tb00646.x.

9. Adapted from Patrick Lencioni, *The Six Types of Working Genius: A Better Way to Understand Your Gifts, Your Frustrations, and Your Team* (Dallas: Matt Holt, 2022).

10. "Underdog Status Can Motivate Teams to Beat the Odds," Academy of Management Insights, June 22, 2021, https://journals.aom.org/doi/abs/10.5465/amr.2019.0336.summary (subscription required).

11. Adam Grant, "The Creative Power of Misfits," LinkedIn, March 5, 2019, https://www.linkedin.com/pulse/creative-power-misfits-adam-grant.

12. Charles R. Evans and Kenneth L. Dion, "Group Cohesion and Performance: A Meta-Analysis," *Small Group Research* 22, no. 2 (1991): 175–86, https://doi.org/10.1177/1046496491222002.

13. Irving L. Janis, *Victims of Groupthink: A Psychological Study of Foreign-Policy Decisions and Fiascoes* (Boston: Houghton, Mifflin, 1972). For a review of applications of his original theory, see M. E. Turner and A. R. Pratkanis, "Twenty-Five Years of Groupthink Theory and Research: Lessons from the Evaluation of a Theory," *Organizational Behavior and Human Decision Processes* 73, no. 2–3 (1998): 105–15, https://doi.org/10.1006/obhd.1998.2756.

14. Adapted from Irving L. Janis, *Groupthink: Psychological Studies of Policy Decisions and Fiascoes* (Boston: Houghton Mifflin, 1982), 35–45.

15. Barry M. Staw, "The Escalation of Commitment to a Course of Action," *Academy of Management Review* 6, no. 4 (1981): 577–87, https://doi.org/10.5465/amr.1981.4285694.

16. For a review of the events that led to the downfall of Mars Hill Church, see *The Rise and Fall of Mars Hill*, a podcast by *Christianity Today*, available at https://www.christianity today.com/ct/podcasts/rise-and-fall-of-mars-hill.

17. Chris Argyris, "Making the Undiscussable and Its Undiscussability Discussable," *Public Administration Review* 40, no. 3 (1980): 205–13, https://doi.org/10.2307/975372.

18. Peter Hawkins, *Leadership Team Coaching: Developing Collective Transformational Leadership*, 4th ed. (London: KoganPage, 2021).

19. For a good overview of this model as well as a more advanced systemic coaching approach, see Peter Hawkins and Eve Turner, *Systemic Coaching: Delivering Value beyond the Individual* (London: Routledge, 2019).

20. A. R. Howard, "Coaching to Vision versus Coaching to Improvement Needs: A Preliminary Investigation on the Differential Impacts of Fostering Positive and Negative Emotion during Real Time Executive Coaching Sessions," *Frontiers in Psychology* 6 (2015): 455, https://doi.org/10.3389/fpsyg.2015.00455.

21. Michael Bungay Stanier, *The Coaching Habit: Say Less, Ask More and Change the Way You Lead Forever* (Toronto: Box of Crayons Press, 2016).

22. Stanier, *Coaching Habit*, 200.

Chapter 7 Conflict Management

1. Adam Grant, "The Science of Productive Conflict," *WorkLife with Adam Grant* (podcast), April 13, 2021, TED, https://www.ted.com/podcasts/worklife/the-science-of -productive-conflict-transcript.

2. Ricky W. Griffin and Gregory Moorhead, *Organizational Behavior: Managing People and Organizations*, 10th ed. (Australia: South-Western College, 2008), 405.

3. Barry Johnson, *Polarity Management: Identifying and Managing Unsolvable Problems* (Amherst, MA: HRD Press, 2014).

4. Henry M. Robert III, Daniel H. Honemann, Thomas J. Balch, Daniel E. Seabold, and Shmuel Gerber, *Robert's Rules of Order Newly Revised*, 12th ed. (New York: Public Affairs, 2020).

5. See the seminal work on this concept, Corinne Bendersky and Nicholas A. Hays, "Status Conflict in Groups," *Organization Science* 23, no. 2 (2012): 323–40, https://doi .org/10.1287/orsc.1110.0734.

6. K. W. Thomas and R. H. Kilmann, *Thomas-Kilmann Conflict Mode Instrument* (Mountain View, CA: CPP, 1974).

7. Adapted from Katie Shonk, "Conflict-Management Styles: Pitfalls and Best Prac- tices," Daily Blog, Program on Negotiation, Harvard Law School, April 6, 2023, https:// www.pon.harvard.edu/daily/conflict-resolution/conflict-management-styles-pitfalls -and-best-practices.

8. David Antonioni, "Relationship between the Big Five Personality Factors and Con- flict Management Styles," *International Journal of Conflict Management* 9, no. 4 (1998): 336–55, https://doi.org/10.1108/eb022814.

9. Neil Brewer, Patricia Mitchell, and Nathan Weber, "Gender Role, Organizational Status, and Conflict Management Styles," *International Journal of Conflict Management* 13, no. 1 (2002): 78–94, https://doi.org/10.1108/eb022868.

Chapter 8 Leadership, Part 1

1. Warren Bennis, *On Becoming a Leader* (New York: Basic Books, 2009).

2. James MacGregor Burns, *Transforming Leadership* (1978; repr., New York: Grove, 2004).

3. George Barna, *The Power of Vision: Discover and Apply God's Plan for Your Life and Ministry*, rev. ed. (Grand Rapids: Baker Books, 2018); and John C. Maxwell and Zig Ziglar, *The 21 Irrefutable Laws of Leadership: Follow Them and People Will Follow You* (Nashville: Thomas Nelson, 1998).

4. See, e.g., Ken Blanchard, Phil Hodges, and Phyllis Hendry, *Lead like Jesus Revisited: Lessons from the Greatest Leadership Role Model of All Time*, rev. ed. (Nashville: W, 2016).

5. John Goldingay, *Men Behaving Badly* (Milton Keys, UK: Paternoster, 2000).

6. For a review of the romance of leadership, see Michelle C. Bligh, "Romance of Leadership," in *Global Encyclopedia of Public Administration, Public Policy, and Governance*, ed. Ali Farazmand (New York: Springer International, 2017), 1–4.

7. See Maxwell and Ziglar, *21 Irrefutable Laws* for this emphasis on the roles of leaders in the success in organizations. Maxwell's entire body of work suggests that this is his guiding philosophy.

8. Edward Lyman Munson, *The Management of Men: A Handbook on the Systematic Development of Morale and the Control of Human Behavior* (New York: Holt, 1921).

9. Warren G. Bennis, "Leadership Theory and Administrative Behavior: The Problem of Authority," *Administrative Science Quarterly* 4, no. 3 (December 1959): 259–301.

10. Fred Edward Fiedler, *A Theory of Leadership Effectiveness* (New York: McGraw-Hill, 1967).

11. Robert K. Merton, "The Social Nature of Leadership," *American Journal of Nursing* 69, no. 12 (1969): 2614–18, https://doi.org/10.2307/3421106; and R. Hogan, G. J. Curphy, and J. Hogan, "What We Know about Leadership: Effectiveness and Personality," *American Psychologist* 49 (1994): 493–504, https://doi.org/10.1037/0003-066X.49.6.493.

12. B. M. Bass, *Leadership and Performance beyond Expectations* (New York: Free Press, 1985).

13. David P. Campbell, "The Challenge of Assessing Leadership Characteristics," *Issues & Observations* 11, no. 2 (1991), https://onlinelibrary.wiley.com/doi/abs/10.1002/lia.4070110201.

14. Wilfred H. Drath, Cynthia D. McCauley, Charles J. Palus, Ellen Van Velsor, Patricia M. G. O'Connor, and John B. McGuire, "Direction, Alignment, Commitment: Toward a More Integrative Ontology of Leadership," *Leadership Quarterly* 19, no. 6 (2008): 635–53, https://doi.org/10.1016/j.leaqua.2008.09.003.

15. Peter G. Northouse, *Leadership: Theory and Practice*, 9th ed. (Thousand Oaks, CA: Sage, 2021).

16. David V. Day and John Antonakis, eds., *The Nature of Leadership*, 3rd ed. (Thousand Oaks, CA: Sage, 2017).

17. While it is beyond the scope of this book to fully explore social constructivism, see the seminal work of Peter L. Berger and Thomas Luckmann, *The Social Construction of Reality: A Treatise in the Sociology of Knowledge* (New York: Anchor, 1967).

18. A. Zaleznik, "Managers and Leaders: Are They Different?" *Harvard Business Review* 44 (1977): 67–78.

19. J. P. Kotter, "A Force for Change: How Leadership Differs from Management," *Management* 11 (1990): 180.

20. Peter Drucker, *Essential Drucker* (London: Routledge, 2018).

21. Burns, *Transforming Leadership*.

22. See, e.g., the aforementioned works Zaleznik, "Managers and Leaders"; and Kotter, "Force for Change."

23. See, e.g., classic books such as Henri J. M. Nouwen, *The Wounded Healer: Ministry in Contemporary Society* (Garden City, NY: Doubleday, 1972); and J. Oswald Sanders, *Spiritual Leadership: Principles of Excellence for Every Believer*, updated ed. (Chicago: Moody, 2017).

24. See, e.g., Barna, *Power of Vision.*

25. For a good example of this, see Justin A. Irving and Mark L. Strauss, *Leadership in Christian Perspective: Biblical Foundations and Contemporary Practices for Servant Leaders* (Grand Rapids: Baker Academic, 2019).

26. S. J. Shondrick, J. E. Dinh, and R. G. Lord, "Developments in Implicit Leadership Theory and Cognitive Science: Applications to Improving Measurement and Understanding Alternatives to Hierarchical Leadership," *Leadership Quarterly* 21, no. 6 (2010): 959–78, https://doi.org/10.1016/j.leaqua.2010.10.004.

27. For an interesting study on leadership folk wisdom in a military context, see W. C. Borman, "Personal Constructs, Performance Schemata, and 'Folk Theories' of Subordinate Effectiveness: Explorations in an Army Officer Sample," *Organizational Behavior and Human Decision Processes* 40, no. 3 (1987): 307–22, https://doi.org/10.1016/0749-5978(87)90018-5.

28. For a full treatment of these and other theories, consider a text such as Northouse, *Leadership.*

29. For a seminal article that takes this early approach, see Ralph M. Stogdill, "Personal Factors Associated with Leadership: A Survey of the Literature," *Journal of Psychology* 25 (1948): 35–71, https://www.tandfonline.com/doi/abs/10.1080/00223980.1948.9917362.

30. T. A. Judge, J. E. Bono, R. Ilies, and M. W. Gerhardt, "Personality and Leadership: A Qualitative and Quantitative Review," *Journal of Applied Psychology* 87, no. 4 (2002): 765.

31. Adapted from Northouse, *Leadership,* chap. 2 ("Trait Approach").

32. See, e.g., Jay A. Conger, "The Dark Side of Leadership," *Organizational Dynamics* 19, no. 2 (1990): 44–55, https://doi.org/10.1016/0090-2616(90)90070-6; and https://www.hogandarkside.com.

33. I am using not the Pentecostal sense of the word "charismatic" but the sense used in Max Weber, *On Charisma and Institution Building* (Chicago: University of Chicago Press, 1968).

34. Paul Hersey, *The Situational Leader* (Escondido, CA: Center for Leadership Studies, 1984); and Paul Hersey, Kenneth H. Blanchard, and Dewey E. Johnson, *Management of Organizational Behavior: Utilizing Human Resources,* 7th ed. (Upper Saddle River, NJ: Prentice Hall, 1996).

35. C. L. Graeff, "Evolution of Situational Leadership Theory: A Critical Review," *Leadership Quarterly* 8, no. 2 (1997): 153–70, https://doi.org/10.1016/S1048-9843(97)90014-X.

36. Adapted from Colin Baker, "What Is Situational Leadership, and How Do You Practice It?," Leaders (website), updated September 7, 2022, https://leaders.com/articles/leadership/situational-leadership.

37. Weber, *On Charisma*; Jay Conger, *Charismatic Leadership* (San Francisco: Jossey-Bass, 1989); Jay A. Conger and Rabindra N. Kanungo, *Charismatic Leadership in Organizations* (Thousand Oaks, CA: Sage, 1998); and Robert J. House, "A 1976 Theory of Charismatic Leadership, Working Paper Series 76-06" (paper presented at the Southern Illinois University Fourth Biennial Leadership Symposium, Carbondale, Illinois, October 26–28, 1976), available at http://files.eric.ed.gov/fulltext/ED133827.pdf.

38. For information on how followers can create a "love story" with a charismatic leader, see Ken Parry and Steve Kempster, "Love and Leadership: Constructing Follower Narrative Identities of Charismatic Leadership," *Management Learning* 45, no. 1 (2013): 21–38, https://doi.org/10.1177/1350507612470602.

39. J. J. Sosik, B. J. Avolio, and D. I. Jung, "Beneath the Mask: Examining the Relationship of Self-Presentation Attributes and Impression Management to Charismatic Leadership," *Leadership Quarterly* 13, no. 3 (2002): 217–42, https://doi.org/10.1016/S1048-9843(02)00102-9.

40. Maximillan Weber, "The Nature of Charismatic Authority and Its Routiniza-tion," in *Theory of Social and Economic Organization*, trans. A. R. Anderson and Talcot Parsons (London: W. Hodge, 1947). Originally published in 1922 in German under the title *Wirtschaft und Gesellschaft*, chap. 3, sec. 10.

41. See "History," The Foursquare Church, https://www.foursquare.org/about/history.

42. Edith L. Blumhofer, *Aimee Semple McPherson: Everybody's Sister* (Grand Rapids: Eerdmans, 1993).

43. Elaine Woo, "Rolf K. McPherson Dies at 96; Longtime Pentecostal Church Leader," *Los Angeles Times*, May 28, 2009, https://www.latimes.com/local/obituaries/la-me-rolf -mcpherson28-2009may28-story.html.

44. Burns, *Transforming Leadership*.

45. Bernard M. Bass and Bruce J. Avolio, *Transformational Leadership Development: Manual for the Multifactor Leadership Questionnaire* (Palo Alto, CA: Consulting Psychologists Press, 1990).

46. Warren Bennis, *On Becoming a Leader* (New York: Basic Books, 2009).

47. For example, James M. Kouzes and Barry Z. Posner, *The Leadership Challenge: How to Make Extraordinary Things Happen in Organizations*, 6th ed. (Hoboken, NJ: Wiley & Sons, 2017), could be considered a transformational leadership approach, though it is not so named.

48. Bruce Avolio, *Full Range Leadership Development*, 2nd ed. (Thousand Oaks, CA: Sage, 2010); and T. A. Judge and R. F. Piccolo, "Transformational and Transactional Leadership: A Meta-Analytic Test of Their Relative Validity," *Journal of Applied Psychology* 89, no. 5 (2004): 755–68, https://doi.org/10.1037/0021-9010.89.5.755.

49. X.-H. (Frank) Wang and J. M. Howell, "A Multilevel Study of Transformational Leadership, Identification, and Follower Outcomes," *Leadership Quarterly* 23, no. 5 (2012): 775–90, https://doi.org/10.1016/j.leaqua.2012.02.001.

50. R. J. Givens, "Transformational Leadership: The Impact on Organizational and Personal Outcomes," *Emerging Leadership Journeys* 1, no. 1 (2008): 4–24.

51. Some readers may balk at the idea of considering Freud, citing both religious or pragmatic objections, and this is understandable. Some consider him, along with certain other controversial figures such as Charles Darwin, to be antithetical to the Christian faith. Freud held religious belief to be a sort of neurosis, and he is seemingly obsessed with sex. To some, his methods and samples are suspect, as he primarily used people suffering from psychological problems for his research. Nevertheless, his influence on contemporary thought is undeniable, and even those in the Christian counseling profession rely on some of his seminal insights about unconscious family-related drives and motives to understand human behavior.

52. For a good introduction to Kets de Vries's work, see Manfred F. R. Kets de Vries, *The Leader on the Couch: A Clinical Approach to Changing People and Organizations* (San Francisco: Jossey-Bass, 2006).

53. Eric Berne, *Games People Play: The Psychology of Human Relationships* (New York: Penguin, 1964).

54. Some look at the virtues of major world religions—e.g., M. Kriger and Y. Seng, "Leadership with Inner Meaning: A Contingency Theory of Leadership Based on the Worldviews of Five Religions," *Leadership Quarterly* 16, no. 5 (2005): 771–806, https:// doi.org/10.1016/j.leaqua.2005.07.007.

55. L. W. Fry, "Toward a Theory of Spiritual Leadership," *Leadership Quarterly* 14, no. 6 (2003): 693–727, https://doi.org/10.1016/j.leaqua.2003.09.001.

56. "Operationalize" is a research term that refers to taking abstract concepts and making them observable and measurable for purposes of doing research.

57. For a good current review, see J. Oh and J. Wang, "Spiritual Leadership: Current Status and Agenda for Future Research and Practice," *Journal of Management, Spirituality and Religion* 17, no. 3 (2020): 223–48, https://doi.org/10.1080/14766086.2020.1728568.

Chapter 9 Leadership, Part 2

1. The phrase "glass ceiling" has been attributed to Marilyn Loden. See Emily Lefroy, "Marilyn Loden, Who Coined the Phrase 'Glass Ceiling,' Dies at 76," *New York Post*, September 6, 2022, https://nypost.com/2022/09/06/marilyn-loden-who-coined-the-phrase -glass-ceiling-dies-at-76.

2. Alice H. Eagly and Linda L. Carli, *Through the Labyrinth: The Truth about How Women Become Leaders* (Boston: Harvard Business Review Press, 2007).

3. Eagly and Carli, *Through the Labyrinth*.

4. M. L. Van Engen and T. M. Willemsen, "Sex and Leadership Styles: A Meta-analysis of Research Published in the 1990s," *Psychological Reports* 94, no. 1 (2004): 3–18, https:// doi.org/10.2466/pr0.94.1.3-18.

5. Lynn R. Offermann and Kira Foley, "Is There a Female Leadership Advantage?," *Oxford Research Encyclopedia of Business and Management*, February 28, 2020, https:// doi.org/10.1093/acrefore/9780190224851.013.61.

6. Adapted from Peter G. Northouse, *Leadership: Theory and Practice*, 9th ed. (Thousand Oaks, CA: Sage, 2021), 709–15.

7. N. J. Adler and S. Bartholomew, "Managing Globally Competent People," *Academy of Management Perspectives* 6, no. 3 (1992): 52–65, https://doi.org/10.5465/ame.1992.4274189.

8. G. Hofstede, "Nationality and Espoused Values of Managers," *Journal of Applied Psychology* 61 (1976): 148–55, https://doi.org/10.1037/0021-9010.61.2.148.

9. Adapted from "Intercultural Management," Hofstede Insights, https://www.hof stede-insights.com/intercultural-management.

10. Robert J. House, Paul J. Hanges, Mansour Javidan, Peter W. Dorfman, and Vipin Gupta, eds., *Culture, Leadership, and Organizations: The GLOBE Study of 62 Societies* (Thousand Oaks, CA: Sage, 2004).

11. Adapted from Peter G. Northouse, *Leadership: Theory and Practice*, 7th ed. (Thousand Oaks, CA: Sage, 2015), 436–39.

12. Robert K. Greenleaf, *Servant Leadership: A Journey into the Nature of Legitimate Power and Greatness* (New York: Paulist Press, 2002).

13. Adapted from Larry C. Spears, "Servant Leadership and Robert K. Greenleaf's Legacy," in *Servant Leadership: Developments in Theory and Research*, ed. Dirk van Dierendonck and Kathleen Patterson (New York: Palgrave Macmillan UK, 2010), 11–24.

14. Larry C. Spears, "Character and Servant Leadership: Ten Characteristics of Effective, Caring Leaders," *Journal of Virtues and Leadership* 1, no. 1 (2010), https://www .regent.edu/journal/journal-of-virtues-leadership/character-and-servant-leadership-ten -characteristics-of-effective-caring-leaders.

15. For a wealth of proceedings for current and past roundtables, see Bruce E. Winston and Kathleen Patterson, "Regent Research Roundtables," Regent University (website), January 9, 2023, https://www.regent.edu/research-dissertations/regent-research -roundtables.

16. For a good review of Southwest Airlines and its practices of servant leadership, see John Milliman, Jeffery Ferguson, David Trickett, and Bruce Condemi, "Spirit and

Community at Southwest Airlines: An Investigation of a Spiritual Values-Based Model," *Journal of Organizational Change Management* 12, no. 3 (1999): 221–33, https://doi.org /10.1108/09534819910273928.

17. Mary Uhl-Bien, Rajnandini Pillai, and Michelle C. Bligh, "The Social Construction of a Legacy: Summarizing and Extending Follower-Centered Perspectives on Leadership," in *Follower-Centered Perspectives on Leadership: A Tribute to the Memory of James R. Meindl*, ed. Boas Shamir, Rajnandini Pillai, Michelle C. Bligh, and Mary Uhl-Bien (Greenwich, CT: IAP, 2009), 265–78.

18. S. Kerr and J. M. Jermier, "Substitutes for Leadership: Their Meaning and Measurement," *Organizational Behavior and Human Performance* 22, no. 3 (1978): 375–403, https://doi.org/10.1016/0030-5073(78)90023-5.

19. Wilfred H. Drath, Cynthia D. McCauley, Charles J. Palus, Ellen Van Velsor, Patricia M. G. O'Connor, and John B. McGuire, "Direction, Alignment, Commitment: Toward a More Integrative Ontology of Leadership," *Leadership Quarterly* 19, no. 6 (2008): 635–53, https://doi.org/10.1016/j.leaqua.2008.09.003.

20. For a seminal work on this approach, see Craig L. Pearce, Charles C. Manz, and Henry P. Sims Jr., *Share, Don't Take the Lead* (Charlotte: IAP, 2014).

21. Charles C. Manz and Henry P. Sims Jr., *Superleadership: Leading Others to Lead Themselves* (New York: Prentice Hall, 1989).

22. Joe Raelin, "From Leadership-as-Practice to Leaderful Practice," *Leadership* 7, no. 2 (2011): 195–211, https://doi.org/10.1177/1742715010394808.

23. The literature on leadership development is vast. I will be adapting many of the ideas that are summarized in David V. Day, "Leadership Development: A Review in Context," *Leadership Quarterly* 11, no. 4 (2000): 581–613, https://doi.org/10.1016/S1048 -9843(00)00061-8.

24. Day, "Leadership Development," 582.

25. David A. Kolb, *Experiential Learning: Experience as the Source of Learning and Development* (Englewood Cliffs, NJ: Prentice Hall, 1984).

26. This model is adapted from Robert J. Sternberg, "WICS: A Model of Leadership in Organizations," *Academy of Management Learning and Education* 2, no. 4 (2003): 386–401.

27. Adapted from Day, "Leadership Development."

28. Liz Ryan, "The Horrible Truth about 360-Degree Feedback," *Forbes*, October 21, 2015, https://www.forbes.com/sites/lizryan/2015/10/21/the-horrible-truth-about-360 -degree-feedback.

Chapter 10 Organizational Culture

1. I do not discuss the interorganizational level in this book.

2. For a review of the early approaches to understanding and theorizing about organizational culture, see Yvan Allaire and Mihaela E. Firsirotu, "Theories of Organizational Culture," *Organization Studies* 5, no. 3 (1984): 193–226, https://doi.org/10.1177 /017084068400500301; and W. G. Ouchi and A. L. Wilkins, "Organizational Culture," *Annual Review of Sociology* 11 (1985): 457–83.

3. See, e.g., Samuel R. Chand, *Culture Catalyst: Seven Strategies to Bring Positive Change to Your Organization* (New Kensington, PA: Whitaker House, 2018).

4. The terms "etic" and "emic" are derived from the seminal linguistic work K. L. Pike, *Language in Relation to a Unified Theory of the Structure of Human Behavior*, Janua Linguarum Series Maior 24 (Boston: De Gruyter Mouton, 1967).

5. Edgar H. Schein, *Organizational Culture and Leadership* (Hoboken, NJ: Wiley & Sons, 2010).

6. Schein, *Organizational Culture and Leadership*.

7. Kim S. Cameron and Robert E. Quinn, *Diagnosing and Changing Organizational Culture: Based on the Competing Values Framework*, 3rd ed. (San Francisco: Jossey-Bass, 2011).

8. Adapted from Stephen P. Robbins and Timothy A. Judge, "Organizational Culture," in *Organizational Behavior*, 18th ed. (New York: Pearson, 2018).

9. John Weaver, *The New Apostolic Reformation: History of a Modern Charismatic Movement* (Jefferson, NC: McFarland, 2016).

10. Association of Related Churches, https://www.arcchurches.com.

11. See, e.g., John P. Kotter and James L. Heskett, *Corporate Culture and Performance* (New York: Free Press, 1992).

12. Henri J. M. Nouwen, *The Wounded Healer: Ministry in Contemporary Society* (Garden City, NY: Doubleday, 1972).

13. For a seminal discussion of this idea, see Chris Argyris, "Making the Undiscussable and Its Undiscussability Discussable," *Public Administration Review* 40, no. 3 (1980): 205–13, https://doi.org/10.2307/975372.

14. Organizational development is a broad and important area of management sciences and lies beyond the scope of this book. It involves a long-range, ongoing, and systematic process with the focus of improving performance. See Charles Lusthaus, *Organizational Assessment: A Framework for Improving Performance* (Ottawa, ON: International Development Research Centre, 2002).

15. Kenneth Leithwood, Doris Jantzi, and Rosanne Steinbach, *Changing Leadership for Changing Times* (Philadelphia: Open University Press, 1999).

Index

FRANK MARKOW has been teaching and leading in Christian higher education for twenty-five years and currently is professor of leadership studies and director of the master of organizational leadership program at The King's University in Southlake, Texas. His calling is to serve leaders through education, counsel, and research. He teaches at the undergraduate, graduate, and doctoral levels, helping students discover more about themselves and expand their capacity to be more effective leaders and have a greater impact on the world for the advancement of the kingdom of God.

He has a PhD in organizational leadership from Regent University School of Leadership and Entrepreneurship, an MA in ministry leadership from Church of God Theological Seminary (now Pentecostal Theological Seminary), and a BA in biblical studies from Patten University. He has been a member of the Academy of Management, the International Leadership Association, the Society for Pentecostal Scholars, and the Foursquare Scholars Fellowship. He has presented numerous times at academic conferences and is published in peer-reviewed journals and edited volumes on leadership.

Connect with Dr. Markow:

Email frankmarkow@gmail.com

 www.linkedin.com/in/frankmarkow